Origins of American Academic Librarianship

LIBRARIES AND LIBRARIANSHIP

An International Series

Edited by

MELVIN J. VOIGT

University of California, San Diego

Associate Editors:

Jane Robbins-Carter
University of Wisconsin, Madison

Evelyn H. Daniel
Syracuse University

Edward T. O'Neill
Case Western Reserve University

Eldred Smith
University of Minnesota

Peter Hernon • Use of Government Publications by Social Scientists (1980)

Allan D. Pratt • Information of the Image (1981)

In Preparation:

Ellen Altman • Problems in Library Supervision

Peter Hernon • Public Access to Government Publications

Alan R. Samuels • Organizational Climate and Public Libraries: A Psychological Approach to Library Management

Douglas L. Zweizig • Public Library User Studies: Applications and Issues

Editorial Board: Ester R. Dyer, Rutgers University; Guy Garrison, Drexel University; Stephen Green, The British Library; Roger Greer, University of Southern California; Alice B. Ihrig, Moraine Valley Community College; W. Carl Jackson, University of Indiana; Paul Kaegbein, Universität zu Köln; Preben Kirkegaard, Royal School of Librarianship; Maurice B. Line, The British Library; Mary Jo Lynch, American Library Association; Carmel Maguire, University of New South Wales; Phyllis A. Richmond, Case Western Reserve University; Basil Stuart-Stubbs, University of British Columbia.

Origins of American Academic Librarianship

by Orvin Lee Shiflett
Louisiana State University

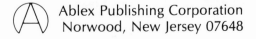
Ablex Publishing Corporation
Norwood, New Jersey 07648

Printed in the United States of America.

Library of Congress Cataloging in Publication Data

Shiflett, Orvin Lee.
  Origins of American academic librarianship.

  (Libraries and librarianship)
  Includes bibliographical references and
index.
  1. Library science—Vocational guidance—
United States. 2. College librarians—United
States. 3. Library education—United States.
I. Title. II. Series.
Z668.S52   020'.7'11   81-14969
ISBN 0-89391-082-1   AACR2

ABLEX Publishing Corporation
355 Chestnut Street
Norwood, New Jersey 07648

In memory of Paul Shaner Dunkin

Contents

Acknowledgements

A study this long in creation owes much to many. I regret that only a few who made it possible can be named here, but recognize my debt to many more. My first obligation is to the committee that nursed this work through its first draft: to Ron Blazek, John Goudeau, Harold Goldstein, and L. V. Rasmussen of Florida State University, my gratitude. I am also thankful to my colleagues in Room 12 and the students of the School of Library Science for their moral support over the years. I am grateful to two "special" members of my committee: Joan R. Yeatmen of the English Department of the University of Wisconsin—LaCrosse forced me to begin and kept me to the main road; Marisol Zapater of the library of Inter-American University offered invaluable aid in the completion of this book.

Jane Robbins-Carter and Francis Miksa of Louisiana State University are owed much for their criticism of the manuscript and support in its final preparation for publication. Ajaye Bloomstone of Louisiana State University's Middleton Library has earned my special gratitude for the compilation of the index to this volume. Without their help, this effort would have been impossible. I also thank Walter J. Johnson for publishing this work.

And, I thank my mother, Elsie Shiflett, who made the work possible in many ways.

Introduction

The Gale Research Company shuttle buses at the conferences of the American Library Association are usually crowded, and those who have seats in the circuit from one hotel to another frequently feel themselves less advantaged than those who have ready access to the doors. I was among the more fortunate at one conference as I struggled to hold onto my day's collection of programs, exhibit materials, and my finds in the shop of a local bookseller who did not realize the value—to me at least—of the 1908 cataloging rules compiled by British and North American librarians. Swinging from side to side, clutching the chrome post provided for the purpose, trying to preserve my dignity as well as the sensibilities of those with whom I was engaged in this peculiar dance, and avoiding the glares of those with seats upon whom we were constantly about to be thrown, I overheard a conversation that echoed the concerns of a large number of academic librarians.

One well-dressed librarian of middle age sat with another. Obviously, some earlier conversation about the situation of academic librarians was being continued. With a look of intense agitation, one leaned over to the other and, emphasizing points with the fist of one hand in the palm of the other, put forth the case:

Damn it! I teach each time I answer a reference question or show the kids how to use The *Reader's Guide*. But, they deny us on the grounds that we have to do it in a class. So, we do it in a class. I teach a one-hour course in library use—and they tell me that research is required of the faculty. Damn it! Every time a librarian tracks down an unknown author or figures out what someone wants at the desk, *they are doing research.*"

As the bus stopped and I was forced out onto the front steps of the wrong hotel, I heard the ultimate question: "Why don't they give us faculty status?"

Concern over their status in the academic community has been a major obsession of academic librarians. Although some have opted for positions in a hierarchy different from that of the faculty, most feel that their preparation and functions in the enterprise of higher education and their major contribution to the objectives of America's colleges and universities entitle them to at least equality with the faculty in the consideration of administrators, teachers, and students. The idea of an academic community that includes faculty members, administrators, and librarians in a cooperative venture to promote the goals of higher education has been a major focus of academic librarians.

What academic librarians think about their role in the academic community has been shaped to a great extent by a series of *myths* that have been promoted through the professional education of academic librarians. The 1936 textbook of William M. Randall and Francis L. K. Goodrich on academic library administration provides an excellent example of the formula by which academic librarians, such as those on the Gale shuttle bus, have attempted to conceptualize their role in higher education. Randall and Goodrich postulated that academic librarians had, by the turn of the century, fallen from a state of grace in which they had had direct communion with the gods of scholarship. Before this fall, to be a librarian one "had first to be a scholar of renown. Added to his encyclopedic knowledge was an insight into some department of learning in which his studies had carried him to the position of an acknowledged specialist." They charged the emphasis on the developing technical aspects of library management with destroying the sympathetic relationship of librarianship and scholarship, but felt that this was only a temporary separation rather than a divorce. Academic librarianship, they assured the student, would overcome the false values of technical efficiency and begin "once more to stress the value of intellectual attainment."

Randall and Goodrich went on to point out that for academic librarians properly to fulfill their function in the academic endeavor, they must "enter into the fellowship of the college faculty." Faculty rank was mandated for academic librarians. By this, the authors meant no hollow titles, but full equality in the amount of free time for study and research and equal access to grants and sabbaticals. The authors realized that true equality could come only when the doctorate became the standard degree for academic librarians, but they accepted more realistic credentials by allowing the minimum requirements of a bachelor's degree, a year of professional training, and a strong background in educational methods.[1]

The authors of this basic text were prescriptive rather than descriptive in their evaluation. Their concerns still appear in the literature of librarianship and in the conversations of academic librarians. The evolution of a true community among librarians and faculty members envisioned by Randall and Goodrich and desired by academic librarians has not come to pass. A mutual distrust and sometimes actual hostility have been the normal interaction between the two groups. Complaints by librarians of outrageous faculty demands on services and materials budgets are conversational gambits wherever academic librarians congregate. When Dr.Dunderhead sends his freshman literature section of 500 students to read the library's one copy of *All Quiet on the Western Front* or demands three-quarters of the college book budget to support his research on William Wycherly, librarians can neither understand nor remain passive in their resistance to what they consider a direct abuse of the library's role in the institutional effort.

Faculty members have their complaints about librarians and frequently these are telling. Jacques Barzun, after disclaiming any animosity toward librarians and, indeed, displaying a strong understanding of many of the problems faced by libraries, finally affirmed the value to students and professors of owning books rather than relying on libraries for basic sources. Barzun took exception to precisely those areas in which academic librarians sought to identify their functions in the educational effort. The practice of making displays of books while denying access to the stacks struck him as ridiculous presumption, intellectual arrogance on the part of librarians. He essentially felt that the emphasis on help to the student was contrary to the true function of the library:

> The librarian composes a little reading list to be pasted up for the edification of undecided readers. This is thoughtful, but while this is being typed and thumbtacked, the student who knows what he is about can get no hearing for his inquiry: the staff is too shorthanded and again he waits in line. It almost seems as if a clear purpose in a student disqualified him from receiving assistance. And too often, when he approaches the high priestess, it is the suppliant who has to guide the ritual. I mean that the librarian who knows only tricks and numbers is made nervous by an unexpected question and turns the tables on the inquirer by implying that he does not know what he himself wants.[2]

Barzun encapsulates many of the complaints of the faculty in this criticism. Librarians, indeed, did focus their attention on the "uncertain reader" to the exclusion of the competent user and sometimes viewed the experienced reader "who knows what he is about" as either naive or in need of no aid.

Several issues need to be examined in order to increase understanding of the profession of academic librarianship. The relationship of libraries and librarianship to scholarship and the academic profession is a crucial one. An essential question is the role of the librarian in higher education during the nineteenth century. The persistent belief that the place of the librarian in the academic community was once much loftier than it is today has fostered a sense of displacement that has engendered numerous attempts to explain the low position of the librarian as the result of the inability of shortsighted faculty members and administrators to understand the role of the library in the academic purpose. The relationship of the values and commitment of librarianship to the emerging academic profession would seem to be a major force in the relative status of academic librarians and faculty members in American higher education. The nature and role of library education in the preparation of academic librarians and the role of the American Library Association in the definition of librarianship as a profession need consideration. This work approaches answers to these questions.

The present status of librarians in the academic community has historical roots that seem to be only imperfectly understood by librarians. The current confusion and diversity of opinion about the proper position of the librarian in the academic hierarchy and the proper role of the library in the academic enterprise derive from traditions established in the development of American higher education that defined the role of the teacher and the role of the library in academic and scholarly life. This work investigates the mythos of academic librarianship in its formative period and how it contributed to the place of librarians in the academic community.

The literature of librarianship has frequently addressed itself to the status of the academic librarian. Few writers have taken a historical approach to the problem. Arthur M. McAnally briefly touched on the topic of this study in an introduction to an article describing what he considered the desirable characteristics of faculty status for academic librarians. To introduce his vision of the perfect state, he took a backward look at the struggle of the emerging profession. McAnally asserted that numerous factors were involved in the slow growth of professionalism in academic librarianship. Among these were the small number of people involved in the operations of the library before the beginnings of the twentieth century, the lack of any distinction between clerical and professional workers in the allotment and performance of tasks, the predominance of women in librarianship and their lack of acceptance in the academic community, the low quality of early library training, a pervasive attitude of the faculty that librarians were not equipped to function as colleagues, the bureaucratic structure of academic library administration, the lack of support of academic librarianship by the American Library Association, growing emphasis by regional accrediting associations and university administrators on the doctorate for faculty members, and a belief held by some important faculty members that librarianship should evolve its own status equal to, but distinct from, that of the teaching faculty.

McAnally's historical sketch, aside from or perhaps because of, being conceived as an introduction to his own analysis of the meaning of "faculty status," failed to come to terms with the crucial realities of early academic librarianship. He condemned early college and university librarians for paying too much attention to "housekeeping" activities and failing to distinguish between clerical and professional tasks without realizing that it was precisely those clerical and housekeeping tasks that professional (full-time) librarians were hired to perform when the job became too time-consuming for the part-time librarian who was also a teacher.[3]

Although McAnally's historical treatment represents only a minor effort offered as background to the true purpose of his article, it is one of only two attempts to come to terms with the evolution of early academic librarianship. His article has attained significance beyond its original intent. It has been collected with several other items on the subject of faculty status by the Association of College and Research Libraries Committee on Academic Status in a publication, *Faculty Status for Academic Librarians*, that was advertised in the publications catalog of the American Library Association as the authoritative word on the subject. It is acclaimed as an "information source" for academic administrators and faculty members "who question the position of the library profession on the issue of faculty status."[4]

Robert B. Downs covered essentially the same ground as McAnally in a bibliographic essay. He examined a sample of catalogs of public and private universities and colleges for the 1870–71 academic year. He found that at that time only library heads who were members of the teaching faculty were given academic titles. Taking another sample of catalogs for the 1900–1901 academic year, he observed a trend toward classifying the head librarian as a faculty member, but not the professional staff. Downs traced the main points of the literature of status to the mid-1960s and concluded that though the struggle was far from over, prospects for eventual equality with the teaching faculty were promising.

A decade after this, Downs examined the problem again and modified his conclusions. He traced the development of academic librarianship from its low status in the classical college to the modern research library and pointed to the development of library education, library research, and the involvement of academic librarianship in professional organizations as having defined the distinctiveness of academic librarianship. But he did not foresee any clear equality of librarians in the academic community.[5]

Edward Holley offered a centennial history on the state of American academic librarianship in 1876. He discussed the transitions in higher education at the time, the financing of academic libraries, the size and quality of collections, the student society library phenomenon, the relationship of the library to the students, library staffing, library buildings, and professional school libraries. He concluded from his survey that the major issues of the role of the academic library in the educational process were emerging in 1876. Holley regarded 1876 as a watershed year separating the placid pond of the nineteenth century from the torrent of the twentieth. The transformations of American society and parallel changes in American higher education infused American librarianship with a new vision of the power of the library in the academic enterprise.[6]

Both Kenneth Brough and Samuel Rothstein have examined the development of service orientations in American academic libraries. If, as McAnally implied, the development of concern with the utilization of books can be equated with professionalization in academic librarianship, Brough's and Rothstein's studies are concerned with the topic.

Brough agreed with this identity by contending that the crucial activity of academic librarianship has been the utilization of the collections: "The MODERN UNIVERSITY librarian has built his role around the urge to increase the usefulness of books."[7] Starting with a description of the library of the classical college, he traced the development of collections and services in the libraries of the University of Chicago, Columbia, Harvard, and Yale. He examined the evolving conception of the library in the university, the clientele of the library, the collections and their accessibility, the development of reference work, and the librarian's role in the research library. Brough viewed the history of academic librarianship as a projection from preservation to utilization of materials and found that the role of the librarian is defined by the manner and degree to which he makes the collections usable.

Rothstein took a narrower view of library services than Brough and limited his study to those activities that are commonly called *reference services*. The rise in the late nineteenth century of American scholarship modeled on Germanic forms and accompanied by demands for increased resources led to the growing necessity for guidance in the use of the library. Rothstein recorded that the development of the reference service was "the transformation of occasional and casual courtesy into a complex and highly specialized service of steadily increasing scope and importance."[8] He found that the growth of reference service was directly attributable to the admission of large numbers of inexperienced readers into the library. The dual character of the emerging American university that attempted to fill the needs of both scholars and undergraduate students placed strains on the library because the former demanded materials and the latter required assistance in using those materials.

Reference service had become established by the end of the nineteenth century in many American academic libraries, but it was almost always in the form of service to undergraduate students: scholars neither felt the need for it nor utilized it. By the end of the First World War, subject specialists in libraries were common and the volume and prestige of reference work had increased significantly. It was, however, still directed toward the inexperienced reader. Not until the late 1920s were attempts made to provide service specifically for scholars. These efforts met with little acceptance. As Rothstein was writing in 1955, he found that the philosophy of "moderate" service prevailed, but he saw expansion in increased service and diversification of services.

The development of education for librarianship has been an important factor in the evolution of modern academic librarianship. Through the forms and rituals of education and the trappings of degrees, academic identity and, ultimately, academic community is established. Carl M. White's historical examination of library education describes the social and educational forces that underlay the impulse to library education in America.[9] White traced the decay of the apprenticeship system and the rise of technical education from the 1860s to the 1890s. He found that the vitality of the American library movement, the limited patterns of transferring professional skills through contact with a few experienced librarians, and the growing acceptance of the idea that education should be related to the needs of the common man were primary factors contributing to the emergence of library schools. White placed Dewey's school and philosophy of librarianship solidly in the technical school movement. Dewey's genius considered the methods of technical education as most appropriate for librarianship, and the establishment of new schools modeled on the Columbia/Albany school spread the idea.

Sarah Vann examined the Dewey to Williamson period of library education. She found that before the *Williamson Report* "divisive and conflicting attitudes toward training were being expressed in the literature, within the American Library Association, and within the Association of American Library Schools."[10] Her strongly documented and detailed account of the various programs existing, levels of sophistication and types of credentials provided, and the attitudes underlying professional thought on library education make this an important study in the history of librarianship.

On a lesser scale, W. Boyd Rayward has investigated the politics involved in the establishment of Dewey's school at Columbia.[11] He concluded that none of the participants in the decision to connect the school with the university did so because they considered library economy an academic discipline. Rather, Dewey wanted the connection as a step in firmly establishing librarianship as a profession. To obtain the support of the American Library Association in the founding of a school, it was necessary for Dewey to accept the prevailing philosophy of librarianship that demanded practical, nonacademic training. Through a series of dissimulations, Dewey, with the help of President Barnard, brought the school to Columbia.

Lloyd J. Houser and Alvin M. Schrader attempted a more central study in their evaluation of the rigorousness of research in librarianship. Their third chapter relates directly to the problem under consideration.[12] Here, they consider the evolution of library education from its inception under the direction of Melvil Dewey to the establishment of Chicago's school under George Works. In subsequent chapters they address the early turmoil at Chicago and its resolution with the placing of Louis Round Wilson at the helm. They demonstrate that the Chicago school, though not particularly successful, represented the first significant attempt to establish librarianship as a scientific study and thus obtain the dignity of academic reputability.

Since this volume went to press, Arthur T. Hamlin's masterful overview of the history of the American university library has appeared.[13] A glance at the bibliographies of both books would lead the casual reader to assume that he and I had tilled the same fields. On the surface, this is indeed the case. Hamlin's work, however, is much more closely related to the work of Louis Shores, Dennis Thomison, and others who present library history as a phenomenon isolated from the larger environment of the society which the institution serves. Further, Hamlin speaks from the perspective of a library administrator who has experienced much of what he writes. I suggest that the two books be read in conjunction: Hamlin's work for a broad perspective on the growth of the university library from its colonial ancestry to the present; mine for its detailed attention of the problems of an emerging academic profession.

Histories of American librarianship have, for the most part, been isolated chronicles of individual libraries and librarians. The examples cited, with a few others, have represented the only serious attempts to evaluate the role of the academic library and librarianship in a context broader than that of the immediate institutional setting. The present study is an analysis of the position of the library and the librarian in American higher education. It is historical in that the author strongly feels that the present status of academic librarians is not really a modern problem, but one that derives directly from the evolution of American higher education and American librarianship. By the time of the Depression, America's colleges and universities and America's librarians had evolved forms of recognition and reward that remain, substantially, unchanged today. Though the rise of true graduate education with the evolution of doctoral programs in library and information science has made an impact on the credentials of librarians, it still has been too insignificant to have had any substantial effect. The modern academic librarian for the most part still holds an undergraduate degree, a fifth-year credential from an accredited library school, and perhaps, a master's degree based on an undergraduate academic discipline.

The plan of the present work is not chronological because, in such a broad area, change is not chronological but cumulative. Only when enough has been said and done, is it evident that a significant change has occurred. The chapters here presented do roughly follow a time sequence. The first considers the nature of the classical college and the place of the library in its educational plan. The second traces the influence of a changing American society on higher education. Chapter three takes up the relationship of the new American scholarship to the emerging profession of librarianship. Next, the profession of American librarianship and the forms of its academic reputability are examined. In the final chapter the place and the role of the librarian as perceived by the academic community is considered.

The present work does not presume to exhaust the topic. I consulted a great number of primary and secondary sources, yet I realize fully that all the evidence in a work of this scope will never be found and that the one rock left unturned may hide the worm. This is only an attempt to point the way toward a more fruitful discussion of the place of the academic librarian in the enterprise of higher education and a suggestion of possible lines of further and more intensive inquiry into the development of modern American higher education. It is also a realization of my deeply held belief that understanding of the past illuminates the present and shows us some of the possible futures. What follows is library history written by a librarian rather than a historian. It is an attempt to come to terms with the present place of academic librarians in the academic community and views the relationship of librarians to the faculty, administrators, and other concerned groups in the academic enterprise as a historical phenomenon rather than a misconstruction of the nature and purposes of American higher education.

Notes to the Introduction

1. William Madison Randall and Francis L. D. Goodrich, *Principles of College Library Administration* (Chicago: American Library Association and the University of Chicago Press, 1936), pp. 113–18.

2. Jacques Barzun, *Teacher in America* (Boston: Little, Brown & Company, 1945), p. 75.

3. Arthur M. McAnally, "Status of the University Librarian in the Academic Community," in Jerrold Orne (Ed.), *Research Librarianship: Essays in Honor of Robert B. Downs* (New York: R. R. Bowker Company, 1971), pp. 19–50.

4. Association of College and Research Libraries, Committee on Academic Status, *Faculty Status for Academic Librarians: A History and Policy Statement* (Chicago: American Library Association, 1976);

American Library Association, *Publications 1976* (Chicago: American Library Association, 1975), p. 14.

5. Robert Bingham Downs, "Status of Academic Librarians in Retrospect," *College and Research Libraries* 29 (July 1968): 253–58; Robert Bingham Downs, "The Role of the Academic Librarian, 1876–1976," *College and Research Libraries* 37 (November 1976): 491–502.

6. Edward G. Holley, "Academic Libraries in 1876," *College and Research Libraries* 37 (January 1976): 15–47.

7. Kenneth J. Brough, *Scholar's Workshop: Evolving Conceptions of Library Service*, Illinois Contributions to Librarianship, no. 5 (Urbana: University of Illinois Press, 1958), p. 160.

8. Samuel Rothstein, *The Development of Reference Services Through Academic Traditions, Public Library Practices and Special Librarianship*, ACRL Monographs, no. 14 (Chicago: Association of College and Reference Libraries, 1955), p. 100.

9. Carl Milton White, *A Historical Introduction to Library Education: Problems and Progress to 1951* (Metuchen, N.J.: Scarecrow Press, Inc., 1976).

10. Sarah Katherine Vann, *Training for Librarianship Before 1923: Education for Librarianship Prior to the Publication of Williamson's Report on Training for Library Service*, (Chicago: American Library Association, 1961), p. 3.

11. W. Boyd Rayward, "Melvil Dewey and Education for Librarianship," *Journal of Library History* 3 (October 1968): 297–312.

12. Lloyd J. Houser and Alvin M. Schrader, *The Search for a Scientific Profession: Library Science Education in the U.S. and Canada* (Metuchen, N.J.: Scarecrow Press, Inc., 1978).

13. Arthur Tenney Hamlin, *The University Library in the United States: Its Origins and Development*, (Philadelphia: University of Pennsylvania Press, 1981).

Origins of
American Academic
Librarianship

The Classical College
and Its Library

Daniel Coit Gilman, librarian at Yale, complained to President Theodore Dwight Woolsey in 1865 of having to pay the salary of his assistant out of his own meager pay, of the injury to his health from "continued exposure to the cold and dampness which prevail in the library much of the year," and of the lack of any substantial improvement in the condition of the library during the nine years he had served as librarian. He was told the college offered little hope for the future: "The place," Woolsey replied, "does not possess that importance which a man of active mind would naturally seek; and the college cannot, now or hereafter, while its circumstances remain as they are, give it greater prominence."[1] Woolsey's answer did not reflect any disregard for the abilities of a man who indeed made his "active mind" quite evident in his position as professor of geography, a planner of the Sheffield Scientific School, and later as president of the University of California and of Johns Hopkins. It was, rather, an honest appraisal of the place of the library in the American classical college.

At the close of the nineteenth century, America's academic libraries could offer little to higher education. Meager collections, severely restricted physical access to the books, and opening only a few hours a week greatly limited the potential usefulness of academic libraries. Even a cursory look through

1

the two comprehensive library surveys of the period, those of William James Rhees and Charles Coffin Jewett, confirms this generalization. A few libraries were like Harvard with its massive collection of 72,000 volumes and liberal open hours— six hours a day Monday through Thursday and four hours on Friday[2]—but many more were in the position of Central College in Blendon, Ohio, which boasted a total of 550 volumes and opened its doors one afternoon every two weeks. Indeed, the entire holdings of the 126 colleges covered in Jewett's survey were only 586,912 volumes.[3] Rhees's study of some years earlier found 1,211,238 volumes in 244 college libraries that reported their size.

The older settled areas of the country had colleges that held proportionately greater numbers of books. Nine of the eleven colleges in Massachusetts reported their holdings to Rhees; they averaged approximately 15,800 volumes each. The eight Michigan colleges of the fourteen that Rhees was able to identify reported an average of only 2000 each. The total discrepancy between the college library resources of the original thirteen states and those admitted to the union before the 1850s is significant. Of the colleges in the east, 110 averaged 7514 volumes each. In the other twenty-three states, 139 colleges reported owning 416,148 volumes, averaging only 2994 volumes at each institution.[4]

Further, it is important to note the proportion of institutions answering Rhees's questions. In the original states, 110 of the 157 college libraries he identified reported for a 70 percent return. In the other states, only 48 percent of the colleges told Rhees how many volumes they owned. The difference probably arose less from the varying diligence of collegiate officers in answering questions about their institutions, but from the fact that many colleges on the American frontier owned few or no books and, consequently, had insignificant libraries to report.

The history of American academic librarianship cannot be properly comprehended without an understanding of the history of American higher education. The college library did not exist in a vacuum but prospered or suffered in proportion to its value to the college. The position of the librarian in the academic community was also directly related to the place of the library in the college.

The reasons for both the general paucity of resources and the discrepancy between the older parts of America and the edges of the frontier are not difficult to determine. Americans were moving west to fill the opportunities and realize the promise that the frontier offered. The movement, though, was not one that created stable population centers till the end of the nineteenth century. Families moved westward, and then moved again, always outrunning civilization. Between 1790 and the 1820s, the trans-Allegheny population increased from about 100,000 to over two million with many families making two or three moves in a brief time. The confidence of the frontiersmen in themselves and the accompanying desire for local self-sufficiency in their capacity to reproduce the civilization of the East made the growth of local institutions inevitable. The frontier colleges were established as a vital part of Western expansion.[5]

It has been estimated that between the Revolution and the Civil War, 903 colleges were founded of which 721, or 80 percent, failed. Sectarian loyalties betrayed many communities into establishing colleges where none, or at best a grammar school, was needed. The founding of one denominational college frequently was followed by the founding of another by a different sect whenever the Presbyterians or Baptists found the Methodists gaining too great a local influence. Trustees' enthusiasms founded two or more colleges where only one could possibly have found a marginal existence. Around the country, colleges were sown and broke the sandy surface of a soil that could only produce a stunted plant. In the college's struggle for survival, education frequently became a secondary consideration to the problem of daily existence.[6]

The evangelical fervor of the second great awakening did much to determine the kinds of colleges that were created. The ardently religious men who founded colleges in America looked to establish agencies of religious purpose in which considerations of doctrine and piety rather than learning and scholarship would be put forth. Denominationalism dominated higher education in America by a confusion of the roles of the church and state in education, and in some cases, exerted direct influence on the few state universities that were founded before the Civil War.[7]

Religion retained a strong and pervasive influence on the activities of the institutions through most of the nineteenth century. In 1838, the Reverend John Maclean, then a professor and later President of Princeton, wrote to Eliphalet Nott, President of Union College, inquiring after details of a religious revival then occurring on the Union campus. He closed by asserting: "We greatly need in our college the presence of the Spirit of God, to quicken the few pious youth we now have, and especially to arrest the attention of the large mass among us, who have no concern about their eternal welfare."[8]

Nott's answer tells the story of a characteristic collegial revival of the antebellum period. The revival being experienced on the campus, Nott reported, had "commenced immediately after the observance of the day of fasting and prayer in February last." A meeting had been held in a local Dutch Reformed church where a number of students who had remained at the college over the vacation had become converted. Nott was attending a meeting of the presbytery in Philadelphia and returned to find a "protracted meeting in progress" that had begun in the Baptist church and moved to the Presbyterian because of its ability to accommodate more people. The meeting was being conducted by the Reverend Mr. Knapp, a Baptist, about whose orthodoxy Nott had reservations. Assured that Knapp was a "forcible and faithful preacher," Nott finally accepted him.

Nott avoided the question of sectarian diversity and advised students to avoid points of minor difference in favor of establishing the validity of their own callings. Nott consulted the religious leaders of Schenectady and they concurred. By late June, the spirit of brotherhood, by which all denominations, "Episcopalians, Presbyterians, Dutch Reformed, Methodists, and Baptists met and worshipped together for several weeks," had cooled, and though the morning group prayer meetings were still held, the converts had separated to repair to the various churches with which they had associated themselves.

Nott cautioned that it was too early to assess the effects of the revival on the college, but he was optimistic:

An unusual seriousness has pervaded almost the entire institution. Numbers are rejoicing in hope and numbers are still anxious. Time alone will show who and how many will endure to the end. From present appearances, a considerable number of candidates for the ministry, at home among the churches, or abroad among the heathen, will be furnished.

Nott concluded with the hope that the blessing would extend from Union and the town through the country "till the nation shall become regenerate, and, our whole land filled with the knowledge of God."[9]

Such religious revivals were as common in America's colleges as they were outside the college walls—and were frequently as fervent. In college after college intense waves of piety washed students off to the ministry and the missions. Though the purpose of the college had changed from the production of ministers to the education of a Christian laity early in the nineteenth century,[10] clearly a reaffirmation of godliness even at the older, well-established, and more secularized colleges was considered a blessing.

The American college, before the Civil War, was a small, self-contained institution enrolling only about 100 male students. Columbia, in the 1830s, dipped below this number several times. As of the 1860s, Harvard, which had been graduating students since 1636, had fewer dead graduates than living. Yale, largest of the American colleges before the Civil War, could boast an enrollment of only 400.[11] With a small student population and a campus of only one building, the American classical college was at best a stunted plant. Tewksbury's study of the founding of colleges before the Civil War in sixteen states found an 81 percent failure rate. He attributed this high rate of failure to several reasons, most of them financial. With the depression of 1837, eastern financial sources upon which many western institutions depended began to decline, leaving the colleges, many of which functioned as a sort of western or southern campus for Yale or Princeton, [12] without support.

Frequently, when a college was lucky enough to receive promises of substantial local support, the community found that, when the afterglow of exuberance had faded and the college was a physical fact, resources for its continuation were nonexistent. Many colleges, like Amherst, founded in 1821, were initially funded with subscription pledges as low as fifty cents a year for five years. Amherst raised its roof with donations of lumber, stone, and labor from farmers and craftsmen in much the same manner as a medieval cathedral was constructed.[13] Agrarian America's heavy reliance on self-sufficient farms and the barter system meant that hard money—even for great purposes—was scarce.

Natural catastrophies, principally in the form of fire, felled many colleges before they could securely establish themselves. In the era before fire insurance, the loss of all or most assets by the burning of a wooden building was a disaster. But the destruction of the moral and social cohesiveness that was the strength of the American classical college was, perhaps, the most serious reason for failure. The college could retain its integrity and validity of purpose only while its goals remained pure. Dissension could not be suffered in an education that defined truth in terms of denominational orthodoxy. It was an era of extreme political polarization over such questions as slavery and the role of the common man in the new Jacksonian enterprise, of great flux in the spheres of control by various competing denominations and heresies, and of a general secularization of American life. Those factors, coupled with an increased awareness among many factions of the academic community that the classical curriculum was not an adequate response to the changing needs of American society, produced many points of contention within colleges that frequently proved too divisive for the delicate structures of the infant institutions.

Frequently, attempts to raise money brought disastrous results. Aside from direct appeals for charity from individuals or such groups as the Society for the Promotion of Collegiate and Theological Education at the West, perhaps the most widespread and popular form of financing was the sale of perpetual scholarships. These were usually sold for about $500 and assured the buyer—and his heirs, one by one—a college education. The expectation usually was that such income would be invested as an endowment, but the necessity for immediate repairs and new facilities, not to mention faculty salaries, often proved too compelling for the trustees, and the money was spent for current expenses. This proved to be an increasing financial embarrassment as sons and then grandsons of purchasers appeared at the opening of the fall term, having fulfilled their part of the contract.[14] The practice even developed of renting the perpetual scholarships. A holder of a scholarship would lease it to a student who would receive a reduced rate of tuition. The holder made a profit, the student saved money, and everyone, except of course the college, prospered.[15]

Colleges that relied on tuition-paying students for continuing financial existence found that increasing numbers of nonpaying students were entitled to the same amenities of education as their paying classmates. The college libraries as well as all other aspects of the institutions' functions were hurt by the discrepancy between the demands for education and the declining resources. Antioch, for example, relied solely on a $2.50 incidental fee assessed each student to buy books for its library. Exempting the perpetual scholarship holders from payment of this fee severely affected the library's early development.[16]

The American classical colleges were similar in more ways than size and poverty. Frequently, the frontier colleges were established as part of a conscious effort to spread denominational orthodoxy by churches and older colleges in the east. The growth of the frontier college was not a movement that arose directly from local needs. The dependency of the American frontier on the culture and society of the east forced the new colleges to model their purpose and development on the established patterns of the eastern colleges.[17]

Princeton and Yale emerged as the two most influential colleges in the country before the beginning of the Civil War. Hampton-Sidney, Washington and Lee, and even the University of North Carolina came under direct Princeton influence during the first third of the nineteenth century when they hired Princeton graduates as presidents, adopted the Princeton curriculum wholesale, and hired Princeton men as professors to insure Princeton orthodoxy. As these schools established themselves, they followed contemporary practice and hired their own graduates—trained in the Princeton curriculum by Princeton graduates—to maintain their traditions.[18]

The indirect influences were as significant as the direct. It was only natural for a new college to look for college-trained men for its presidency and professorships. New England, as the oldest area of the country, provided such resources. About 40 percent of the 276 antebellum American college presidents were born in New England. A great many more were of New England parentage and had been born into a New England environment.

Even more indirectly, the colonial colleges perpetuated their traditions on the American frontier. The new denominational colleges looked to their older counterparts in the east for models. The local Congregational minister, in his capacity as an influential member of a new board of trustees, would naturally remember his years at Yale and tend to look with favor on applicants who subscribed to his own values in education when he searched for a president and faculty for a new college being founded in Illinois or Tennessee.

The influence of older colleges on the newer ones often thwarted significant moves toward curricular diversity and reform. Joseph Caldwell came from Princeton to the University of North Carolina in 1797. He found there a liberal curriculum that provided for electives and an unusual array of courses in history, political science, and the natural sciences. This curriculum, established by local leaders, was gradually replaced by the Princeton plan of classical studies so that when he left North Carolina in 1835, Caldwell could look with satisfaction on a properly orthodox institution—a new Princeton in the South.[19]

The classical curriculum of the eighteenth-century American college that was carried out into the wilderness of the West and South by the men trained in eastern colleges, was one of the most striking aspects of homogeniety in the American college. Though the question of the appropriateness of extreme emphasis on Latin and Greek in the curriculum was raised with increasing frequency and fervor throughout the period, the colleges and the new state universities insisted upon their fundamental necessity if a student was to take his place among educated men at the end of four years. Even colleges such as West Virginia University, established under the 1862 Morrell Act, offered a rigidly classical curriculum with only grudging and superficial attention to agriculture and military science until 1895 when an elective system modeled on that of Harvard was introduced.[20]

At institutions as distant from New England as Knox College in Illinois, Ohio Wesleyan, and the numerous small colleges in Michigan, the students studied the classical languages and mathematics and observed the wonders of the universe—or at least as many of them as were known by the professors of natural science—by memorizing their textbooks, reciting their lessons, and observing the manipulation of the philosophical apparatus. Under this system, "the good student was one who spotted the ablative absolute, and excellence consisted in snappy recognition of that subtlest of all distinctions: the one between the gerund and the gerundive."[21]

The circumscribed and almost ritualistic quality of the classical curriculum was conditioned by the current concept of faculty psychology. This theory of human function viewed man as "a bundle of Desires, Natural Affections, Intellect, Reason, and Moral Affections, each of which possessed a certain bodily abode." By introspectively examining these faculties, man could discover his purpose. The moral imperative of realizing his abilities compelled him to fulfill these God-given potentialities.[22]

American academic men of the nineteenth century held a holistic view of man's place in a world where there was a purpose to be discovered and a faculty by which that purpose became clear. They realized this in a curriculum designed not to convey a specific body of knowledge, but to exercise the capacities of the mind. Mental discipline rather than proficiency at any one intellectual activity or mastery of a specified body of information was the goal. Consequently, the purpose of the college was character building. Curricular matters did not unduly excite either the president or the faculty. They had at hand a system of education in which three years of study developed the mind of the student to come to grips with Moral Philosophy in the fourth year. This system produced the final product—a virtuous Christian citizen of the republic.[23]

As a direct result of this purpose, controversy was avoided and the virtues of social peace were affirmed. The original purpose—and the prime purpose in the frontier colleges—was to produce clergymen, but a college of a hundred students drawing upon a population of several thousand for support could not rely upon the demand for sectarian ministers. By the 1840s, the religious purpose had shifted from the professionally religious to the worldly religious. The education of ministers had been replaced by the education of moral citizens.

Jonathan Blanchard, president of Knox College in the 1850s, was a Congregationalist who wished to infect the land with

Christian fervor—of his own persuasion. In 1858, he was replaced, after a bitter struggle with a local Presbyterian faction,
by Harvey Curtis. Curtis, in his inaugural address, affirmed the
necessity for intellectual innocence in the classical curriculum:
"My own settled convictions are," he proclaimed, "that the college is not the place, and this early stage of education not the
fitting time, in which to inculcate distinctive opinions on doubtful or contested points, either in religion or morals." The college, he affirmed, was the place where foundations were to be
laid for religion and morals as well as intellectual development:

> Let pupils be trained to a clear apprehension of their personal
> responsibility; let a higher sense of honor be inculcated, and an in-
> flexible regard for truth and right; let pure sentiments, and a
> quick and correct moral sense be cultivated; let the principles and
> practical teachings of the Word of God be made familiar to the
> mind; and then; super-added to this, let gentlemanly manners and
> a courteous deportment and address be formed; and withal a
> habit of independent thought, and bold, frank, manly utterance,
> so let it be also kind and consiliatory [sic]; and we may safely
> leave the rest to time and free individual action.[24]

Intellectual, moral, or religious heterodoxy was to be avoided.
The task of the college was to provide education for Christian
gentlemen and that was difficult enough without confusing
issues.

After three years of strenuously exercising the student's
mental musculature on Latin, Greek, mathematics, and the
natural sciences, the culmination of the classical curriculum, the
senior course in moral philosophy, provided a capstone. This
was usually taught by the president of the college in his role as
father of the institutional family. The course covered all of what
have emerged as the several modern social sciences. The forms
that moral philosophy took as a classroom experience appear—
like many of the intercollegiate forms—quite regularized. After
an orientation to the content of moral philosophy, the motives
of human existence were examined. Upon this necessary foundation, a generalized ethics like Bentham's calculus of pleasure
was erected. This led directly to consideration of social institutions and interactions as exemplars of the highest moral law.[25]

Although this description seems to indicate some degree of
freedom of thought at least in the senior year, the appearance is

largely illusory. Moral philosophy, coming after the student's mind had been sharply honed on Greek, Latin, and mathematics, and taught by the president of the college, could lead to only a circumscribed set of alternative answers to questions of man's role in the universe.[26]

The picture of the classical curriculum that emerges is a formal, almost ritual, series of exercises intended to form the whole man. Pressures were, however, developing toward increasing the college's relevance to the American experience. By the 1840s, the sciences, at least in their theoretical forms, had become entrenched in the classical curriculum. The practice of most colleges simply to add courses—all required—to the existing array became increasingly difficult. By the 1850s, there was a general recognition that the traditional four-year course of study could contain only so much. In response to this, systems of partial curricula were established in which a student not interested in a degree could take science courses. The results of this solution were mixed, and it was found that the better students, having spent the time, wanted the degree awarded for the classical curriculum. Further, it was generally acknowledged that the students who chose the scientific courses were those who found the regular course, the classics, too difficult. A partially satisfactory alternative was the establishment of semiseparate scientific schools attached to established colleges, like the Lawrence Scientific School at Harvard, which was well established before the Civil War. But most colleges merely kept adding courses to the requirements; not until the general acceptance at the end of the nineteenth century of the concept of major and minor areas of study was the problem resolved.[27]

Other colleges arrived at different solutions. One of the more progressive thinkers in American education, Francis Wayland, president of Brown from 1827 to 1855, confronted his trustees in 1849 with the necessity for curricular reform and, with the threat of his own resignation, won the decision.[28] In 1850, Brown adopted an elective system that provided for alternative courses of study leading to degrees. Wayland's scheme was modeled on the curriculum of the University of Virginia and was a direct outgrowth of his recognizing the necessity for a closer relationship between higher education and the practical needs of the nation. The new programs introduced the Bachelor of Philosophy degree and changed the Bachelor of Arts degree to a three-year program offering a wide latitude in elective courses in modern languages and the sciences. The classical course was retained, with the Master of Arts degree to be awarded in course.

The system did not work well. The Reverend Barnas Sears, a Brown graduate of 1825, who succeeded Wayland as president in 1856, immediately had to modify the system. Sears's report to the Brown executive board on July 5, 1856, noted that Brown's reputation had suffered greatly because of the revisions. Sears asserted that the faculty thought that the university's reputation had suffered grave harm because of its low standards for the bachelor's and master's degrees. Indeed, Brown was losing potential students to other colleges with better reputations. It was not only the students that were affected by the program: "Even the personal relations of our professors are humiliating, so that their intercourse with officers of other colleges is a source of mortification rather than of Pleasure." Sears went on to note that the graduates of the classical program with MA degrees carefully referred to themselves only as "graduates" for fear of drawing "upon themselves the scorn of the graduates of other colleges, who believe that their literary honors have not been earned."

Sears had no real quarrel with the curricular reforms but felt that the degrees awarded were inappropriate. Accordingly, the granting of degrees was revised to reflect the practices current at other colleges. Changes in requirements followed; by 1861, the curriculum for the BA—with the MA to be awarded in-course—progressed in its traditional four-year march from the Greek historians to moral philosophy.[29]

Most attempts at reform in higher education were thwarted by the pervasive belief that the American college's purpose was to educate the total man and that the mechanism by which that could be best accomplished was the classical curriculum. Perhaps the most important document of this period in higher education was the Yale Report of 1828. The report was designed to end criticism of the classical system and to curb attempts at the radical reform of substituting modern languages for Latin and

Greek. Its wide dissemination and authoritative origin gave it a high degree of acceptability.[30]

It was to counteract sentiments such as Albert Gallatin expressed at the meeting to found New York University that the Yale Report was designed. Gallatin affirmed egalitarianism in the "republic" of knowledge. The emphasis upon Latin and Greek in the curriculum was a manifestation of elitism that had outlived any purpose it once may have had. He argued that unless the artificial insistence on "education" as synonymous with possession of the ancient languages was abandoned, there could be no improvement in higher education.[31]

The committee that produced the Yale Report was explicitly charged with examining the place of the ancient languages in the Yale curriculum. It concluded that the classics were the proper object of collegiate instruction. They rejected as inappropriate any substitution of modern languages for the ancient: "Modern languages, with most of our students, are studied and will continue to be studied, as an accomplishment, rather than as a necessary acquisition."[32]

The insistence of the report on retaining the classics was directly related to the faculty theory of learning in a curious way that is almost incomprehensible in the light of modern linguistics:

> Such study carries the young pupil back to the earliest era in the history of mental efforts, lays open to him the most simple and original operations of the mind and acquaints him with its brilliant and unrivalled productions. It stimulates to industry and severe and faithful application, by proving to the student that the mines of learning can be penetrated only by unceasing exertion, while it admonishes him of the inutility and fate of genius when unaided by deep and laborious research. The student's memory is thus rendered retentive; his recollection quick, and his power of discrimination more accurate. Beginning with language in its primitive simplicity and tracing its progress to its present state, the student can hardly fail to improve his taste and to enlarge his capacity to think and to communicate thought.[33]

The report puts forth two ideas that must be understood in order to appreciate the classical college: first, the notion that human history and thought represent a linear progression—the language of Homer somehow is simpler than that of Shakespeare because it is from a more primitive time—second, the material of education—the group of things studied—was less important than its effect in improving the student's mind. The highest function of education was to lay the foundations for further learning. Grounding the students in the classical forms and the basics of the sciences fulfilled the colleges' function.[34] The report addressed itself specifically to the purposes of collegiate education by stating that the college is not to produce professional men or to train farmers or those in the mechanical or commercial occupations. Rather, it was to lay the foundations for such work.[35]

The Yale Report allowed for curricular change by recognizing that the range of subjects to be presented was not absolute but was tied to circumstances; yet its insistence on the validity of the classical curriculum betrayed the basic conservatism of the document. In the final analysis, it was not the strength of the classical curriculum but the lack of any proven alternative that provided the most telling argument for the committee. The college, it concluded, "has much to expect, and nothing to fear" from staying with the old ways. The report did not so much affirm faith in the classics as express fear of tampering with a mechanism that was, albeit marginally, working. The college "by deserting the high road which it has so long travelled, and wandering in lanes and bypaths, . . . would trifle with its prosperity, and put at hazard the very means of its support and existence."[36] The Yale Report was essentially an affirmation of the college's commitment to educate the total man. Against the forces of change that were pushing the college into the mainstream of American life, it proclaimed a higher purpose than service to the emerging industrial state. The cry for specialized knowledge in a developing American technology was pointedly ignored in favor of giving the mind "the fair proportions which nature designed."[37]

Nevertheless, the committee did not totally deny the value of specialized knowledge, rather, it affirmed generalization. The college's function was to educate all aspects of the mind. The report divided the purposes of education into mental discipline and the provision of mental furniture. Of the two, the discipline was the most important. The furnishings were to be provided partially through the collegiate course, but more importantly in later life through the practice of the discipline that the colleges provided.[38] With the Yale Report, the classical college renounced any role in the preparation of specialists beyond training in the intellectual discipline that would enable the graduates to acquire specialized knowledge wherever they could.

The raw material from which the colleges attempted to hew the total man was frequently flawed. The Yale Report itself admitted difficulties. Yale's age of admission was fixed at fourteen, but frequently applicants were able to pass the entrance examinations at a much earlier age.[39] Columbia had a similar problem in that the age of its students in the 1830s was not much greater than that of modern high school students.[40]

In rural areas, students tended to be older than they were in the "urban" colleges because of economic exigencies.[41] But the frontier colleges had somewhat different problems. The slow growth of lower schools and academies in many parts of the country forced the frontier colleges to reduce standards in order to maintain enrollments until they were offering work comparable to the level of the ordinary academies: "This circumstance, with the multiplication of institutions capable of conferring degrees, has been attended with the additional evil, that, in some, the highest honours have been, and are conferred for acquirements, which would scarcely enable the possessors to enter the lowest class of others."[42] One study of the antebellum colleges in Michigan found that the denominational colleges studied—Albion, Adrian, Hillsdale, Kalamazoo, and Olivet—offered work that was equivalent to only two years of study at the then embryonic University of Michigan.[43]

Many frontier colleges found early that they had overreached their capabilities. Communities established universities when they had support only for grammar schools and had to readjust their plans radically. Knox College in Galesburg, Illinois, was founded in 1842. Its first catalog proclaimed: "Candidates for admission to the freshmen class will be examined in English Grammar, Adams's Arithmetic, six books of Virgil's Aeneid, the Four Gospels of the Greek Testament, Graeca Minora, and Day's or Lacroix's Algebra through simple equations." The school found few who could qualify. In 1842, when the college opened, ten students were admitted to the freshmen class and 147 to the preparatory department.[44]

Even in the later period of the educational frontier, the land grant period, this condition obtained. In a letter of May 7, 1897, Professor A. J. Hare complained to the president of West Virginia University:

> ... that there came into my Latin class last September, and the class this year forms no exception to that every year, some who are mere children, who really could write only with the greatest difficulty a miserable baby scrawl that could scarcely be read; who are almost entirely ignorant of the most common rules of grammar and who were as likely to begin a sentence with a small letter as a capital.[45]

Throughout the nineteenth century, physical as well as mental discipline was a primary function of the classical college. The youth of the students and the manners of the age did not fit well with the sometimes harsh asceticism of college life, and rebellions, both individual and collective, were not uncommon. James Fenimore Cooper's expulsion from Yale in 1805 may have directly resulted from an unfortunate incident involving the explosion of gunpowder in another student's room, but he had been in trouble before for more minor infractions and abandoned New Haven leaving many unpaid bills for books and clothing.[46] Drunkenness was common, especially before the intense religious awakening in the 1830s brought temperance forward as a positive value. A trustee ruling at Williams College in 1823 forbade any alcohol to the students. Wine was excepted but was allowed only by special dispensation to a student obtaining commencement honors. This came about because of a particularly unfortunate end to a commencement evening that found the college privy burnt. The students' fondness for liquor at the University of Virginia led to the adoption of a dress code that proscribed wearing boots. For students sent them out for mending with empty bottles and the cobblers returned them with full ones.[47]

The Yale Report recognized that the age of the students demanded some restraining influence. The kinds and diversity of untried experience would be too tempting for the young student newly released from his parents' control. The report asserted that "it is necessary that some faithful and affectionate guardian take them by the hand, and guide their steps."[48] It concluded that as the college should act as substitute for the parent, the system of collegial control should resemble that of the family.

In practice, the concept of the college operating *in loco parentis* went far beyond direct physical discipline. At the University of Virginia, a rule was enacted whereby a student was required to deposit all of his money with the proctor. The proctor, for his services in holding it, received a commission of 2 percent of the students' money. Each student, upon leaving the university, was required to sign a declaration that he had made the required deposit. If he claimed to have withheld anything, the proctor was entitled to assess him, including the amount already received in commissions, a total of $12.00. If the student did not sign the declaration and did not report all of his assets, the fact was made known to the Chairman of the Faculty (president), the faculty in general, the Visitors (trustees), and, of course, the student's parents.[49] Thus, there emerged in the American college a system of organization that almost directly and by design paralleled the family. The father, the president, watched over the household: the uncles, the professors—some brothers to the president, other older sons—undertook to instruct the children in the facts of life—Latin, Greek, mathematics, and the natural sciences. The children learned to become good men.

The president, as head of the collegial community, was the most important figure in the American academic community. Education, as a matter of human contact rather than mastery of subjects, relied heavily on the presence of the college president. As the usually autocratic head of the faculty and the professor of moral philosophy, he had a profound effect on the college and the students. A man of long tenure in the presidency sometimes in a real sense became the college. Mark Hopkins, a year before his death in 1887, discovered while going through the records of the college, that he had taught 1695 of the 1726 living alumni of the college. As Williams approached its centennial, Hopkins found that he had had three-quarters of all Williams graduates, living and dead, before him in the classroom.[50]

Eliphalet Nott's inability to unperplex the financial affairs of the college from his own gave his enemies enough ammunition to almost send him down in total disgrace at the end of his own career as president of Union College. Nott tried to remove John Austin Yates, Professor of Oriental Languages, from the college in 1848 while attempting to transform Union from a college into a university. Nott wanted to remove an enemy from the faculty who was about to prove an embarrassment with his insistence upon marrying a woman of suspect reputation. This led to one of the nastiest battles in the history of American higher education. Yate's connections in Albany opened an investigation into the financial affairs of the college that threatened to leave both Nott and Union devastated. With the weapons of calumny, invective, and falsified evidence, Nott's opponents demonstrated that he had over the years, converted almost a million dollars of college funds to his own ends. The bemused Dr. Nott, as incapable of understanding the distinction between the college's finances and his own as he was of understanding the difference between the college and himself, was eventually cleared of the charges before the state legislature committee conducting the investigation in 1853. Nott then gave to the college property valued at $600,000, certain lands that figured significantly in the charges against him, and forgave the college debts that the accounts showed were clearly owed him. In short, at the end of his life, he left everything to the academic family.[51]

As part of the collegiate family, the faculty assumed a major role in the disciplinary process. Faculties, in the early part of the century, usually consisted of a few professors supplemented by a larger group of transient tutors. The tutors were usually young graduates of the colleges at which they were teaching. Since graduate schools as training grounds for college teachers did not yet exist, any college graduate was immediately qualified to teach—just as he would be qualified to follow a number of other professions. Frequently, the young tutor would continue some sort of informal study under one of the older professors, but the necessity for holding advanced degrees or for advanced study did not exist.[52]

In light of the purposes of the early American colleges, the logic of retaining the college's own graduates is clear. The assumption that the colleges' purpose was to pass on to the student a specific form of "truth" made it necessary that the teachers have unshakable faith in what they taught. Appointing a faculty who had proved its ability to accept the truth in the form the college accepted when they were students was a guarantee of the purity of the effort. The quality of the faculty member was measured by his religious orthodoxy as much as or more than by his Latin and Greek. Even the most eminent American man of letters of the time, Ralph Waldo Emerson, was unacceptable to Harvard. In addition to never being offered a professorship there which would have been due him, he was never invited back to speak at Harvard after offending the faculty and administration with his Phi Beta Kappa oration, "The American Scholar," on August 31, 1837, and his address to the Harvard Divinity School on July 15, 1838, in which he discussed the mythos of Christianity. Thomas Cooper, probably the most capable scientist in America at the time, found it impossible to gain a teaching position in a college because of his liberal religious views. Not even the intercession of Thomas Jefferson on his behalf was enough to overcome the antipathy of the officials of the University of Virginia to Cooper's radicalism. Cooper finally was offered the presidency of the University of South Carolina in 1821, but his administration quickly became a series of constant squabbles with the local clergy.[53]

Scholarship was not a requirement for teaching in the American college, and the wrong kind of scholarship could be a definite detriment to an academic career. George Bancroft, while still an undergraduate at Harvard, was urged by Edward Everett and President Kirkland to pursue Biblical studies in Germany. To this end, the Harvard Corporation awarded him a $700 scholarship for three years study. Bancroft, hoping for an appointment to the Harvard faculty on his return, assured his supporters that he would not allow his faith to be shaken by Germanic Biblical criticism. He received the PhD from Göttingen in 1820, but did not get the appointment he expected because of the obvious influence Germany had had on him. Indeed, his affectation of Continental manners was found so obnoxious that he alienated most of his friends upon his return.[54] He, of course, later made a career as a politician, ambassador, and historian.

Through the nineteenth century, German learning was generally recognized as the acme of scholarship.[55] By 1837, the influence of German scholarship was making itself felt in America's classical colleges. But prior to the 1850s, few Americans had been exposed to Germanic scholarship. From 1789 to 1851, Göttingen had enrolled only forty American students. Halle had only sixteen from 1826 to 1849. Leipzig had but two. Royal Friedrich Wilhelm's forty-nine American students enrolled from 1825 to 1850 included two that had transferred from Halle and four from Göttingen.[56] These early seekers brought back small commitment to arcane knowledge. The early American explorers into the realms of Germanic criticism were not prepared to face the realities of German *Lehrfrieheit* and retreated into the safety of studying the ancient languages.[57]

Occasionally, there appeared a man like Francis James Child who studied in Europe from 1840 to 1851 and whose remarkable scholarship was considered an asset to Harvard which appointed him Boylston Professor of Rhetoric and Oratory on his return from Europe. But a far more typical reaction to the idea of scholarship was that received by a candidate for a professorship at Illinois College. When the man told the trustees that he wished time for study, he was rejected, "for the board said that they wanted no man who had to study his lessons. They wanted a professor who already knew all that he had to teach."[58]

The established degree held by college professors was the in-course master's degree. These credentials were conferred upon graduates of a college after they had been awarded a bachelor's degree and had paid a small fee. Frederick A. P. Barnard, in lamenting the low quality of the degree, observed "that the degree of Master of Arts is significant of nothing at all, except of the fact that the recipient has been graduated before."[59] Harvard was probably the first school that required work beyond the BA for the MA. It began requiring one year of study beyond the baccalaureate in 1872. This was the same year it established a PhD program.[60] The other colonial schools, Princeton, Yale, Brown, the University of Pennsylvania, and Columbia, soon followed in awarding the master's degree only on an earned basis.[61]

The group of academics that came closest to representing any real specialization, the science professors, reflected the disregard for intensive study in a limited area in the classical college. Science professors were a transient group in the American college and held comparatively low status in the academic hierarchy. Their salaries were almost always less than those of other professors; financial difficulties of the schools frequently caused them to be dropped in order to save the ancient languages which were regarded as essential to the college.[62] They, however, probably had more options than their generalist colleagues. Developing American industry and government had more need for scientists than for translators and teachers of the ancient languages.

Although discipline took a great part of the teacher's time, it was only a part of his duties. The lack of any intense specialization in the classical curriculum, and the rigid and traditional means by which it was taught, meant that one man could teach a wide variety of subjects.[63] The small size of the student population on each campus and the general poverty of the colleges made it mandatory that he do so. At the first meeting of the Regents of the University of Michigan, June 6, 1837, it was resolved that there should be a professor of mental philosophy who would also be in charge of moral philosophy, natural theology, rhetoric, oratory, logic, and the history of *all* religion. A professor of mathematics who also had charge of engineering and architecture was appointed at the same time.[64]

The lack of specialization in the antebellum college is not surprising. The highest earned degree that college teachers held was the same as that for which they were educating students—the bachelor's and the in-course master's. Because of the patterns of influence in the development of the American college, the curriculum that the professor taught was the same as that he had taken at his college, and he was perfectly prepared to teach what he had learned. In addition, the emphasis on character building rather than the transfer of information and skills made the teacher's example of the *total man* more important than any specific body of knowledge he might have to disseminate.

Perhaps because any college graduate was considered qualified, assuming his denominational orthodoxy, to teach virtually anything the classical college offered, the salaries of the unspecialized and interchangeable professors was low. The low pay of the professors was necessary for the survival of the classical college. The increasing rift between the education offered by the colleges and the needs of the nation was reflected in their decreasing enrollments. Students were necessary if the colleges were to remain open and were offered lowered or even free tuition when it became evident that the college and the classical curriculum could not attract those willing to submit themselves to the discipline. In a real sense, the professors began to subsidize the colleges.

There were two major reasons for the development of a system by which the students rather than the professors were paid. The public interpretation of the classical curriculum as an elitist and aristocratic symbol led directly to attempts by the colleges to adopt a popular appearance. Also, the number of available students who wished to pursue the classical curriculum and who could afford it was much lower than the capacity of the colleges to educate them. Since the major source of funding for professorial salaries was tuition, any cut in tuition was reflected in corresponding cuts in salaries. The states felt at best only sporadic obligation to allocate money to support colleges, and the munificence of private benefactors more often led to the erection of monumental buildings or the establishment of scholarships for poor boys than to endowments for faculty salaries.

Even the inadequate salaries were frequently not paid in full. Paying professors in arrears, or having the faculty share what might be left over when all other obligations of the college had been met were general practices. Paying in produce donated by local farmers or relying on the charity of a professor's friends to keep him day to day were also frequently used to ease the financial strain. In addition to salary cuts, dividing a dead or retired professor's teaching assignments among his colleagues with no increase in their own compensation was a common practice. Exhibiting a spirit of Christian sacrifice, the faculty of Indiana University in 1848 apportioned the responsibilities of a vacant mathematics chair among its members and requested the governing board to use the money thus saved to purchase books and scientific apparatus. Occasionally, a man of independent means felt the call to teach. Assuming he was a good Christian and his orthodoxy of the sort that the trustees found pleasing, his offer was accepted. Edward Lasell, Professor of Chemistry at Williams College from 1835 to 1852, accepted a salary of $200 a year which he returned to the college in the form of books and scientific equipment that the college could not afford.[65]

It was generally understood that the purpose of the college and the position of the professor in society were such that the prestige was in some way a more adequate reward than money for this Christian labor. The notion that the professor's salary should be in some way based on his success at teaching was rejected by at least one 1831 commentator:

> This is plausible in theory, and doubtless has occasionally been found to be the fact. It is not likely to occur, however, if the professor be held rigidly responsible, and if the tenure of his office be on good behavior instead of for life. It is to be calculated, likewise, that every professor is a gentleman, and that the honour of the situation is a part of his emolument. There should be sufficient guarantee that his duties will be performed energetically, and that his behavior will be courteous. Should this not be the case, he is unfit for his situation, and the trustees should have moral courage enough to remove him.[66]

Without tenure, and frequently underpaid—if he was paid—the college professor had to make much of "the honour of the situation." Professors at the University of Michigan relied on the prospects of the institution to carry them through the 1840s and 1850s when their salaries of $700 a year paid in warrants had to be sold below face value because the regents lacked the resources to redeem them at full value. The faculty finance committee felt that the prestige was enough at Wheaton College that the faculty could be paid at an average rate of 86 percent of official salaries through the last two decades of the nineteenth century.[67]

The methods of instruction employed by these teachers relied heavily upon common textbooks and the lectures of the faculty. From 1800 on, earlier modes of textbook reading and recitation were increasingly replaced by the lecture method. The lectures were felt to be a better method than recitation because "they give that light and spirit to the subject, which awaken the interest and candor of the student. They may place before him the

principles of science in the attractive dress of living eloquence."
But frequent—even daily—examination and recitation were required to insure that the student had not merely listened
passively to the lectures and thus "his steady and earnest efforts" were secured.[68]

Even commentators who considered the textbook to be of
minor importance in the educational effort insisted that the
forms of recitation and examination be adhered to rather than
the modern forms of discussion. The ideal of education remained
the receipt of authoritative knowledge whether delivered by an
author or a lecturer. Though the lecture method became increasingly popular as the century progressed, the lecture was viewed
as simply a more democratic alternative to the textbook: "The
student will, of course, be understood to come prepared for the
examination on the subject of the lecture, as delivered *ex
cathedra.*" The method reduced the necessity for reading but retained the ritual by which textbook reading was measured.

The same anonymous reviewer of *The Journal of the Proceedings of a Convention of Literary and Scientific Gentlemen*, who
required such attention of the students also affirmed the value
of memorization and the principle of drill:

> We believe the very best system of instruction, where it can be
> adopted, is:—to recapitulate the subject of the previous lecture,
> and, after the lecture of the day, to examine the class thoroughly
> on the last lecture but one. In this manner, the facts and theories
> of a science are impressed three times, upon the memory of the
> pupil; and if, after this, he is unable to retain them, he must be
> pronounced incorrigible. This plan we consider to be the superla-
> tive; and to this conclusion we are led, not from theory simply,
> but from practice.[69]

That pedagogy relied heavily on the textbook and on the pronouncements of the professors. The emphasis was placed on the
memorization of received knowledge; the analysis of divergent
opinion and conflicting facts was unknown.

The attitude and methods of the American college militated
against the concept of academic freedom. A curriculum that
allowed no divergent views; a faculty that had no need for
freedom of inquiry because it did not engage in research; and a
necessity to pass on to the students a unified vision of the world

unencumbered by contradictions and bearing the distinctive impress of the college made conflict of opinion intolerable.[70] The one course offered that would seem by nature to encourage thought in the form of analysis of alternatives—moral philosophy—shared the intellectual constrictions. The American moral philosophers affirmed man's competence to perceive right through reason. No authority was necessary to find universal laws because all men possessed the means to discover them by application of reason to nature.[71] As natural law was universal, however, only one correct solution could be drawn. Mark Hopkins drew upon "a reservoir of faith, an abiding conviction, [and] a capacity for transferring his confidence in God's rule to others" in his ardent opposition to David Hume. When one Williams professor, unable to find the works of Hume at the college, discovered that Hopkins had never read the philosopher, Hopkins was undisturbed. Later Darwin and Huxley were among the authors unread by Hopkins though repeatedly attacked from his pulpit.

Hopkins found early in his career that teaching moral philosophy had little to do with learning and could be antithetical to true scholarship because that might confuse issues. After a desultory attempt at the German philosophers, Hopkins abandoned learning to rely on his own reason and ability as a teacher. Hopkins's antiintellectualism stemmed from an attempt to set aside the theological construct of Calvinism and return to experience as the basis of action.[72] Emphasizing thought rather than reading in developing the *total man* resulted in few demands by the students and few more from the faculty for adequate college libraries.

Other antebellum presidents shared this view of the educational process. Eliphalet Nott once opened a class in moral philosophy by announcing:

> Young Gentlemen. Your studies are intended to be such as are calculated immediately to improve the mind... There are many, I have no doubt, in this class, as there are in all classes, who can't be persuaded to think. Them I could probably forward most by giving them longer lessons. But it has been my endeavor these twenty years, since I have had the care of youth, to make men rather than great scholars. I shall not give you long lessons, but shall lead you to exercise your own minds in much thought.

Seniors should act for themselves. . . . It is easy to read, nothing
is easier. The folly of most people is that they read too much. You
should read but little, and turn that to the best account.[73]

Francis Wayland, although classifying himself as a Calvinist,
admitted he had never read Calvin—or anything else of contro-
versial theology. (He advised a student having difficulty
reading Paley, Chalmers, and Butler to take a long walk and
forget theology.[74])

Reading occupied a small place in the educational process of
the old colleges, and the library occupied a small place in the college's life. Until well after the Civil War, what research was accomplished at the American colleges and universities was done
in special departmental collections or the private libraries of the
professors. The college library was regarded largely as a book
museum. President Arthur Twining Hadley of Yale remembered in 1909 having had "one of the more enlightened professors of the old school" say to him, "I conceive that the chief
educational use of a university library is to lend an occasional
book to a professor who does not happen to have that book in
his own library."[75]

Even in cases where reading by students was in some degree
encouraged, the alternatives were extremely circumscribed. Intellectual curiosity was not of high positive value in the American college[76], and the kind of intellectual expansion encouraged
by large and diversified collections was actively discouraged in
the few cases where the college library was large enough to
allow satisfaction of a wide range of reading interest. In 1832,
the Harvard Board of Overseers Visiting Committee to Examine the Library reported back to the board their view of the
proper role of the library in undergraduate education. They
strongly disapproved of "indiscriminate use of the library by
Undergraduates." Undergraduates, they felt, were more often
lured to books "by the splendor of their binding, or the beauty
of the engravings" than by the importance of the contents.
Rather, students should be given a selection of the library's
treasures. Five hundred volumes suitable for undergraduate
use should be all they would be allowed save with the written
permission of a member of the faculty.[77] Aside from exhibiting a
basic distrust of the quality of undergraduates and their intel-

lectual powers, the committee's recommendation points out a basic assumption of college life of the period: students' reading should be circumscribed and prescribed by the faculty. The student who went beyond the established curriculum had to be controlled carefully.

The combination of poverty, reliance on highly structured and frequently ritualized methods of instruction, and an anti-intellectualism that rejected both broad reading and specialization in favor of acculturation had an obvious effect on nineteenth-century college libraries. The library of the classical college was a marginal ornament to most institutions. Buildings, scientific apparatus, and even faculty salaries took precedence in line for the pittance with which most colleges had to function. Even when the governing boards of the newer state colleges attempted to gain marginal support for their libraries, they were overruled by higher budgeting authorities. From its founding in 1868, the West Virginia University Board of Regents habitually requested from the state legislature the munificent sum of about $2000 for a library. They received little or nothing to that purpose and in 1882 complained to the governor that the opinions of the regents and the state legislature were at odds. They had asked for $2500 for the library the year before and only $300 was given. It would be good, they thought, to have more support in this area: "While the sum asked for this purpose is not essential to the life of the institution, as all the amounts asked for most other purposes, an extensive library is necessary to its healthful activity."[78] The regents did not get the money and the college limped along for many years.

In the private institutions, the regents took on the role of the state legislatures in appropriating money. North Central College in Plainfield (later Naperville), Illinois was founded in 1861 by the Evangelical Society of North America. By 1868, the library counted forty-five volumes. In 1869, the members of the board of trustees realized that they must act on the situation. They requested that the faculty have their photographs taken and sold to provide funds for the library. Finding that this did not generate sufficient income, they appointed a committee of the faculty to investigate the situation at the library. The committee reported in November, 1885. It recommended that an appeal be made to congregations and ministers for books and money and that a fund be established; anyone giving $1.00 would have either his name written into a book in the library or receive a certificate for the gift.[79] This, at least, was a more positive response than that of Bucknell University. Bucknell's trustees—all men raised in the traditions of the classical college—could see no real need for a library. Their typical response to library funding well into the twentieth century was to authorize the president to raise money by soliciting donations.[80]

The colleges' responses to the need for a library was usually inadequate, yet many people recognized that a strong library was vital to higher education. Samuel Osgood, delegate from the Providence Athenaeum, addressed the 1853 conference of librarians held in New York with a common complaint:

> Proud as we are of our four or five great libraries, there is not one of them, not even that of Harvard University, my own cherished Alma Mater, that affords the requisite means for the thorough study of any one topic of recondite learning, even, if of practical science. Any scholar who tries to investigate any ancient or historical subject will find, to his regret, that no library in the country has a plummet that can sound its depths.

Reasons for this were apparent even to contemporary observers. Edward Edwards defended Americans against those who[81] ascribed the lack of resources to a "disregard of literature of the higher order." Edwards perceived that the real reason was the obvious necessity for Americans to clear the frontier before erecting cultural monuments. The frontier society of antebellum America simply lacked the resources necessary to finance both survival and cultural parity with the Old World.[82]

Even had budgets been adequate and the impulse to scholarship extant, it is unlikely that the situation of the American college library would have been much improved in any immediate way. Until the end of the first quarter of the nineteenth century, bookselling and publishing were essentially local businesses. Retail stores operated by publishers were the principal means of distribution, and publishers exchanged their products with one another to give their stores a more diverse stock. As the century progressed, publishing and bookselling increasingly became more specialized, separate activities, and direct purchase from publishers became the standard method of stocking, along with various import channels. But for most of the antebellum period, books were difficult to acquire, especially by frontier colleges founded far from the paths of commerce. When the University of Mississippi opened its doors in 1848, for example, it was so far from the established lines of trade that even textbooks were unobtainable.[83]

The practice of appropriating specific sums for the library (although not providing continuing funds for growth) and the difficulties of identifying specific items for purchase because of the inadequacies of nineteenth-century trade bibliography made it necessary for colleges, when they had money for books, to send someone to buy them. A $10,000 gift to Ohio Wesleyan sent the president, Edward Thomson, to New York and Europe in the summer of 1854 to purchase books. He returned with approximately 3000 volumes and a curious philosophy of building a college library. He avoided purchasing current materials in favor of "rare and valuable works." The former could always be procured, but it was important for the college to acquire the latter. Common books could be found anywhere, but the rare was the proper object of collecting for the college library: "If one goes to the library for Gibbon, he is disappointed if he do [sic] not find it; but the disappointment is not a serious one; for he may find the books, perhaps, in the first respectable house he enters." But in case of rare items, this is not true and it was the duty of the college to obtain them.[84]

The attitude that the college library was for reference rather than reading and for supplementing professors' libraries rather than operating as an active force in the education of students was reflected in the kinds of libraries that were built. Hence, Thomson returned with books related to the curriculum, but hardly suitable for Ohio Wesleyan students. Mathematics texts in French, highly technical treatises on various subjects, many travel books, and little history or literature characterized his selections. Thomson had exhausted the funds for continuing acquisitions, so he circulated a letter asking American authors for copies of their books. Clearly his belief that the more common books "can be purchased at any time" was not accurate in this case. For almost twenty years, all that the college bought were a few periodical subscriptions that were cancelled and resubscribed with abandon.[85]

One of the more interesting cases in building collections was that of the University of Michigan. The first purchase for the library was made by the regents in 1839, when $970 was authorized for Audubon's *Birds of America*. It was not discovered until much later that the copy purchased had only four volumes of the work. The text volumes which had been published separately to avoid the depository requirements of British copyright were missing. The appropriateness of such a purchase for an embryonic college library, of course, depends on subsequent acquisitions. In the case of Michigan, acquisitions at least continued.

Michigan's early regents did not feel that one book—no matter how valuable—was sufficient for their college, and Asa Gray provided them with the opportunity to expand their collection. Gray had been hired as professor of botany and zoology in 1838 from Harvard but insisted on a year's leave first to tour Europe before assuming his position. The regents commissioned him to purchase books for the library. For this, they gave him $5000 for books and $1500 for travel expenses as well as his salary of $1500 for the year. Gray wanted to purchase scientific equipment with this money, but was finally persuaded to return with a balanced college library collection. When he reached London, he commissioned George Palmer Putnam, a partner in the publishing firm of Wiley and Putnam, to select and acquire the library at a 5 percent commission. When Gray completed his tour of Europe, he returned to New York with the purchases and had them sent on to Michigan. Since the university had not yet opened its doors, Gray remained in New York occupying his time with a variety of activities on suspended salary until he returned to Harvard in 1842, never having assumed his duties at Michigan.

Granting Gray a commission was a necessary inducement to persuade him to come to Michigan, but his firm belief in the need to emphasize the sciences at all levels of education and his view that the entire allocation of $5000 should be spent on scientific books and apparatus made him a poor choice at best to entrust with the development of a library for what was essentially a classical college. So, perhaps, it was fortunate in the end that Putnam's services were available to Gray. Aside from some unnecessary duplication of titles, the collection Gray assembled was an appropriate one for the University of Michigan beginnings.

As in other cases, the Regents of the University of Michigan felt that their initial efforts were sufficient and failed to make subsequent appropriations to the library for many years. By the late 1840s, professors found themselves increasingly burdened by having to purchase their own copies of new publications and having to maintain their own subscriptions to standard periodicals.[86]

After the initial purchases, most college libraries were maintained—if at all—by gifts. Even the largest library in the country suffered. John Langdon Sibley reported that when he became librarian of Harvard in 1856, the total fund for binding and purchasing books and periodicals was $250 per year. A substantial sum compared to the funds available to most other colleges, it was hardly enough to sustain Harvard's collection of approximately 75,000 volumes and 3000 unbound pamphlets. Sibley, like many other librarians and college presidents of the period, was forced to resort to mendicancy:

> I began to beg for the library. Appeals were made to authors for their books and pamphlets. I asked people to send whatever they had that was printed, whether they considered it good for anything or not. "Clean out your garrets and closets, send me the contents." And with such earnestness did I plead, that I literally had boxes and barrels sent to me, and once I received a butter-firkin. Almost always I got something precious which I had for years been trying to obtain. . . . I acquired the name of being a sturdy beggar, and received a gentle hint from the College Treasurer to desist from begging, which I *as gently* disregarded. Long before the century closed, it was found necessary to shelve the galleries of Gore Hall, to fill all the vacant places, and provide a larger building.[87]

Sibley's collection development practices probably contributed to his eventual fall from grace with President Charles W. Eliot. Eliot, upon viewing the small but well-selected collection of 8000 volumes of the University of Colorado in the mid-1890s, is reported to have lamented that Harvard had not started with a view toward usefulness in collecting books. He felt that the sins of the past had placed Harvard at a disadvantage in its facility: "Let the administration be never so perfect, Harvard Library must always confuse the average student with its collections of incongruous donations begotten in the relic period of library economy."[88]

Even when the amount of useless material received by a library was not sufficient to create confusion from sheer clutter, the attitude of establishing memorials rather than useful collections tended to obscure the purposes for which books were used. In 1837, the Board of Trustees of the University of Georgia acknowledged a gift of sixty-two volumes from William D. Watkins and entered into the minutes of their meeting that the collection was "considered more valuable on account of the meritorious and respectable source from which it emanates."[89] Ohio Wesleyan's reliance on gifts and its attitude toward both books and donors caused them to keep all bequests of private libraries together, each in its separate alcove inscribed with the donor's name.[90]

Alternatives to establishing large libraries were frequently explored by cost-conscious boards of trustees. The necessity for local self-sufficiency was recognized in the period before widespread interlibrary cooperation, but poverty frequently made this impossible even with the circumscribed curriculum and self-contained teaching methods of the time. When Ohio State University was founded in 1873, the presence of the state library in the same town was considered by the Board of Trustees in planning the facilities of the university. The state librarian was very cooperative in allowing both students and faculty members access to the library. The library was four miles from the campus, however, and the rules did not allow for the circulation of books. This arrangement proved quite inadequate and did not improve until the university developed facilities of its own.[91] Wheaton College solved the problem in a slightly different manner. The Reverend John Calvin Webster was Professor of Rhetoric, Logic, and Belles-Lettres, a chair largely endowed by his friends in the East. He came to Wheaton with a 1000 volume personal library that he made available to students and faculty. His arrival in Wheaton, Illinois, doubled the facilities available to the college.[92]

In addition to limited or marginal resources, access was a major problem in the early college library. John Boll found in his study of antebellum college libraries in New England, that the college library was "designed to keep readers and books apart."[93] The librarians of these colleges were most frequently not consulted in planning and constructing new buildings and facilities; had they been, the results would probably not have been appreciably different. Preservation rather than access was the major design criterion, and both the men acting as librarians and those designing the buildings held this view realizing it in the design of library buildings. A faculty committee at Harvard appointed to consider the situation of the library reported, April 18, 1859, on access to the books:

> Just beyond Mr. Sibley's office, there is a spacious and hand-some hall, about twenty roomy and comfortable alcoves, all well lighted, ventilated and warmed, furnished with many convenient tables and desks, but showing in many places an advertisement in large type, conspicuously posted up, announcing that "No person is allowed to enter," &c. Without obtaining the special leave from the Librarian, a student may not even seat himself at one of the tables in order to read or write, though most of them are unoccupied nine tenth [sic] of the time . . . The students' privileges in the body of the building are limited to a permission to walk up and down the long hall in the centre, consult the alcove lists, and admire the President's busts.[94]

Boll reported that Mr. Sibley approved of the arrangement, though the students did not.

Amherst in the 1840s kept its books in cases covered with white netting so they could not be touched by the casual student reader. The library was opened one hour a week when the students could obtain books. Amenities like tables or a reading room were absent.[95] Marshall College in Mercersburg, Pennsylvania, solved the problems of appointing a librarian and providing an accessible library room by distributing the books to the various professors in charge of the departments.[96]

There was a great deal of confusion between the reference and the circulation functions of college library. The dominant view that the library was a facility much like the chemical equipment or the collections of specimens maintained by the botany or geology professors was in direct conflict with the demands that were increasingly being made throughout the nineteenth century for reference help and the circulation of materials. The professor-librarian of the early period could not open the library for more than a few hours each week and still attend to his teaching and other duties. Student demands for books meant that they had to be allowed to remove books from the library room or building. But the removal was strictly controlled.

The college library, then, had clearly a marginal role in the educational enterprise of the American college. But this was not a role that even the most conservative educators considered best. Speaking through the medium of the influential Society for the Promotion of Collegiate and Theological Education at the West, Noah Porter of Yale deplored the situation of college libraries and urged their support. He compared libraries to mechanics' tools and deplored that, whereas, no one questioned the necessity for expensive and complicated tools at best ill understood by the nonpractitioner of the trades, some denied the need for college libraries. Porter affirmed the educational value of books and libraries in terms that may seem familiar to followers of the modern Library-College movement: "When the student-teacher seats himself in his library, all the good and wise men who have thought, and lectured, and written, on the subjects to which his mind and life are devoted, are present to converse with him."[97] Porter recognized the necessary relation of books to scholarship, but further, founded his plea on a principle of contingency. Admitting that college libraries were rarely used by undergraduates, he focused on the fact that they were sometimes so used, therefore the lack of books at a crucial moment in an undergraduate's intellectual life was more to be feared than the expense of collecting a large library.

Porter's argument, however, loses force when one examines his audience and the particular type of need for libraries that he envisioned. The society, as an organization formed for the promotion of Christian education, was a major force in the financial life of many frontier colleges. It was the Christian purpose that Porter emphasized in his plea: "If our Western colleges are to be saved from being seats of disorganization and fanaticism, of rash speculation and heretical dogmatisms, their libraries must be well furnished." He pointed to the large libraries of the

Jesuit colleges and asked how the Protestant colleges could be respected in the community with such splendid centers of learning available for comparison.[98]

Infidelity and Romanism, according to Porter, were the great antagonists of the frontier ministers and both had weapons stronger than the pure belief and divine inspiration available to the Protestant preacher:

> Infidelity and Romanism understand how to use their learning so as to produce a strong and deep impression on the people. They do not lock it up in libraries, nor confine it to books which scholars and recluses only will read; but they can make it intelligible and attractive to the common people. Audacious theories which turn the Old Testament into ridicule, and the New into a mythic nothing, are translated into English as vigorous as Cobbett's, and so illustrated and enforced that they sink deep into the minds of men of plain but strong sense, and half shake the faith of the devout believer.[99]

It was not a concern with the needs of scholarship and freedom of inquiry that Porter pled. It was rather for libraries as tools in the eternal struggle against evil. Protestantism must prevail and vanquish the heretics with their own weapons—learning.

The professor-librarians of the nineteenth-century American college have become a commonplace in the mythos of American librarianship. But assigning the care of the library to a professor was not universal in the classical college and did not derive from any feeling that the job of a librarian was in any way comparable to that of a professor. In the small colleges of nineteenth-century America, each participant in the educational endeavor had to assume whatever tasks were necessary. Care of the books owned by the college became the responsibility of whoever was available. Professors, tutors, students, and even college presidents assumed the job. But, for the most part, professors were the one group who were available and who were reliable enough to be entrusted with what represented a major portion of the college's wealth.

In most American colleges until the last quarter of the nineteenth century, there was no real distinction between the members of the faculty and the man who served as librarian. The academic community was for the most part a homogeneous group of men. President, professors, and tutors shared, to a high degree, a similar background and more importantly, a virtually identical education, usually at the same college.

Robert Downs's survey of college catalogs of the 1870s revealed that unless librarians were also members of the teaching faculty, they were listed with miscellaneous officers, such as museum curators and registrars. Downs found, though, that even at this date, joint appointments were common.[100] Earlier in the century, they were much more common. A college on the frontier with a collection of a few hundred volumes, a faculty of perhaps two with a president, attempting to educate a small group of semiliterate frontier youths in the intricacies of algebra and Latin gerunds had little need for a full-time librarian and less money to pay one. Accordingly, a member of the faculty took on the task as a natural addition to his teaching duties. The academic librarians in attendance at the 1853 librarians conference operated their libraries as a minor part of their academic occupation. Most of them took over the libraries as a matter of necessity—to supplement their meager salaries by the small amount given for such tasks as were necessary to keep the libraries of their various colleges open.[101]

When Longfellow came to Bowdoin in 1829, the Board of Trustees, staunchly Calvinist, distrusted his Unitarianism to such an extent that, although they did ultimately hire him, they offered him only $800—the salary of an instructor—rather than the salary that would have been due his position as professor of modern languages. To mollify him, the trustees appointed him librarian at an additional $100 a year. Longfellow's concern with the library reflected on the manner by which he was chosen for the task. Aside from a few complaints to those to whom he wrote on the time consumed in his duties—one hour each day during the week—the library found little mention in his correspondence of the period.[102] The salary appended to the library was not always as high as that awarded Longfellow. Robert Stewart Thomas, Professor of Metaphysics and English Literature at the University of Missouri, accepted the position of librarian as an additional duty in 1849 at $50 a year. His salary was paid from student fees until they were abolished in 1851 and he was paid from regular college funds.[103]

A number of colleges, however, had no salary appropriated

for the job. It was expected that the extra duties would be assumed as part of the natural duties of the faculty. Even though the Board of Trustees' Library Committee argued in 1845 and 1851 that adopting such a course would cause a lessening of the sense of responsibility of the appointee, the Prudential Committee of the Trustees of the University of Georgia voted that care of the library would rotate among the faculty each term. Even the president served. Roanoke College, through the antebellum period, rotated the library custodianship frequently. It was required that each member of the faculty serve as caretaker of some part of the college property each term. At the University of Mississippi, the post of librarian rotated among the faculty on a yearly basis from 1851 to 1885 with only two brief changes in 1876–82, when the job was taken by August Blomgren who also served as corresponding secretary and janitor for the college, and in 1883–84, when a senior student, John Howard Schumaker, accepted the job.[104]

Harvard was an exception to this rule. The modern academic librarian who knows nothing else of the distinguished history of his trade has heard the tale of John Langdon Sibley's meeting Harvard's President Charles W. Eliot in 1858. Sibley became the first assistant librarian at Harvard in 1825 after his graduation at a salary of $150 a year. The librarian, Charles Folsom, was paid $300. At the end of the year, the two salaries were combined and Benjamin Peirce was appointed librarian at about $600 a year. Peirce's wife supplemented the family income by boarding students.[105] Sibley turned to the Unitarian ministry for a time and then to the editorship of the *American Magazine of Useful and Entertaining Knowledge*. He enjoyed success at neither occupation. Happening to be in Cambridge during the movement of Harvard's library from Harvard Hall to the newly constructed Gore Hall in 1841, Sibley accepted the temporary position of assistant librarian again when it became evident that the design of the building made employment of a full-time assistant necessary. Harvard's library expanded quickly in Gore Hall and within a few years after Librarian Thaddeus William Harris died in 1856 and Sibley ascended to the post, the staff numbered at least five people including a few women.[106]

Sibley conducted the business of the library in much the same way as his contemporaries. The hours of opening were longer than most college libraries, but borrowers were not as a rule allowed direct access to the shelves and had to rely on the frequently unreliable card catalog for finding books. But Sibley, when confronted with a man of true scholarship, could abandon his rules to make the library more useful. He even bent those rules for the occasional exceptional undergraduate as when he visited a new freshman, Justin Winsor, in his rooms in 1849 and, impressed by the scholarship displayed by Winsor (later to become the preeminent academic librarian of the century) in his history of Duxbury, extended him unusual privilege in the library as a man of letters.[107]

Sibley, however, was not generally recognized as equal to the other members of Harvard's faculty. Only with difficulty did he convince the library board in 1847 that it should allow him at least to continue to take half of each college vacation—he had previously enjoyed the entire vacation—to travel to purchase books. Modern scholars have attempted to resurrect Sibley's reputation by the evidence of his scholarship as displayed in his *Harvard Graduates*.[108] Contemporary reception, particularly the comments of the trenchant James Russell Lowell, differed in the evaluation of Sibley's work. Lowell wrote to Jane Norton on September 19, 1874, that aside from efforts in learning Old French and Old English,

> My only reading has been Mr. Sibley's book of "Harvard Graduates," which is as unillumined, dry, and simple as the fourteenth-century prose of the Early English Texts. But it interests me and makes me laugh. It is the prettiest rescue of prey from Oblivion I ever saw. The gallant librarian, like a knight-errant, slays this giant, who carries us all captive sooner or later, and then delivers his prisoners. There are ninety-seven of them by tale, and as he fishes them out of those dismal *oubliettes* they come up dripping with the ooze of Lethe, like Curll from his dive in the Thames, like him also gallant competitors for the crown of Dulness. It is the very balm of authorship. . . . I do not know when the provincialism of New England has been thrust upon me with so ineradicable a barb.[109]

Clearly Mr. Sibley's contribution to the world of letters was not greatly appreciated by all his colleagues on the Harvard faculty.

A number of academic librarians functioned without any real

connection with the faculty. Thomas Jefferson tried to interest a professor at the University of Virginia in taking the duties of librarian for an additional reward of $50 a year. Jefferson had to settle for John Vaughn Kean at a salary of $150 a year in 1825. Jefferson's idea that the librarian should serve as a guide as well as a guard to the collection had to be abandoned. Kean became an effective guard, but a professor had to sign permission for a student to withdraw a book.

Kean was replaced the next year by a student, William Wertenbaker, who served—except for the periods 1831–35 and 1857–65—until 1881. Wertenbaker had few real duties as librarian and began taking on other jobs around the campus to supplement his income. At various times, he held almost every non-teaching position available at the University including assistant proctor, university postmaster, and bookstore manager. When he was appointed librarian, he was also given the position of secretary to the faculty. There was objection to the appointment of a student, but Wertenbaker's seriousness made him acceptable. Indeed, he was so stern that he aroused violent opposition when attempting to perform some of his diverse duties. Attempting to discipline students of approximately his own age was difficult, and his tendency to act as a martinet intensified the problem. Violent language and attacks directed against him were frequent in the earlier part of his career. A student was expelled in 1831 for repeatedly threatening to flog him.[110]

Henry Colclazer was appointed the first librarian of the University of Michigan in June, 1837, primarily because of his close friendship with the family of the president and his acquaintance with most of the members of the board of regents. After he came to Ann Arbor, he kept the library in his home for a time. By the time the Grey purchases arrived, Colclazer had been transferred by his denomination to Detroit and the regents hired a reformed newspaperman and bookseller, George Corselius, to catalog the collection. The catalog was completed in 1841 when Colclazer returned to take up his duties again. By 1845, Colclazer's inattendance to duty was so marked that the regents dismissed him in order to appoint a professor to the post. The work performed at the library during Colclazer's term of office was done by students acting as assistants to Colclazer.[111]

Perhaps the best known clergyman-librarian of the nineteenth century was the Reverend Beverley Robinson Betts who served Columbia from 1865 until his replacement by Melvil Dewey in 1883. Betts was a minister and the son of one of Columbia's trustees. Though he resigned his post as rector of a church in Maspeth, Long Island, in 1869, he never devoted his total attention to the Columbia library. He remained active for many years in the New York Genealogical and Biographical Society serving at various times as its librarian, editing its quarterly *Record*, and serving on its Publications Committee as well as writing numerous papers on genealogy and heraldry. The trustees, when hiring Betts, conceived his role as custodial. Betts was to see that specified books were purchased from the limited funds available and that the library was kept open for a few hours each week. Although Betts had no special qualifications for the post, the trustees felt this to be no problem.[112]

Betts took no part in the major professional movement of his time, the founding of the American Library Association, and had little or no contact with other librarians. He viewed his job as principally helping students and considered his role in the academic scheme as teaching about books.[113] Superficially, this may seem to be a modern attitude, but there is evidence that Betts's commitment to the library's role in education was unrealized. When John W. Burgess came to Columbia to teach political science in 1876, he was disappointed in the library. Though the college was over a century old, there were only about 25,000 volumes in the library, few of which, he felt, were worth the space in which they were stored. The building was completely inhospitable for library use; the catalog of the collection was completely inadequate. Worse, the sole caretaker of the library was Betts "who crept up to the building about eleven o'clock in the morning and kept the library open for the drawing of books about one hour and a half daily." To Burgess, Betts typified all that was evil in librarians. He "seemed displeased when anyone asked for a book and positively forbidding when asked to buy one."

Betts made the mistake of telling Burgess with some pride that he had returned $500 of the year's appropriation for books to the trustees because it was unneeded. Burgess was upset. He had recently been before the trustees asking for several thousand dollars to modernize the history and political science collections. Burgess immediately went to President Barnard and asked that the money Betts had returned be given over for the binding of Hansard's *Debates in Parliament.* Barnard complied without comment and Burgess made an enemy of Betts who considered him "disloyal to the college." The "old school" as represented by Betts was so well entrenched that it took Burgess's "new school" seven years to win the battle.[114] The aggressive demand for resources was not yet strong enough at Columbia even past the 1870s to change the view of the library as a storehouse for the college's books presided over by a guard. But the end was near for Betts and the enmity of Burgess, to a great extent, caused it.

Students represented a major source of nineteenth-century academic librarians. It would seem logical that a student working his way through school should assume the duties of librarian as a part-time position. Although many of the students working in nineteenth-century libraries were to some degree under the direction of a faculty member who retained the title of "Librarian," a number enjoyed the position of professor-librarian and reported directly to the president or faculty library committee.

From its beginnings through the 1850s, the library of Antioch College was cared for by a series of impoverished students. When Horace Mann died in 1859 and was replaced as president by Thomas Hill, the faculty and president took an increasing role in the library routines. Hill took the book selection duties that Mann had exercised and the faculty extended its influence in the daily operations by voting to extend borrowing privileges, recalling overdue books, withholding degrees for the payment of library fines, and establishing hours of operation. For the fall of 1860, the faculty appointed a professor to take charge of the library and allowed him a student assistant. The faculty retained tight administrative control, though.[115]

Nepotism was also a major determinant in the choice of a college librarian, as was frequently apparent in many academic relations. At Waco University (later Baylor), the only recorded librarian until 1879 was Richard B. Burleson an 1843 graduate of the University of Nashville, a minister and former president of Moulton Female Academy, professor of moral and mental philosophy and belles lettres at Waco from 1856 to 1861, and the younger brother of the president. From 1861 to his death in 1879, he was vice-president of the university and professor of natural sciences as well as serving as librarian.[116] The librarian of the University of Michigan during the 1850s was John L. Tappan, son of the reformer president, Henry L. Tappan. Both Tappans left the college when Henry was exiled.[117]

After twenty years of operating with only a small collection of a few hundred books, the library of the University of Washington received as a gift the collection of the Seattle City Library in 1881. This, coupled with a slight increase in revenue for books, made it necessary that a librarian be hired. The president of the university, being assured that the library had support, had his son, Louis P. Anderson, a member of the junior class, appointed librarian. He held the post until his graduation in 1882.[118]

Whatever their other roles in the colleges and universities, librarians displayed little or no professional awareness or consciousness that they filled a distinct position in American higher education. The 1853 librarians' conference attracted a total of eighty-three attendees. Only twelve of these were associated with academic institutions. Only nine institutions were represented and only nine of the academic men present were acting as librarians.[119]

Charles Coffin Jewett wrote to Seth Hastings Grant on August 16, 1853, while planning the 1853 conference and expounded his view of the typical American librarian:

> The fact is our fraternity are generally very quiet, unostentatious men, not accustomed to public speaking, or fond of exhibiting themselves. Besides, our pursuits are not of such nature as to reward our labors by brilliant discourses, or results that will resound in the busy world. We must work hard and long, with small visible effect, and in the track where hundreds, more learned than ourselves perhaps, have worked before us. More than all this, there are but few—very few—who have devoted themselves professionally to bibliography. This is taken up by the young man for a few years till he can "get something better to do" or assumed as an extra labor to eke out the income of some half paid professor.[120]

Clearly, Jewett harbored no illusions about the readiness of American librarians to form a vital professional association at the time of the conference. As it came about, he was quite correct.

The part-time academic librarian had little or no control over the operations of the library for most of the nineteenth century. His task was to carry out the directives of the official governing agent—usually either the faculty library committee or the president of the college. These bodies exercised close control over library business. The library committee of Columbia in the 1870s met quarterly to deliberate on such matters as lists of books recommended for purchase by the president to the librarian. Usually, if the prices of the books were given, the lists were approved, but frequently enough, the decision was deferred till the next meeting three months away. Periodical subscriptions and appropriations for binding books were also approved or rejected by the committee.[121]

The president's direct influence on the library was greater than that of any other member of the academic community. Horace Mann, president of Antioch from 1854 to 1859, was a strong library supporter who assumed almost complete responsibility for book selection and purchase. Because of the limited budget for such purposes, he wrote directly to authors requesting autographed copies of their books. Occasionally, these requests were answered. Mann's view of the function of the college library was such that he purchased only nonfiction, and most of that biographical works and a few books of poetry. Fiction and scientific works were avoided.[122]

Occasionally, the presidential hand in book purchasing led to potential or actual disaster. When $1250 was appropriated by the Board of Trustees of the University of Missouri in 1849, the president, John Hiram Lathrop, a Yale graduate, was sent to St. Louis to buy books. He spent $350 in various shops for items that were in stock and placed $900 in a bank to await the arrival of other titles ordered through a bookseller. The bank was immediately robbed. Fortunately, the money was ultimately recovered and the books purchased. Less fortunate was Roanoke College President David F. Bittle. Bittle also served as libarian for the college and was an avid collector of books for the library. Toward the end of the Civil War, he found that the college creditors refused to take the approximately $1000 in Confederate currency that represented the institution's solvency. He set out for Richmond to purchase books with it, but as he rode into town, the Confederacy collapsed.[123]

Even in the best of circumstances, the practice of placing total responsibility for book selection in the hands of one man could easily lead to unfortunate results. When the library and philosophical equipment of the University of Georgia were destroyed by fire in 1831, the president, a minister, was sent North by the trustees who had appropriated $3000 for replacement. The president returned with a library appropriate for a theological seminary, but hardly suitable to a state university.[124]

At times the president's role in the library went beyond his nominal responsibilities as patriarch and filled a necessary position in the college library. Though Western Maryland College in Westminster, Maryland, was founded in 1867, it was not until 1872 that an official college library was established. The trustees, apparently considered the libraries collected and maintained by the student literary and debating societies sufficient even though their collections were mostly novels. The Reverend J. T. Ward, a minister who had retired because of failing health, filled the gap when he accepted the presidency of the college at its founding and opened his private library to students. Ward even went so far as to circulate his books and bought a set of *Living Age* and the ninth edition of the *Encyclopaedia Britannica* because they would be useful to the students.[125]

But the president's varied roles in the classical college only infrequently included any direct contact with the library. The librarian, as a rule, could not bring the kind of autocratic power exercised by the college presidency to bear on the problems of the library. The nineteenth-century academic librarian had, aside from the clerical responsibility of keeping track of the books and assuring that the rules of the college were followed, little or no responsibility for, or influence on, the policies that he followed. Whether chosen from the ranks of professors, students, presidential relatives, or general lackeys around the college, he faithfully followed the directions handed down to him.

This is nowhere more apparent than in the librarians' involvement—or lack of involvement—in the planning of library buildings. John Boll's study of the first library buildings at Harvard, Yale, Williams, Amherst, Wesleyan, Mount Holyoke, and Brown concluded that the administrative hierarchy of the nineteenth-century American college isolated the librarian from the decisions that determined his working conditions. Boll found that, in each case, it was usually a committee of trustees that determined the shape and planned the building. The trustees, as the controlling force in the New England college, took responsibility and authority for financial and building matters. Frequently, this activity went beyond the mere provision of money and authorization for new projects and projected into areas that later would become controlled by faculty committees, administrators, contractors, and even librarians.

The Western college departed from this pattern somewhat but still allowed the librarian little or no influence in the realm of planning. When Ohio Wesleyan received a gift of $10,000 for books, provided that $15,000 could be raised for a building, a building committee was formed composed of Dr. Edward Thomson, the president, and the Reverend Frederic Merrick, a professor, who was appointed chief fund raiser for the project. The college architect, Morris Caldwalleder, was sent East to visit a number of college library buildings to aid in formulating his plans. The building was dedicated in the fall of 1854 and marked not only a change in the location of the library, but a change in librarians. But neither Tullius Clinton O'Kane who served from 1852 to 1854 nor Samuel Wesley Williams who took over in the new building and served till 1857 seem to have been consulted in planning the new facility. Indeed, they probably did not take part in or even attend the dedication ceremonies. Expert advice in planning the new building would probably have made the facility much more useful. Not until 1872 were chairs available for readers and at least forty years passed before the librarian had anything other than a small cabinet to use for a desk. The building housed the college library, the library and meeting rooms of the four literary societies, and the painting gallery.[126]

* * * * * *

The position of the librarian in the classical college that dominated higher education in America until the last quarter of the nineteenth century was a minor one. There was little or no feeling on the part of college officers that any special qualifications were necessary in the person chosen as librarian. Further, and perhaps more importantly, there was little or no feeling by those who served as college librarians that any special qualifications were necessary or that there was any special distinction in being the librarian.

There seems to have been a slight tendency to prefer that a responsible person be charged with the task of caring for the library, perhaps because the books represented a substantial portion of the college wealth. Partially for this reason, appointing a professor to serve as librarian as an additional part of his duties became standard practice. But this practice was far from universal. Convenience was of more concern to the appointers of academic librarians. If it was easier to use a student, a janitor, or an unemployed clergyman, this was done. Every college had professors that could be counted on to be reliable and available to serve. It was not from any concencus that care of the library was in any way equivalent to teaching that the appointment of professors to serve as librarians became standard in the nineteenth century, but from mere convenience.

The academic hierarchy of the classical college had no specified place for a librarian. It was a necessary task and one that was assumed as part of the natural duties of a professor like other necessary tasks, such as counseling or registering students or cleaning the philosophical apparatus. The small size and the poverty of colleges made the versatility mandatory for the faculty. One man often assumed teaching duties in several diverse areas and administrative and other duties as needed by the college. Care of the library was an obviously necessary minor task for a professor to take on, but only because the books represented a major financial asset of the institution.

The small classical colleges were committed to educating students to assume Christian citizenship in the American republic. To this end, the classical curriculum, an almost ritualized progression from the Greek historians through the wilderness of mathematics and the natural sciences to reach the abode of the moral philosophers, was central. It was a course of study designed to train students' minds rather than to provide them with any specific body of knowledge.

The curriculum was taught by men who themselves had been taught by the same scheme. The professors of the classical colleges were usually graduates of the college at which they taught or, especially in the case of the newer colleges on the southern or western frontiers, graduates of the college's mother institution in the East. They were men whose qualifications to teach were not represented by any high degree of scholarly attainment. Indeed, the degrees conferred by the faculty upon the students were the same as those the faculty themselves held—Bachelor of Arts and Master of Arts given incourse. The professors were chosen for their orthodoxy and their ability to impress on the students the particular character of the college.

In the early years of the nineteenth century, the methods of instruction were rigidly tied to the textbook. Memorization and recitation were the forms used to educate the students. As the century progressed, the lecture method came into use and gradually supplanted rote memorization of assigned textbook passages. The lectures of the faculty were not designed to draw together diverse opinion into a whole. Rather, the advantage of the lecture method was thought to be its forcefulness and immediacy. Students were still required to memorize and recite at each class meeting on the lecture as delivered *ex cathedra*.

The organization of the classical college was consciously modeled after that of the family. The students of the nineteenth-century college were in most cases significantly younger than those of the twentieth century. The youth of the students and the manners of a frontier society made discipline a major occupation of the colleges. Training a group of children ill-prepared in Latin and Greek to become moral citizens required, in addition to the mental conditioning provided by drills and recitations, physical and moral conditioning. The exuberance of youth frequently found outlets in destructive and immoral ways that the faculty had to guard against.

The colleges relied heavily on their presidents as fathers of the institutional families. They were ultimately responsible for every facet of the colleges' life and could only be overruled by the boards of trustees. Their duties included deciding whether to suspend or simply rusticate the student for individual acts of misconduct, fund raising, hiring and firing faculty, doling out money to the college's creditors, and even selecting and ordering books for the college library. The president exercised autocratic control over the college. Below him, the few professors and tutors of the college trained the students in the moral life and gave them the orthodox mental furnishings and discipline necessary to approach the acme of the classical curriculum—the president's senior course in moral philosophy.

A wide range of reading was not required by the classical curriculum. Indeed, in most cases, it was discouraged. The rigid forms followed required rigid adherence to a circumscribed set of values and truths. Introduction of alternative and conflicting ideas to the students was avoided in favor of giving them a consistent view of the world and the properly developed mental faculties needed to gain more specialized knowledge that would fit them for their eventual professions.

The place of the library in such a scheme of education was a minor one. Libraries were small, inadequately funded, and opened only a few hours a week. The books represented rather a memorial collection of donation than any well-planned utility of the college. Though there was some early agitation for reform of the colleges and a general recognition of the inadequacies of their libraries, the lack of any compelling need for numerous books in the classical curriculum and the methods of instruction by which that curriculum was taught prevented any serious diversion of scarce money from the more pressing needs of the colleges for the purpose of developing strong library collections. The library was an ornament to the college. Though occasionally useful for reference, it was not considered a vital necessity for the function of the college. Consequently, the librarian provided no vital service to the college in his capacity as caretaker of the books comparable to the service of the faculty and his status in the collegiate family derived from other duties he performed. If he was also a professor, a tutor, or even president of the college, his status in the academic community was high. If he was drawn from the ranks of students or janitors, his status was not enhanced by his role as librarian of the college.

Notes to Chapter 1

1. Gilman to Woolsey, June 1, 1865, and reply in Fabian Franklin, *The Life of Daniel Coit Gilman* (New York: Dodd, Mead & Company, 1910), pp. 77-78.

2. William Jones Rhees, *Manual of Public Libraries, Institutions, and Societies, in the United States, and British Provinces of North America* (Philadelphia: J. B. Lippincott Company, 1859), pp. 22, 29.

3. Charles Coffin Jewett, *Appendix to the Report of the Board of Regents of the Smithsonian Institution Containing a Report on the Public Libraries*, 31st Cong., 1st sess., Sen., Misc. Doc., No. 120 (Washington, D.C.: Printed for the Senate, 1850; reprinted Arlington, Va: Carrollton Press, 1967), p. 120.

4. Rhees, p. xxvi.

5. Richard Hofstadter, *Anti-Intellectualism in American Life* (New York: Alfred A. Knopf, 1963), p. 76; Carl Russell Fish, *The Rise of the Common Man 1830-1850*, A History of American Life, vol. 6 (New York: Macmillan Company, 1929), p. 132; Donald George Tewksbury, *The Founding of American Colleges and Universities Before the Civil War, with Particular Reference to the Religious Influences Bearing Upon the College Movement*, 1932; Reprint (Hamden, Ct: Archon Books, 1965), p. 17.

6. Frederick Rudolph, *The American College and University: A History* (New York: Alfred A. Knopf, 1962), p. 47; George Paul Schmidt, *The Old Time College President*, Columbia University Studies in the Social Sciences, no. 317 (New York: Columbia University Press, 1930), p. 61.

7. Hofstadter, *Anti-Intellectualism*, p. 72; Tewksbury, p. 164.

8. Maclean to Nott, June 21, 1938, in Cornelius Van Santvoord, *Memoirs of Eliphalet Nott* (New York: Sheldon and Company, 1876), p. 222.

9. Nott to John Maclean, June 25, 1838, in Van Santvoord, pp. 222-24.

10. Tewksbury, p. 78.

11. Stephen Edward Epler, *Honorary Degrees/A Survey of Their Use and Abuse* (Washington, D.C.: American Council on Public Affairs, 1943), p. 13.

12. Tewksbury, pp. 24-28.

13. Thomas Harold Andre LeDuc, *Piety and Intellect at Amherst College, 1865-1912* (New York: Columbia University Press, 1949), p. 2.

14. Frederick Rudolph, "Who Paid the Bills," *Harvard Educational Review* 31 (Spring 1961): 148-50.

15. Richard W. Giffin, "Student Days at Davidson College, 1838-1857, in Letters to the Rev. G. F. W. Petrie," *Presbyterian History Society Journal* 40 (September 1962): 184.

16. Judith K. Meyers, "A History of the Antioch College Library, 1850 to 1929," Master's thesis, Kent State University, 1963, pp. 41-42.

17. Tewksbury, p. 13.

18. Donald Robert Come, "The Influence of Princeton on Higher Education in the South Before 1825," *William and Mary Quarterly* (3d ser.) 2 (October 1945): 366-86.

19. Schmidt, *Old Time College President*, pp. 40, 96-97, 146-47.

20. Don Cameron Allen, *The Ph.D. in English and American Literature* (New York: Holt, Rinehart and Winston, 1968), p. 2; Robert Ferguson Munn, *West Virginia University Library, 1867-1917*, unpublished doctoral dissertation, University of Michigan, 1961, pp. 26-27, 34-35.

21. Thomas A. Askew, Jr., *The Liberal Arts College Encounters Intellectual Change: A Comparative Study of Education at Knox and Wheaton Colleges, 1837-1925*, unpublished doctoral dissertation, Northwestern University, 1969, p. 14; Maurine Irwin, "History of the Ohio Wesleyan University Library, 1844-1940," Master's thesis, University of California, 1941, p. 13; William C. Ringenberg, "College Life in Frontier Michigan," *Michigan History* 54 (Summer 1970): 91; George Paul Schmidt, "Intellectual Crosscurrents in American College, 1825-1855," *American Historical Review* 42 (October 1936): 61.

22. George E. Peterson, *The New England College in the Age of the University* (Amherst, Mass.: Amherst College Press, 1964), pp. 32-33.

23. Frederick Rudolph, *Mark Hopkins and the Log: Williams College, 1836-1872* (New Haven: Yale University Press, 1956), p. 45.

24. Quoted in Askew, pp. 36-37.

25. Gladys Bryson, "The Emergence of Social Sciences from Moral Philosophy," *Ethics* 42 (April 1932): 306.

26. Wilson Smith, *Professors and Public Ethics: Studies of Northern Moral Philosophers Before the Civil War* (Ithaca, N.Y.: Published for the American Historical Association by The Cornell University Press, 1956), pp. 8-10.

27. Stanley M. Guralnick, *Science and the Ante-Bellum American College* (Philadelphia: The American Philosophical Society, 1975); American Philosophical Society, Memoirs, vol. 109. 119-37.

28. Peterson, *New England College*, p. 15.

29. Walter C. Bronson, *The History of Brown University 1764-1914* (Providence: Published by Brown University, 1914), pp. 271-82, 321-26.

30. Schmidt, *Old Time College President*, p. 99.

31. *Journal of the Proceedings of a Convention of Literary and Scientific Gentlemen, Held in the Common Council Chamber of the City of New York, October, 1830* (New York: J. Leavitt and G. and C. and H. Carvill, 1831), p. 179.

32. "Original Papers in Relation to a Course of Liberal Education," *American Journal of Science and Arts* 15 (1828): 298, 333.

33. *Ibid.*, pp. 346–47.
34. *Ibid.*, p. 343.
35. *Ibid.*, pp. 309–310.
36. *Ibid.*, p. 337.
37. *Ibid.*, p. 301.
38. *Ibid.*, pp. 300–301.
39. *Ibid.*, p. 317.
40. Epler, p. 13.
41. Rudolph, *Mark Hopkins*, p. 70.
42. "College Instruction and Discipline," *American Quarterly Review* 9 (June 1831): 285.
43. Ringenberg, p. 91.
44. Askew, p. 9.
45. Munn, p. 38.
46. James Fenimore Cooper, *Letters and Journals*, ed. James Franklin Bears, 6 vols. (Cambridge: Belknap Press of Harvard University Press, 1960–68), 1:5.
47. Rudolph, *Mark Hopkins*, pp. 122–23; "College Instruction and Discipline," p. 301.
48. "Original Papers," p. 303.
49. "College Instruction and Discipline," p. 299.
50. Rudolph, *Mark Hopkins*, p. 41.
51. Codman Hislop, *Eliphalet Nott* (Middleton, Ct.: Wesleyan University Press, 1971), pp. 439–94.
52. Sister M. St. Mel Kennedy, *The Changing Academic Characteristics of the Nineteenth Century American College Teacher*, unpublished doctoral dissertation, St. Louis University, 1961, p. 16; Michael Chiapetta, *A History of the Relationship Between Collegiate Objectives and the Professional Preparation of Arts College Teachers in the United States*, unpublished doctoral dissertation, University of Michigan, 1950, p. 15.
53. Askew, p. 86; Van Wyck Brooks, *The Life of Emerson* (New York: E. P. Dutton, 1932), pp. 74–48; Schmidt, *Old Time College President*, p. 191.
54. Jerry Wayne Brown, *The Rise of Biblical Criticism in America, 1800–1870: The New England Scholars* (Middletown, Ct.: Wesleyan University Press, 1969), pp. 42–44.
55. Richard T. Ely, "American Colleges and German Universities," *Harper's Magazine* 61 (July 1880): 256.
56. B. A. Hinsdale, "Notes on the History of Foreign Influence Upon Education in the United States," in U.S. Commissioner of Education, *Report of the Commissioner of Education for the Year 1897-98*, vol. 1 (Washington, D.C.: Government Printing Office, 1899), pp. 602–603; 610–13.

57. Carl Diehl, *Americans and German Scholarship, 1770-1879* (New Haven: Yale University Press, 1978), pp. 148-50.

58. George Lyman Kitteridge, "Francis James Child," in Francis James Child (Ed.), *The English and Scottish Popular Ballads* vol. 1, 1882-1898. Reprint. (New York: Dover Publications, 1965), p. xxiv; David Starr Jordan, "The Evolution of the College Curriculum," in David Starr Jordan, *The Care and Culture of Men: a Series of Addresses on the Higher Education* (San Francisco: The Whitaker and Ray Company, 1896), p. 36.

59. Frederick Augustus Porter Barnard, "On Improvements Practicable in American Colleges," *American Journal of Education and College Review* 1 (January 1856): 279.

60. Mary Vernace Bean, *Development of the Ph.D. Program in [sic] United States in the the Nineteenth Century*, unpublished doctoral dissertation, Ohio State University, 1958, pp. 97-98.

61. Carroll Atkinson, *Pro and Con of the Ph.D.* (Boston: Meador Publishing Company, 1945), p. 13.

62. Guralnick, p. 142.

63. John S. Brubacher and Rudy Willis, *Higher Education in Transition: A History of American Colleges and Universities, 1636-1956*, 3d ed. (New York: Harper & Row, 1976), p. 85.

64. Andrew Ten Brook, *American State Universities, Their Origin and Progress: A History of Congressional University Land-Grants, a Particular Account of the Rise and Development of the University of Michigan, and Hints Towards the Future of the American University System* (Cincinnati: Robert Clarke and Company, 1875), p. 156.

65. Rudolph, "Who Paid the Bills," pp. 153-57; *Mark Hopkins*, p. 140.

66. "College Instruction and Discipline," p. 289.

67. Ten Brook, p. 175; Askew, p. 201.

68. "Original Papers," pp. 203, 304.

69. "College Instruction and Discipline," pp. 310-311.

70. Peterson, *New England College*, p. 90.

71. Schmidt, *Old Time College President*, p. 115.

72. Rudolph, *Mark Hopkins*, p. 28; John Hopkins Denison, *Mark Hopkins: A Biography* (New York: Charles Scribner's Sons, 1935), p. 180.

73. Quoted in Schmidt, "Intellectual Crosscurrents," p. 50.

74. Schmidt, *Old Time College President*, p. 224.

75. Arthur Twining Hadley, "The Library in the University," *Public Libraries* 14 (April 1909): 116.

76. Schmidt, *Old Time College President*, p. 195.

77. Quoted in John Jorg Boll, *Library Architecture 1800-1875: A Comparison of Theory and Buildings with Emphasis on New England College Libraries*, unpublished doctoral dissertation, University of Illinois, 1961, p. 119.

78. Munn, pp. 104-105.

79.   Clarence N. Roberts, *North Central College: A Century of Liberal Education 1861-1961* (Naperville, Ill.: North Central College, 1960), pp. 3, 46, 104.

80.   J. Orin Oliphant, *The Library of Bucknell University* (Lewisburg, Pa.: Bucknell University Press, 1962), pp. 91-92.

81.   "Proceedings of the Librarians' Convention Held in New York City, September 15, 16 and 17, 1853," in George Burwell Utley, *The Librarians' Conference of 1853: A Chapter in Library History*, ed. Gilbert H. Doane (Chicago: American Library Association, 1951), p. 154.

82.   Edward Edwards, *Memoirs of Libraries Including a Handbook of Library Economy*, 2 vols. (London: Trübner and Co., 1859), 2:164-67.

83.   Hellmut Lehmann-Haupt, *The Book in America: A History of the Making and Selling of Books in the United States*, in collaboration with Lawrence C. Wroth and Rollo G. Silver, 2d ed. (New York: R. R. Bowker and Company, 1951), p. 131; Mary Elizabeth Nichols, "Early Development of the University of Mississippi Library," Master's thesis, University of Mississippi, 1957, p. 5.

84.   Edward Thomson, *Letters from Europe: Being Notes of a Tour Through England, France, and Switzeland* ed. D. W. Clark (Cincinnati: D. Swormstedt and A. Poe, 1856), pp. 12-13.

85.   Irwin, pp. 72-75.

86.   Ten Brook, pp. 165-67; Russell Eugene Bidlack, *The University of Michigan General Library: A History of Its Beginnings, 1837-1852*, unpublished doctoral dissertation, University of Michigan, 1954, pp. 116-39, 149-52; A. Hunter Dupree, *Asa Gray 1810-1888* (Cambridge, Mass.: The Belknap Press of Harvard University Press, 1959), pp. 65-73; Bidlack, pp. 145-46; 285.

87.   John Langdon Sibley, "Address Delivered Before the A.L.A. at Boston," *Library Journal* 4 (July-August 1879): 307.

88.   C. E. Lowrey, "University Library: Its Larger Recognition in Higher Education," *Library Journal* 19 (August 1894): 266.

89.   Elizabeth La Boone, "History of the University of Georgia Library," Master's thesis, University of Georgia, 1954, p. 31.

90.   Irwin, p. 93.

91.   James Everett Skipper, *The Ohio State University Library, 1873-1913*, unpublished doctoral dissertation, University of Michigan, 1960, pp. 113-14.

92.   Askew, p. 48.

93.   Boll, p. 37.

94.   Quoted in Boll, p. 120.

95.   Boll, p. 244.

96.   Theodore Wesley Koch, *On University Libraries* (Paris: Librarie Ancienne Honore Champion Edouard Champion, 1924), p. 22.

97.   Noah Porter, *A Plea for Libraries. A Letter Addressed to a Friend in Behalf of the Society of the Promotion of Collegiate and Theological Education at the West* (New York: S. W Benedict, 1848), p. 6, 10-11; 21-22.

98.   *Ibid.*, pp. 19, 15.

99.   *Ibid.*, p. 23.

100. Robert Bingham Downs, "The Role of the Academic Librarian, 1876–1976," *College and Research Libraries* 37 (November 1976): 491.

101. Utley, p. 64.

102. Robert Michener, "Henry Wadsworth Longfellow: Librarian of Bowdoin College, 1829–35," *Library Quarterly* 43 (July 1943): 218; Henry Wadsworth Longfellow, *The Letters of Henry Wadsworth Longfellow*, ed. Andrew Hilen, 4 vols. (Cambridge, Mass.: The Belknap Press of the Harvard University Press, 1966–1972), 1:319–482.

103. Henry Ormal Severance, *History of the Library, University of Missouri* (Columbia: University of Missouri, 1928), p. 25.

104. La Boone, pp. 31–33; Jeanne Peery Hudson, "A History of the Roanoke College Library, 1842–1959," Master's thesis, University of North Carolina, Chapel Hill, 1963, p. 14; Nichols, pp. 9–10.

105. Sibley, p. 307.

106. Clifford Kenyon Shipton, "John Langdon Sibley, Librarian," *Harvard Library Bulletin* 9 (Spring 1955): 236–37; Boll, p. 151.

107. Joseph Alfred Borome, *The Life and Letters of Justin Winsor*, unpublished doctoral dissertation, Columbia University, 1950), p. 328.

108. Shipton, p. 238; Borome, p. 289.

109. James Russell Lowell, *Letters of James Russell Lowell*, ed. Charles Eliot Norton, 2 vols. (New York: Harper & Brothers Publishers, 1894), 2:130–31.

110. Harry Clemons, *The University of Virginia Library, 1825–1950: Story of a Jeffersonian Foundation* (Charlottesville: University of Virginia Library, 1954), p. 95.

111. Bidlack, pp. 43–45; Ten Brook, p. 167.

112. Winifred Linderman, *History of the Columbia University Library, 1876–1927*, unpublished doctoral dissertation, Columbia University, 1959, pp. 44–45.

113. *Ibid.*, pp. 62–63.

114. John W. Burgess, *Reminiscences of an American Scholar: The Beginnings of Columbia University* (New York: Columbia University Press, 1934), pp. 174–75; 217–18.

115. Meyers, pp. 36–40.

116. Roscoe Rouse, Jr., *A History of the Baylor University Library, 1845–1919*, unpublished doctoral dissertation, University of Michigan, 1962, pp. 66–67.

117. Bidlack, p. 319.

118. Jessica Chandler Potter, "The History of the University of Washington Library," Master's thesis, University of Washington, 1954, p. 12.

119. Utley, pp. 118–28.

120. *Ibid.*, p. 29.

121. Linderman, p. 50.

122. Meyers, pp. 19–26.

123. Severance, p. 21; Hudson, pp. 9-10.
124. La Boone, pp. 24-25.
125. Alethea Hoff, "A History of the Library of Western Maryland College," Master's thesis, Drexel Institute of Technology, 1954, pp. vii-x, 1-7.
126. Boll, pp. 429-30; Irwin, pp. 17-40.

two

The University Movement

During the last quarter of the nineteenth century, a radical new force transformed American higher education. The dissatisfaction many felt with the limitations of the classical colleges focused on what became known as "the university movement." This movement resulted in the establishment of graduate education and professional schools, the development of specialization at the undergraduate level, and the emergence of an academic profession. The university movement was never organized or directed, but represented the culmination in the modern university of the thinking and innovations of individuals searching for solutions to the problems of the colleges. The university movement represented a direct response of the colleges and educators to the basic transformation occurring in American life after the Civil War.

In the half-century from the end of the Civil War to the early decades of the twentieth century, America came of age. The nation passed the test of survival in the Civil War and, with a new meaning of the word "united," encountered the growth pains of adolescence. To be sure, it was an awkward youth that presented itself to the world at the turn of the twentieth century: the wisdom of the Great Depression of the 1930s had yet to dispel the brashness and self-confidence of its aggressive suc-

57

cess in the world. But, it was a youth formed in all its parts and prepared for its approaching maturity.

In contrast to the frontier isolation that characterized the antebellum period, a more urban population entered the new century. By 1920, over half the people in the United States lived in urban centers. The population density of the continental United States had increased to 35.5 per square mile from 8 in 1850. More importantly, communication and transportation were linking the islands of population in the country. By 1920, America's 30,626 miles of railroad that had served the nation in 1850 had grown to 250,146 miles; by 1922, 14,347,395 telephones were reported in the country.[1]

This was an era characterized by one historian as an *Age of Energy*—energy in the sense of both mechanical and personal force.[2] The Carnegies, Rockefellers, and Goulds transformed American industry. The Dreisers, Cranes, and Sinclairs moved American letters into new realms. The Kitteridges, Jameses, and Turners established a new tone for American scholarship. The period saw the reshaping of American institutions and ideas to conform to a new and potent role in the world.

It was the age of the machine. The demands for power quickly outstripped the capacity of muscle and the efforts of man and animal were surpassed by new forces. Henry Adams attended the Paris Exposition of 1900 and felt a new presence in the hall of dynamos that rekindled an interest he had felt at the Chicago Exposition of 1893:

> As he grew accustomed to the great gallery of machines, he began to feel the forty-foot dynamos as a moral force, much as the early Christians felt the Cross. The planet itself seemed less impressive, in its old-fashioned, deliberate, annual or daily revolution, than this huge wheel, revolving within arm's-length at some vertiginous speed . . . Before the end, one began to pray to it; inherited instinct taught the natural expression of man before silent and infinite force.[3]

Adams, perhaps, went too far in proclaiming the rise of a new god, others had been just as obsessed as he about the massive power displayed by the machine exhibit of the centennial a quarter-century earlier.[4]

Power and its growth had become, by the 1920s, an integral part of American consciousness. It was a real and concrete phenomenon. By 1923, the primary horsepower of American industry was 33,094,228. In 1869, it had been only 2,346,142. But power also involved a mental and moral aspect that manifested itself in celebrations of militarism and conquest—or liberation.[5] This sense of power forced sometimes radical revisions in American thought and institutions in the latter half of the nineteenth and early twentieth centuries.

Concurrent with the rise of American power was a general awareness of the process of development and the self-conscious realization that America had a history. As the century moved on, Americans developed an intense interest in antiques and antiquaries. The sanitary fairs held by women in the Northern states during the Civil War had a profound side effect. One fair held in Poughkeepsie, New York early in 1864 had, as its most popular attraction, a rural colonial room where for fifty cents a visitor could be served tea in the country style of a century before. The idea spread and interest in colonial America during the last half of the nineteenth century became epidemic.[6]

In an America increasingly disposed to view the world as a developing rather than a static entity, Darwinism found fertile ground. By the eighties, the arguments inherent in the clash between science and religion had been resolved so that no reputable Protestant theologian could dispute Darwin. As evidence for biological evolution accumulated, rejection, except by the most fundamentalist sects, became increasingly impossible and reconciliation of theology to science increasingly necessary. Interpreting evolution as a manifestation of divine purpose became the mechanism through which belief in the value of both science and the Bible could be left intact.[7]

Although Darwin's proofs and theories aroused concern on the religious side, they gained wide acceptance from many Americans. Religion, at least of the blind fundamentalist variety, was gradually losing ground. Though *typical* Americans were still believers, it was becoming increasingly difficult to find them among the hoards of immigrants with strange accents and alien creeds that formed the mass of humanity on the continent.

Americans listened raptly to the silver tongue of William Jennings Bryan and envisioned the diamonds of Russell H. Conwell's fields, but the bleak picture that Mark Twain painted of the human condition could earn him popular remunerative support and even professional agnostics like Robert Ingersoll won platforms and widespread acceptance.[8]

Progress was an aspect of the notion of developing and growing power. The idea that the world was becoming better as a natural process appealed to a people used to the idea of freedom from government intervention. Progress, after Darwin, came to be viewed as inevitable. Change, when occasioned by a benevolent Providence, ceased to hold terror, and man could only wait for divine will to be worked out. Darwin's cause was helped in America by John Fiske, whose optimistic enthusiasm in looking to the future divinity of man as he evolved toward godhead reassured Americans that all was for the best.[9]

But Darwin's limiting natural selection to a biological process was insufficient for most Americans. They wanted and needed something to justify the manifestations of power they felt in their daily lives and eagerly embraced the social evolution theories of Herbert Spencer. Spencer's philosophy could satisfy everyone from the agnostic to the Godfearing. Under one rubric, Spencer united the world in a holistic procession toward an ultimate good. Spencerian social Darwinism dominated the thought of America's middle class through the end of the nineteenth century, teaching it that the betterment of society was inevitable and that social wrongs would be corrected in the natural order of things. By postulating a deterministic universe, Spencer withheld the stimulation to the social sciences that was given to the natural sciences by Darwin's theory. Natural scientists found new horizons in the phenomenon of evolution. Spencer's application of evolutionary principles and the assumption of the natural amelioration of human society limited the potential of research in the social sciences. It took the pragmatism of William James and John Dewey, which held scepticism to be essential to research and truth to be ultimately unprovable, and the work of Veblen, Turner, Holmes, and Ward in the eighties and nineties to bring about the view that the study of society could be fruitful.[10]

The forces working to transform American society into the

modern age left their imprint on American higher education.
Reform in America's colleges had never really been a popular
issue before the Civil War. Reformist energies were too committed to the abolitionist cause to allow for less urgent matters.
The final solution of the war and Darwin's damage to the religious purposes of education opened the way for far-reaching
reform. It became overwhelmingly clear that life was intensely
competitive, and in the struggle for survival, education must be
of a type to produce men who could win.[11]

It was widely apparent that the classical college was ineffec-
tive in the antebellum period. Francis Wayland, president of
Brown, observed in the 1850s that the industrial classes had, at
least in the North, become the most important social group in
America. He deplored the lack of any forms of education specifically directed toward industrial and merchantile America.
The classical college did not offer the kinds of education that
merchants, manufacturers, and mechanics wanted for their
sons. Though parents may have been willing and able to provide
for educating their offspring, the only kind of education
available "beyond that of the common academy" was that that
would prepare them for the professions.[12] Wayland, with many
antebellum educators, realized that the methods and purposes
of the classical college by which young boys were subjected to a
rigidly prescribed curriculum and system of discipline in order
to make gentlemen of them were increasingly inappropriate to a
developing America. The simple and single-minded colleges
could not encompass the growing complexities of an emerging
American civilization; their attempts to survey the whole of
knowledge were becoming obviously more absurd. As the century progressed, more and more Americans looked toward
Europe as a source of educational opportunity. It became a
point of national disgrace that America could not and had not
provided a system of education and facilities that would enable
its youth "to secure to them equal and the best possible advantages for gaining a thorough knowledge of the principles that
underlie the several leading pursuits in life."[13]

Germany provided a model that was frequently regarded by
Americans concerned with higher education. The differences between the American college and the German university were
widely recognized. It was as widely apparent that America had

no universities, no matter what some colleges chose to call themselves. Universities had libraries, laboratories, and professors who work at the limits of knowledge and "treat of every subject with the freshness of thought not yet taking its final repose in authorship, and which often present discoveries and views in advance of what has yet been given to the world."[14]

The differing purposes of the American college and the German university were clearly perceived by most writers, and the plethora of colleges that littered the American landscape were felt sufficient, even by the 1830s to support the higher work called for by a university.[15] Combined with a growing feeling of the general inadequacy of American culture, this awareness broke out in sometimes impassioned pleas for establishment of higher learning on American soil. Henry E. Dwight of Yale addressed a meeting concerned with the founding of New York University in 1830 with a glowing description of the wonders of the German university. He ended his appeal by asking the convention to consider the benefits:

> The feeling is very general in the United States, that we need a university like those of Germany. The present time is particularly favorable to try the experiment. Our country is now in its youth and fortunately, we have yet to encounter prejudices which have been gaining strength for many centuries. The present generation must provide for the wants of those which are to come; their fortunes are entrusted to us, and it is for us to describe whether they shall assume that elevated character in literature and morals, which is so essential to our national prosperity. Let such a University, as those we just contemplated, be established in this city, and the sympathies of all the friends of literature will be enlisted in its favor. It will become the prominent object of interest to every stranger visiting this metropolis, and from its walls the light of science and learning will be shed, not only over our great country, but over our mighty continent. With intense interest shall we observe its growth and its increasing influence, and as we behold its blessings widening and deepening with each succeeding year, we shall remember with gratitude those who have been instrumental in its formation and enrol [sic] their names among the benefactors of mankind.[16]

New York University was founded as a classical college; not until 1893 were the elements of a university as proposed by Dwight incorporated into its efforts.[17]

A number of other attempts to reform higher education in the Germanic image were made in America before the Civil War, notably at Harvard, Yale, Columbia, and Michigan. There were even attempts, or at least talk, about founding purely graduate institutions in various places including the University of the South at Sewanee, Tennessee, but these came to nothing.[18]

Industrial education had not been totally neglected in the antebellum period. The Peoples' College Association was founded in 1851 largely through the efforts of Harrison Howard with the support of Horace Greeley. It held annual conventions for several years, raised money and even got as far as the laying of a cornerstone for a college building in Havana, New York, in 1858. But internal dissent and lack of financial backing doomed the college. Hardly more successful was the Farmer's College at College Hill near Cincinnati. It was founded in 1846 by Freeman Cary Grant, an ardent supporter of technical education, who was attempting to broaden the scope of the classical college. Resources again were inadequate and the college was unsuccessful.[19]

A more visionary scheme was proposed to the territorial government of Michigan in 1817. A bill placed before that body called for the founding of a "Catholepistemiad" as a state university that would consist of thirteen professorships including a professor of catholepistemia who would act as president, a professor of intellectual sciences who would serve as vice-president, five professors of various subjects including medicine, professors of economics, history, moral philosophy, mathematics, the literature of all languages, and a chair of military science. These professors were to be a self-governing body empowered to control all the educational efforts of the state. It was to establish academies, museums, and libraries wherever it felt them necessary. The territory at that time had, however, fewer than 7000 inhabitants and the plan was discarded as unnecessary.[20]

The most persistent unrealized dream in American higher education has been the desire for a national university. The idea was first formally proposed by Benjamin Rush in 1787 at the Constitutional Convention. Rush, a medical doctor educated at Edinburgh, and member of the Continental Congress, felt that the classical curriculum should be abolished and that an institution of practical instruction was a basic need of the new nation.

He was voted down from a general feeling that education was a provence of the individual states. George Washington supported the idea during his presidency and even willed a portion of his estate for its establishment. He disliked Americans having to study abroad because of fear lest they become tainted by exposure to foreign forms of government.[21]

Throughout the nineteenth century, the idea of a national university as a capstone to American higher education persisted. In 1856, Alexander Dallas Bache, outgoing president of the National Association for the Advancement of Education, gave his support to the founding of a national university that incorporated elements derived from the best of the German universities. Bache's vision of the national university offered specialized instruction based on the educational foundations laid down by the classical colleges. The national university would provide "that the engineer, the miner, the chemist, the metallurgist, the mechanician, the teacher, the farmer, should have special modes of training—that history, English literature, moral and mental science, political economy, education, should all receive a higher treatment than is possible in our colleges." Further, the research conducted by professors pushing forward the frontiers of knowledge was not only to be encouraged, but to be considered an important function of the university.[22] Even though the idea gained the widespread support of such influential groups as the National Association of State Universities in the United States in 1890 and was still being seriously considered as a project into the 1960s, it was effectively pushed aside by the end of the nineteenth century. The great expansion of America's colleges and universities after the Civil War, the strong opposition of many educational leaders like Charles W. Eliot and Nicholas Murray Butler, and the emphasis on federal aid to broaden educational opportunities kept the national university movement from any more concrete realization than as focus of a national educational vision.[23]

The only permanent collegiate institution founded before the Civil War that was radically different from the classical college was the experiment of the University of Virginia. That was the work of one man, Thomas Jefferson, whose educational philosophy basically differed from that current in the early federal period. In designing the curriculum, Jefferson insisted on avoiding a prescribed set of courses. He placed emphasis on a highly unstructured group of electives that would prepare the student directly for success in a variety of vocational and professional areas. In addition, Jefferson deplored the highly developed disciplinary mechanisms common in colleges and insisted that discipline be held to a minimum.[24]

Jefferson realized that such a course as he proposed would require an exceptional faculty. Rather than search for Christian gentlemen, he sought the best specialists he could find. He wrote Richard Rush from Monticello on April 26, 1824, about his plan, telling him that the trustees would only consider a man "of the first order of science in his line" for the faculty. Jefferson realized that there were few of these in America and was willing to look abroad, "preferably in Great Britain, the land of our Languge, habits, and manners," for them.[25] The groundwork that Jeferson laid in the establishment of the university persisted. In 1841, James Joseph Sylvester was appointed to the chair of mathematics at Virginia. Sylvester was professor of natural philosophy and astronomy at the University of London. The young graduate of St. Johns College was regarded as the preeminent mathematician of the age. Sylvester was also Jewish. The Richmond population thought his religion an affront to the purposes of the university. At first, his supreme competence overshadowed this to the university and to the community, but ultimately, his extreme sensitivity to real and imagined slurs forced his resignation over the discipline of an insufferably rude student. Though the times were frequently against it, the Virginia college maintained the philosophy of attempting to acquire the best men available—and not merely those who were orthodox Christians.[26]

Technical and scientific education also had antebellum manifestations in the classical college.The two notable examples were the Sheffield Scientific School at Yale and the Lawrence Scientific School at Harvard. Both date their founding from 1847. The Lawrence School was originally conceived by President Edward Everett as being modeled after the German university but it soon became a program at the undergraduate level that completely ignored literature in favor of the sciences.

Lawrence's Bachelor of Science degree was not a popular program at Harvard—only twelve were awarded before 1869. The Sheffield School was more successful. There the program in sciences was combined with high-level instruction in the languages and mathematics and the PhD was awarded by Yale after 1860.[27]

The early attempts at educational innovation were only partial successes even when they were not beset by a lack of interest or funding. The first major turning point in the history of American higher education came when Charles W. Eliot was appointed president of Harvard in 1869. Eliot has been credited with the introduction of the elective system to the United States, though actually, he was not the first even at Harvard. Electives at Harvard began at least as early as 1824 when George Ticknor introduced the study of French and German into the curriculum. Neither was required of all students. This mild beginning was halted with Ticknor's resignation in 1836 and it was not attempted again until President Thomas Hill took office in 1860 and made the study of some subjects optional.[28]

Eliot's contribution was in magnitude. Under his administration, the elective system achieved its fullest form. Eliot believed in the elective system as a vehicle for promoting graduate education. He had first tried to encourage graduate work through a series of lectures given to Harvard graduates by visiting lecturers. When this proved ineffectual, he fell back on an elective system in the undergraduate curriculum. By broadening and diversifying undergraduate offerings, he made it possible for the student to specialize and go farther in the mastery of limited areas of knowledge. Early in his career, Eliot affirmed the equality of all areas of study. He considered the study of science to have the same intellectual value as the study of the classics or mathematics. He merely insisted that since they were equal, their study at Harvard must be of the highest quality.[29]

Eliot's firm belief in the capacity of the Harvard undergraduate and the evils of forced study led him to affirm the elective system as the salvation of the classical college. In his announcement of the new plan at his inaugural, he explained:

The elective system fosters scholarship, because it gives free play to natural preferences and inborn aptitudes, makes possible enthusiasm for a chosen work, relieves the professor and the ardent disciple of the presence of a body of students who are compelled to an unwelcome task, and enlarges instruction by substituting many and various lessons given to small lively classes, for a few lessons many times repeated to different sections of a numerous class.[30]

Eliot felt the traditional classical curriculum lacked the diversity necessary to make true learning possible. He insisted that in a true university, the various departments "of instruction taken together ought to cover all fields of human knowledge in which it is possible to give systematic instruction." He also insisted on a hierarchy of courses in each subject arranged from a comprehensive basic introduction through courses of increasing intensity "until the summit is reached in the conferences or seminaries which take advanced students to the limits of knowledge in that subject."[31]

In application, the elective system at Harvard came under some sharp criticism. Eliot expanded the options until, by 1872, courses given by one subdivision of Harvard were open to the students of all other departments and students of law or medicine could enroll in history or Greek classes at the college without paying extra tuition. By 1884, the system at Harvard was virtually complete. Required courses were almost totally abandoned and Eliot's feeling that any intellectual activity when pursued to its highest level, was as valid an object as any other held the day. Electives at Harvard did not, however, become the intellectual anarchy that critics foresaw. Early in his tenure, Eliot changed the system of honors at Harvard so that a student could, by taking six or seven courses in classics, modern languages, philosophy, history, mathematics, physics and chemistry, or natural philosophy and distinguishing himself in them, graduate with honors. Thus, a system of departmental majors was effected.[32]

The system spread quickly to other colleges. Only four years after Eliot announced the new program at Harvard, Wesleyan accepted a modified system that gave considerable latitude at the junior and senior levels and even some at the sophomore level.[33] A survey of colleges and secondary schools made in 1901 sent out questionnaires to 130 college presidents. Of the ninety-seven returned, thirty-four reported that at least 70 percent of the work required for graduation was elective. Twelve reported between 50 percent and 70 percent was elective and fifty-one reported less than 50 percent.[34]

In some cases, the adoption of an elective system was traumatic. Conservative President Noah Porter of Yale repeatedly refused to consider the requests of the faculty for a liberalization of the classical curriculum until Professor William Graham Sumner, leading a faculty committee, cornered Porter in his office in 1884 and refused to leave until Yale had an elective system. After several hours of negotiation, Porter capitulated. Yale achieved a limited reform that only affected upper division students and did not allow them complete selection of course work, but did allow selection of areas of concentration and specialization.[35]

The infection was spread west by carriers such as David Starr Jordan. When Jordan was made president of Indiana University in 1885, he abolished the fixed classical curriculum in existence there by pushing most of the required subjects taught into the freshman and sophomore years. A system of departmental majors was adopted for the upper division students. When he went to Stanford in 1891, he had a clean slate and sketched on it a system of major professors. A student chose a discipline when he entered Stanford and was assigned the courses to be taken by the professor in charge of that department.[36]

The elective system, by the end of the first decade of the twentieth century, had supplanted the classical curriculum and vitalized American colleges and universities. It raised the level of scholarship to heights impossible under the old order and transformed the character of American higher education. At the same time, it tended to make the education process trivial by encouraging vocationalism and offering paths of least resistance toward degrees. Such developing academic disciplines as social work and engineering, or education and American literature, could only be considered as reputable as the classics much later when a significant body of research had accumulated. Eliot's elective system was predicated on the assumption that all subjects were equal only if instruction was of the highest quality. He believed not only that the principal task of the college professor was to teach, but also that "the strongest and most devoted professor will contribute something to the patrimony of knowledge; or if they invent little themselves, they will do something toward defending, interpreting, or diffusing the contributions of others."[37] In many of the emerging academic and vocational areas, there was neither enough basic research nor researchers to sustain valid comparisons between the relative merits of Biblical criticism and agriculture as areas of study.

A wide diversity of reforms and new forms that were instituted in America after the Civil War have been subsumed under the rubric, *The University Movement*. It was a movement, however, so diffuse and unfocused as to be more the result of osmotic pressure than of any sustained drive toward change. The introduction of electives was only one aspect, albeit a major one, of the modernization of American higher education. The expansion into realms of popular and vocational training and into graduate study and research were equally significant developments.

By the end of the nineteenth century, the synthesis that characterized the American classical college had been destroyed. The sense of universal purpose that excused the persistence of the classical curriculum had shattered and left a diversity of widely varying and sometimes contradictory purposes. It was no longer valid for students to use their colleges as a definition of their identity. The particular impress that marked a graduate of Williams or Brown had become far less important than the student's major and minor subjects of study.

The religious purposes that were a foundation of the antebellum college eroded under the new search for truth as a body of scientific and factual information and the increasing awareness that there was more than one path toward a state of social and moral cultivation. Christianity became disassociated from American higher education and theology, a minor department— if a department at all—competed with chemistry, engineering, and the humanities for funding. Where the classical college felt a high sense of Christian purpose, the developing university was basically secular.[38] It was so unconsciously secular that Daniel Coit Gilman expressed surprise at the furor attending the dedication ceremonies of Johns Hopkins University in 1876. Thomas Huxley, the British Darwinist, delivered the opening speech at the ceremony and there was no call upon God to guide the new enterprise:

> Many people who thought that a university, like a college, could not succeed unless it was under some denominational control, were sure that this opening discourse was but an overture to the play of irreligious and anti-religious actors. . . . Huxley was bad enough; Huxley without a prayer was intolerable.[39]

Of course, Huxley with a prayer would have been a preposterous hypocrisy.

Just as Darwin's theory was gaining in popularity through its applications by Herbert Spencer to the social problems attendant upon American industrialism, it was also attracting increasing numbers of serious thinkers in academic circles. Harvard was the first American college to offer lectures on evolutionary thought with a course given by John Fiske in 1869–70 and again the following year. Fiske, as an undergraduate only a few years before, had been threatened with expulsion because of his radical views. But the arrival of Eliot as president and the immediate changes made in the atmosphere of the institution brought him back as a lecturer. Though Fiske failed to obtain a permanent appointment at Harvard because of opposition from the Overseers that undoubtedly had much to do with his religious views, that he was allowed the opportunity by Eliot marks a turning point in American colleges.[40]

As ev. 'nce mounted, more and more educational leaders embraced the theory of the mutability of species and reconciled the Bible to Darwin or abandoned it altogether. Francis Snow, president of the University of Kansas from 1890 to 1901, had been trained at Andover but turned toward science as a career. After the early 1880s, he found the evidence for Darwin overwhelming and became a champion of the theory. He found, however, that he could not abandon Christianity and lived out his life with an uneasy harmony among his beliefs. During his tenure at Kansas, he delivered numerous extension lectures on the subject of evolution that enjoyed wide popularity even though they aroused the active ire of Kansas ministers.[41]

David Starr Jordan was converted during a summer school of science workshop on the island of Penikese when he was studying under the antievolutionary Louis Agassiz in 1873. Jordan began by fully accepting Agassiz's view that species had divine origins and that their forms were permanent. As the summer progressed, his faith crumbled. He was not converted to Darwin's theory by argument, but by the physical evidence that was, to Jordan, irrefutable.[42] The evidence, to any thoughtful and thorough researcher—and the new scholarship was both thoughtful and thorough—was insurmountably in favor of Darwin. Critics like Victor Agassiz who could find no evidence for the Darwinian hypothesis were quickly becoming scientific anachronisms.

There were, of course, reactions to the new scientificism. Alexander Winchell was known to be a conservative evolutionist when he was hired by Methodist Bishop Holland N. McTyeire, president of the Board of Trustees of Vanderbilt. But the publication of his book, *Pre-adamites*, in which he considered the origins of man before Adam was offensive to the Methodist faithful and led to his dismissal. Yet it is difficult to attribute this entirely to his view of evolution. His basic argument that Blacks were so racially inferior that they *must* have had different origins than Adam probably had much to do with the controversy aroused.[43]

Darwin and the rise of Biblical criticism put the religious controversies of American higher education on a higher level. It was no longer a matter of minor sectarian differences—whether or not to dunk—but a fundamental matter of defining the limits of human knowledge. Darwin proved a direct link between man and microbe, and the emerging fields of anthropology and comparative religion proved a link between the Bible and mythology. It was not so much that the university movement abandoned religion. It was simply that religion was at best irrelevant and at worst a hindrance to productive scholarship. The opinion of a Mark Hopkins that whatever contradicted the Bible was false science failed to find many adherents among men who had experienced reality in a direct way and observed the contradictions. Andrew D. White expressed the irrelevance of religion to the university movement in describing his hiring of the first faculty at Cornell:

It required no great acuteness to see that a system of control which, in selecting a Professor of Mathematics or Language or

Rhetoric or Physics or Chemistry, asked first and above all to what sect he belonged or even to what wing or branch of a sect he belonged, could hardly do much to advance the moral, religious, or intellectual development of the mind.[44]

Scholarship rather than orthodoxy became the criterion by which a man was measured.

Through the 1870s and 1880s, the secularization of the New England colleges became evident in their selection of presidents. New England's traditional mixture of religion and education was weakened by a new breed of college president who, while probably a minister, renounced evangelical fervor and adopted a more thoughtful and rational religion. It was a fundamental change in temper that abandoned the rigid prescription of divine law in favor of a more intimate and personal relationship between man and God. It signaled the end of the attempt to build an orthodox American society through the colleges. The evolution of complex organizational schemes made the skills of administration far more important than piety. The men who rose to the challenges offered them, the Gilmans, the Whites, the Harpers and Butlers, were far closer to the Rockefellers and Carnegies than to the Notts and Woolseys.[45]

The composition of the boards of control was also changing. In 1869, almost half the members of the boards of trustees of America's colleges were clergymen. By 1930, only a little over 7 percent were. The proportion of financiers and businessmen was ascendant. In 1860, about one-fourth of the trustees were involved in finance and business. By 1930, two-thirds to three-quarters were.[46] Men of affairs rather than caretakers of the soul were the new lights of twentieth-century higher education.

In their search for new forms, American innovators looked to Germany for models. It was a natural choice. From the early nineteenth century to World War I, it has been estimated that 10,000 Americans studied at Germany's universities.[47] These included many men who emerged as the prime movers in American higher education. These men who, after searching for learning and failing to find it in America, were forced to go abroad. Even though some American colleges did, in theory, offer some further work to graduates, the approach was often desultory.

Daniel Coit Gilman remembered trying to find further instruction at the two leading colleges of the 1850s:

> After taking the degree of Bachelor of Arts at Yale College, I was undecided what profession to follow. The effect of the collegiate discipline, which "introduced" me, according to the phrase of the day, to not less than twenty subjects in the senior year, was to arouse an interest of about equal intensity in as many branches of knowledge. I remained a year in New Haven as a resident graduate. President Woolsey, whom I consulted asked me to read Rau's political economy and come and tell him its contents; I did not accept the challenge. I asked Professor Hadley if I might read Greek with him; he declined my proposal. Professor Porter did give me some guidance in reading, especially in German. I had many talks of an inspiring nature with Professor Dana—but, on the whole, I think that the year was wasted. The next autumn I went to Cambridge and called upon President Sparks, to learn what opportunities were there open. "You can hear Professor Agassiz lecture," he said, "if you want to; and I believe Mr. Longfellow is reading Dante with a class." I did not find at Cambridge any better opportunities than I had found in New Haven.[48]

Clearly, this made a profound impression on the man who became probably most responsible for the transformation of American higher education.

The demonstrable practicality of the research coming from German universities especially after 1870 was appreciated by Americans. Applications of new ideas to the areas of agriculture, medicine, and industry were drawing increased attention, and the return of growing numbers of well-trained men from Germany to American colleges made the German university a symbol of what American education lacked—rigorous specialized training.[49]

The freedom of the German universities appealed to men like Gilman, Butler, and Burgess who brought back ideals of rigorous scholarship to America. The way was difficult, for America lacked the facilities for the kind of scholarship that was being promoted. John Burgess's attempt at Amherst to develop a school of political thought in 1873 had to be realized in the context of the undergraduate curriculum. It was a great success with the students, seven of whom petitioned to be allowed to stay another year after graduation that they might study the history of the United States and Europe after the

French Revolution, yet the enmity of the faculty and the lack of resources at Amherst forced him to go to Columbia in 1876. There he found more fertile ground in the encouragement of Nicholas Murray Butler. But it was a struggle even there.[50]

The idea emerged that the university was to be dedicated to the advanced specialized education of men "who have been prepared for its freedom by the discipline of a lower school." Although methods would differ from study to study, "the freedom to investigate, the obligation to teach, and the careful bestowal of academic honors" were to emerge as the essential functions of the university.[51] It was an idea that eschewed the comprehensive in favor of the specialized, the authoritarian in favor of freedom, and the hollow ritual of in-course degrees for the recognition of substantive achievement. But it was also a movement that of necessity stressed the practical. The German insistence on the search for truth as its own rationale proved unsatisfactory for the emerging American university. The impulse for the transformation of American higher education derived from a necessity for democratic reforms that insisted on the practicality of education and research.[52]

The attainment of secular control of the universities through the boards of trustees and the presidents was only one manifestation of the growing tendencies of American higher education. The new forms of education and research demanded much larger sums of money for facilities and salaries than did the old classical colleges. American businessmen became increasingly aware of the needs of higher education and the contributions that training and research could make and were making to industry and business through the applied sciences and, later, through the emerging social sciences. Sensing the economic value of higher education, they began actively to aid it. The most dramatic instances of philanthropy were, of course, those of Rockefeller's $34 million, the Stanfords' $24 million and Johns Hopkins' $3.5 million. But there were many others.[53] The University of Rochester, for example, benefited from the munificence of George Eastman. A modernization program begun by David Jayne Hill, president from 1888 to 1895, turned Rochester from a small classical college with an associated Baptist seminary into a nascent university offering work on the master's level, a strengthened program in the social sciences, and an elective system. When Rush Rhees became president in 1900, though, the university had a faculty of only seventeen and 187 students. Rhees approached George Eastman. Though Eastman believed education to be useless in general, he had become convinced that trained chemists were essential in photographic research and consequently was persuaded to endow a science building in 1904. Eastman, for a time, could not be moved to contribute more, though he was instrumental in persuading his friends to do so. By 1912, he was providing matching funds for various projects on the campus and continued his support in the Eastman School of Music and Theatre, a dental clinic for local children that was attached to the university, and the medical school.[54]

Three main reasons emerge for the vigor of the university movement. Dissatisfaction with the forms and rituals of the classical college accounts for the early search for new methods. The supplanting of authoritarian knowledge by a new skeptical empiricism that searched out and found new frontiers of human knowledge focused the general dissatisfaction on the university form. The growth of utilitarianism because of the need for technicians and new industrial techniques created a demand for specialized training and the application of research.[55] Response to these pressures was varied. New forms of strictly vocational and technical education emerged in land grant and state universities. Procedures were developed for training and certifying research scholars and scientists. And, an ever-widening group of disciplines and applications of study were considered proper subjects for the attention of American scholars.

One of the most significant responses to the need for reform in higher education was that of the federal government through what have become known as the Morrill Acts of 1862 and 1890. Justin Morrill claimed sole responsibility for the legislation he proposed, but it is evident that he was greatly influenced by educational thought about reform current in the period before the Civil War. The use of public lands for supporting higher education was not a radically new idea. Before the Civil War, Harvard, Yale, Princeton, William and Mary, and Dartmouth had all received grants of land from their respective state legislatures, but the legislation proposed by Morrill specifically provided land or scrip by which the settled Eastern states could claim land in the West to the amount of 30,000 acres for each senator or representative that the state was entitled to under the 1860 census. Further, it specified that it was to be used to provide support for one or more colleges where "the leading object shall be, without excluding other scientific and classical studies, and including military tactics to teach such branches of learning as are related to agriculture and the mechanic arts . . . in order to promote the liberal and practical education of the industrial classes in the several pursuits and professions in life." By directing use of the funds in this manner, Congress took a significant step toward compelling higher education to acknowledge and support the developing patterns of a growing United States. By 1892, there were fifty-seven colleges and universities receiving benefits from the land grants.[56]

A coherent national program was not developed earlier than 1862 because of opposition from the two areas of the country, the South and the West, that seemingly had the most to gain. It was felt early that the elitism of American higher education made it an inappropriate object for the support of the state in a democratic society. A land grant act that made no provision for popular education was opposed by Tennessee Congressman David Crockett with impressive rhetoric in 1829:

> The grant for the support of colleges drained us [his constituency in the wilderness of southwest Tennessee] of fifty-two thousand five hundred dollars in cash. Ay, sir, in hard cash wrung from the hands of poor men, who live by the sweat of their brow. I repeat, that I was utterly opposed to this: not because I am the enemy of education, but because the benefits of education are not to be dispersed with an equal hand. This College system went into practice to draw a line of demarcation between the two classes of society—it separated the children of the rich from the children of the poor. The children of my people never saw the inside of a college in their lives, and never are likely to do so.[57]

But this early proposal did not provide for the specific kinds of education that the Morrill Act did.

Opposition to the first Morrill Act focused on the dispersion of the scrip. The frontier states in the South and West had less population and consequently fewer representatives in Congress. They stood to gain proportionately less than the established Eastern states. Further, the scrip to be issued to the Eastern states was for land located in frontier states that had already had numerous bad experiences with land speculators and scrip.[58]

Southern opposition was withdrawn with the formation of the Confederate States of America and the legislation was passed. The way was clear for the realization of a dream that the advantages of higher education could be made available to the humble through the application of reason and science to the tasks of everyday life.[59] But Morrill's charge only ordered the states to provide for such education as would be suitable for agriculture and the mechanic arts without offering any direction as to how this should—or even could—be accomplished. The scores of small denominational colleges that littered the American landscape immediately held out their emaciated hands for the spoils. With little or nothing to offer, they demanded a share of the wealth.[60]

The founding of Cornell, a peculiar combination of private philanthropy and the land grant, almost failed because of quarrels over the money. Private sectarian colleges across New York, most on the verge of financial collapse, clamored for a share in the land grant that Cornell had attracted. Before Ezra Cornell could get a bill through the state legislature to combine his donaton of $500,000 with the federal land grant in order to found a university, he had to appease Genesee College with the $25,000 that the administration of the college had calculated to be its share of the money in order to satisfy a provision that opponents of Cornell's bill had forced onto it as an amendment. Cornell paid rather than risk failure of the legislation. The money was eventually returned to Cornell University by the state when the details of the extortion became generally known.[61]

The founding and expansion of colleges under the terms and benefits of the Morrill Act and the closely related founding of state universities, many of which benefited from the land grants, helped to realize the idea of providing popular higher education. But there was great uncertainty about what kinds and forms of instruction could satisfy the terms of the land grants. Whether agriculture meant the application of chemistry to the improvement of soils and crops, the technique of plowing a straight furrow, or instruction in the pure sciences, and whether mechanical arts were to include instruction in the physics and mathematics necessary to design a bridge, or carpentry and the techniques necessary to machine metals were questions that had to be answered if the new education was effectively to serve the country.[62]

Cornell was a glowing exception to this confusion. Though a land grant institution, the particular interest of Ezra Cornell and Andrew D. White gave the college a form and direction that served as a model for other state universities and land grant colleges. Other institutions relied in their early years on men drawn from the same pool of ministers from which the classical colleges drew.[63] Andrew D. White brought to Cornell a strong awareness of the inadequacies of American education, a strong commitment to reform, and the experience as a man of affairs that would enable him to realize his vision of a new higher education. As an undergraduate at Hobart College, his dissatisfaction found focus when he chanced upon Victor Aime Huber's book, *The English University*. White compared the campus of Hobart with the "engraved views of quadrangles, halls, libraries, chapels—of all the noble and dignified belongings of a great seat of learning" and found it lacking. When White observed this discrepancy he was saddened: "Every feature of the little American college seemed all the more sordid." White's subsequent travels and study in England, Russia, and Germany further influenced him. His years at the University of Michigan under the presidency of Henry Tappan completed his vision of the true university.[64]

In Ezra Cornell, White found a man who felicitiously combined a firm belief in the equality of all studies with the resources to realize that belief. The legend surrounding Cornell's portrait on the seal of the university, "I would found an institution where any person can find instruction in any study," was no rhetorical fabrication but a sentiment often expressed by the founder.[65]

There were, however, points where White and Cornell did not completely agree. Early in the planning, Cornell developed the idea of combining the necessity for student aid with the mechanical arts program mandated by the Morrill Act. He wanted to build factories on the campus in which shoes and furniture the students would produce to profit the college. White insisted that work at Cornell was to produce industrial leaders, not workers. But he acknowledged that Cornell graduates must be men with intimate knowledge of the best technical work. Out of his own pocket, he set up a small machine shop and introduced the students to it. When the trustees saw how well it worked, they appropriated money to furnish the rest of the equipment and eventually one of their number donated the money for a mechanical arts college.[66]

White, however, was anything but a radical popularizer of education. His opposition to granting free tuition at Cornell derived from a sincere belief that it would attract men really fit for menial occupations to the professions. He wanted to avoid creating bad doctors, lawyers, and engineers from what would have been good farmers, mechanics, or laborers. Further, he feared creating a class of anarchists like that he had found in Russia formed of "young men and women tempted away from manual labor and advocations for which they are fit into 'professions' for which they are unfit."[67]

Like the other land grant colleges, Cornell University had many critics who considered it academically disreputable because of its lack of emphasis on the classics. But in a competition held among several of the leading colleges and universities in the country a few years after Cornell's founding, the success of Cornell students, who took the preponderance of first places in Latin, Greek, and mathematics, made further criticism in this direction hollow.[68]

Most other land grant and state universities had neither the leadership of a White nor the financing of a Cornell. Since the states were not allowed to touch the principal of the money generated from the land grants and could use only the interest, the early history of these institutions show them to have been as impoverished as the classical colleges on the frontier. The typical institution was a single building in the wilderness with little or no equipment. The tendency toward erecting monumental buildings at the expense of teachers and equipment hindered the flowering of the institution. Most colleges failed to find a synthesis, so the classics and the industrial and agricultural arts were ill at ease together. As long as vocational educators kept their place, the classicists tolerated them. The teachers of practical subjects were unified only in their opposition to the classics. The scientists believed in teaching theory; the instructors of agriculture, in producing working farmers. There was no consensus as to what an agricultural and mechanical college should be or what exactly the 1862 Morrill Act was about. Further, farmers' distrust of the possibilities of applying science to their problems was an inhibiting influence on the growth and development of the institutions. The agricultural specialist had to prove himself to the farmer before the colleges could gain the support of their primary constituency.[69]

Although there was much confusion about how to translate the land grant philosophy into a curriculum, there was some degree of unanimity that it really meant collegiate education for the working classes rather than vocational education. Accordingly, even the early curriculum called for English composition, sciences, mathematics, moral philosophy, and history as well as the more technical applied subjects. The effect of the emphasis on scientific applications was felt by an increased regard for the natural sciences and biology, the spreading of the laboratory method, and strange adaptations of social science and literature courses to what were thought to be the interests of technical students.

As the land grant curriculum groped for a form, engineering emerged as a dominant force. America's development from an agrarian to an industrialized society corresponded with the period of development of agricultural and mechanical education. Because of increasing opportunities in the field of engineering, it quickly became more popular than agriculture as a course of study. At the end of the Civil War, there were only six reputable engineering schools in the United States. By 1915, the Society for the Promotion of Engineering Education counted almost 1500 individual members representing 194 institutions teaching some form of engineering.[70]

Through the 1890s, the land grant colleges expanded their functions. At the beginning of the decade, agricultural interests convinced the colleges of the legitimacy of preparing teachers for rural schools. By the turn of the century, the colleges had taken steps toward becoming universities by offering preparation for a broad spectrum of academic and semiacademic programs as well as training for a wide variety of occupations.[71]

It quickly became apparent, when instructors of the new vocational areas began teaching, that much of agricultural science was an unknown area. When Isaac Roberts went to Cornell in the 1870s to teach agriculture, he decided that future farmers should be able accurately to determine the ages of horses. Learning that a number of young horses had recently died of an epidemic near Ithaca, he engaged two farm laborers to exhume them and preserve their heads "and some special parts and such limbs as had been malformed by disease." Roberts was able to determine the age of each of the specimens thus uncovered and set to work: "arranging my materials on a work bench in the open, I placed the class on the windward side and taught them the fundamental principles of horse dentition." Finding this an important but difficult subject to master, Roberts paid particularly detailed attention to it in his book on the horse.[72]

Research became a primary function of the land grant colleges. The lack of basic information about agriculture made the advancement of knowledge and its distribution mandatory if the colleges were to fulfill their functions. The colleges, as they established their roles in the educational world, responded. Faculty members of land grant colleges had published fewer than 100 books by 1895. But almost 300 were produced from 1895 to 1907. With the establishment of agricultural experimental stations at the colleges by the Hatch Act of 1887 and the development of engineering experimental stations beginning at the University of Illinois in 1903 and expanding with the demands of World War I, research became a major function of the land grant colleges. Research in engineering lagged behind that in agriculture for precisely the reasons that it was so popular as a field of study. Discoveries in engineering were patentable and meant money to industry. Industry, utilizing well-paid graduates of engineering schools, preferred to conduct their own research and reap the rewards.

The Hatch Act of 1887 did much to encourage agricultural experimental stations at each of the colleges benefiting from the Morrill Act. It required the publication of an annual report, a periodic bulletin of information, and reports on research in progress. From 1887 to 1903, 6143 bulletins, circulars, and reports had been published. The Adams Act of 1906 broadened the scope of the Hatch Act that specifically charged the stations with conducting original research in applied agriculture to approve financing any original research.[73]

The most dramatic manifestation of the university movement was the development of postgraduate training. The complexity of disparate facts that increasingly characterized the realm of knowledge as the nineteenth century drew to a close allowed of no pantology. The expert in whatever area became supreme. Moral philosophy degenerated into a plethora of disciplines under the rubric, *social sciences,* and no economist was expected to comprehend the intricacies of political science or anthropology. Knowledge became fragmented and it was all one man could do to devote his life to a small corner of the exploding universe.[74] It became evident that study beyond the general survey of knowledge represented by the undergraduate curriculum was necessary if anyone was thoroughly to master any subject.

Yale was the first institution in America to attempt to solve the problem by offering significant work beyond the bachelor's degree and awarding a certificate for it when it gave the first American PhD in 1861. But Yale's graduate school was never more than a minor affair until the present century. It was supported directly by the undergraduate faculty and the scientists of the Sheffield School who taught what they pleased when they pleased. There was no effective administration or coordination of graduate programs and the men teaching courses to graduates did not form a graduate faculty, but worked from their various undergraduate departments. It was not until 1907 that Yale's situation enabled the university to allow a graduate faculty to work as a unit by removing the financial dependence on the undergraduate departments, thus marking the first steps toward an autonomous graduate school.[75]

Eliot's early attempts at Harvard to provide education for

resident graduates by inviting guest lecturers to the campus was a failure. By 1872, he had concluded that this could not keep Harvard graduates in Cambridge. What was needed was not a disjointed series of lectures, but systematic instruction by paid teachers.[76] Eliot's attitude toward graduate education was ambivalent. In his inaugural address, he stressed the value of specialization and deplored the dilettantism of the general teacher:

> As a people, we do not apply to mental activities the principle of division of labor; and we have but a halting faith in special training for high professional employments. The vulgar conceit that a Yankee can turn his hand to anything we insensibly carry into high places, where it is preposterous and criminal. . . . This lack of faith in the prophecy of a natural bent, and in the value of a discipline concentrated upon a single object, amounts to a national danger.[77]

But Eliot's concern was with specialization at the undergraduate level and he had at best a poor understanding of graduate work as it was developing in the minds of other educational leaders. He wanted to develop a graduate program at Harvard not from any confirmed belief in the value of such education, but because the graduate students would offer a challenge to the teachers of undergraduates and thereby improve instruction at the lower level.

Eliot also had an imperfect idea of the value of research. Charles Loring Jackson reported that as a young teacher of chemistry at Harvard, he had approached Eliot with a request to be excused from teaching one of his classes so that he could pursue his research in a specialized area. Eliot inquired as to what would become of the results of these experiments and was answered that they would be published. When Eliot was told in answer to his next question that they would appear in a German chemical journal, he dismissed the matter: "I can't see that that will serve any useful purpose here."[78]

True graduate education awaited the development of an institution totally committed to the idea of research and divorced from the obligations of undergraduate education. Undergraduate instruction at existing colleges absorbed too much institutional energy to allow redirecting of existing purposes and functions. The founding of Johns Hopkins University represented the first realization of the dream of a university on the German model in the United States. From its inception, it was conceived as an institution dedicated to the encouragement of research in highly specialized areas.

Responsibility for the establishment of an institution that would become an archtype for graduate education in the United States lies with Daniel Coit Gilman. When the trustees of the estate of Johns Hopkins sought advice on how best to fulfill the vague terms of the Hopkins will, they naturally turned to educational leaders around the country for help. Eliot of Harvard, White of Cornell, and Angell of Michigan all endorsed a college with an elective system and some small provision for graduate level training. But more importantly, all independently endorsed Daniel Coit Gilman as the man to head it.[79]

The selection met with immediate popular approval. The editors of *The Nation*, announcing that Gilman was under consideration for the position, reported that the trustees put to him the question of the direction the new institution should take. Gilman answered "that he would make it the means of promoting scholarship of the first order." He insisted that the work at Johns Hopkins should be at the graduate level; undergraduate instruction should be left to other institutions. This work would demand for a faculty, "men now standing in the front rank of their own fields." By giving these men only advanced students whose work would be a constant stimulation and a salary large enough so that they could forget "the commoner and coarser cares," he could "exact from them yearly proof of the diligent and faithful cultivation of their researches." The editors applauded the trustees' offer of the position to Gilman.[80] Local pressures prevented Gilman from completely ignoring undergraduate education at Hopkins. But his persistent view that "professional work implies voluntary, self-impelled enthusiasm in the acquisition of knowledge," and that undergraduate education should involve a system of prescribed rules and forms whereas graduate education should be completely free in its conception, led him to devise a system of seven groups of undergraduate courses designed to prepare the young scholar for more advanced work. But Gilman did not pay much attention to the problems of undergraduate students and expected them to perform with much the same intensity as the graduate students. The Hopkins was to be a place for producing research—not gentlemen.

Gilman believed firmly that the ultimate purpose of teaching and research was to produce something needed in everyday life.[81] But he was not concerned with directing research to purely utilitarian ends. To him, ultimate utility was inherent in all knowledge. In an address delivered at Hopkins on February 22, 1885, "The Utility of Universities," he expounded:

> It is the business of a university to advance knowledge; every professor must be a student. No history is so remote that it can be neglected; no law of mathematics is so hidden that it may not be sought out; no problem in respect to physics is so difficult that it must be shunned. No love of ease, no dread of labor, no fear of consequences, no desire for wealth, will divert a band of well-chosen professors from uniting their forces in the prosecution of study.[82]

It was this insistence on a high level of research activity combined with Gilman's refusal to limit investigation in any way that contributed directly to the immediate success of the university.

His faculty of renowned scholars attracted forty young men who enrolled as students at the opening in 1876. All had graduated within the past ten years from American colleges; six held medical degrees; six had PhDs; and twelve had studied abroad.[83] These men found a new type of educational setting at Hopkins. Ephraim Emerton wrote to Charles W. Eliot on May 17, 1881, commenting on the satisfaction of the number of men he had known who had been connected with Hopkins asserting "their testimony is unanimous as to the quick and generous sympathy extended to every scholarly effort." The Hopkins students felt themselves judged by objective standards based on their productive work. It was not a process of acculturation by which quirks of sectarian or personal idiosyncracy could bar a man from academic recognition, but a test of scholarly merit that formed the culture of Hopkins.[84]

Hopkins early developed a spirit of community unlike that of the classical college. It was a sense based not on the shared experiences of the students, but on the nature of their disparate experiences. There was an earnestness of purpose and a mode of academic intensity that was unmatched at other institutions. It was also a mode that outlasted the first flush of excitement at the founding of such a novel institution.[85]

Edward A. Ross remembered his seminar of forty students in history, politics, and economics in the 1890s as being a "dead-earnest group." The thousands of books that filled the shelves of the seminar room were a constant reminder to the students that they had but an imperfect grasp of only a small part of their field of study and each labored intensively on his current seminar papers and theses.[86] It was not a community of boys seeking to thwart the authority of an autocratic faculty or based on a sense of Christian service, but of mature students and researchers seeking to extend the boundaries of human knowledge.

The influence of the Hopkins was great. Gilman's attempts to entice scholars from other colleges were largely unsuccessful, but he did force other institutions to examine their own role in the advancement of knowledge. Through Gilman's and the Hopkins's influence, research came to be recognized as a major concern in higher education. In an educational world that was sharply feeling the need for highly trained specialists, the Hopkins filled a major role. In the first ten years of its existance, sixty-nine people were granted the PhD in various fields. Of these, fifty-six took teaching positions at thirty-two universities and colleges.[87] By the 1880s, the Johns Hopkins was recognized as the leader in American graduate education. George E. Howard of the history department of the University of Nebraska wrote to Herbert Baxter Adams of the Hopkins on May 30, 1883:

> You certainly have great cause for satisfaction. Johns Hopkins, and not Ann Arbor, Cornell, or even Harvard, is now regarded by the more intelligent, as the best conception of the University for America which has yet appeared. In the Department of History and Political Science we of the west are looking constantly to Baltimore as our guide.[88]

The approach of Gilman and the Hopkins to graduate education pointed toward the resolution of a long-felt problem in

American higher education and began the evolution of a new profession in America—that of the scholar.

The University of Chicago represented a different departure from the classical college. The old University of Chicago, a Baptist college with an attached theological seminary, was forced to discontinue operations in 1886. John D. Rockefeller, a supporter of the Baptist educational efforts who had been a generous contributor to the seminary, was prevailed upon, by the Baptist Education Society, to finance a new University of Chicago. Rockefeller approached William Rainey Harper in 1888 about planning for the new university. Harper had been connected with the old seminary at the university and was then teaching at Yale. Harper advised Rockefeller to go through with the plan but envisioned a much more elaborate institution consisting of a college with a fully developed graduate school.

Harper was considered by Rockefeller and the trustees as destined for the presidency from the beginning of the planning, though, at first, he refused the overtures of the men involved. After much negotiation which involved a substantial increase in the donation of Rockefeller to support Harper's vision, Harper accepted the post and on September 18, 1890, was officially named president by the Board of Trustees. Harper came to Chicago as a man of vast energy and accomplishment. He had entered Muskingum College in New Concord, Ohio, at the age of ten and graduated at fourteen. After serving for a time as a clerk in his father's store, he entered Yale and received the PhD at nineteen. After serving time as the principal of Masonic College in Macon, Tennessee, and a year teaching at Denison, he was recommended for and accepted the chair of Hebrew at the seminary of the old University of Chicago, in 1879. At twenty-three, he was felt too young to be offered a professorship and was appointed as an instructor but was promoted the next year. During the early 1880s, he was also principal of the College of Liberal Arts of Chautauqua. In 1886, he was called to Yale as professor of Hebrew and went on to serve the college as Woolsey Professor of Biblical Literature, as an instructor of graduate courses, and in the divinity school.[89]

Chicago's graduate school partook of the same spirit of intellectual community as the Hopkins. Edgar Goodspeed, son of one of the prime movers of the founding of the university, recalled, "An extraordinary atmosphere of high hope and expectancy prevailed, a great deal of which was later realized," when the university opened. Many graduate students were already writing or planning books in the first year and "the spirit of research and publication was in the air."[90]

Like Gilman, Harper insisted that research was to be the prime function of the university. In the notes for his unfinished first annual report, Harper affirmed the transcendence of research over mere teaching. Here Harper explicitly provided for research sabbaticals and made clear that "promotion of younger men in the departments will depend more largely upon the results of their work as investigators than on the efficiency of their teaching." Research, for its own sake and not for the sake of improving undergraduate teaching, was the essential purpose of the university from its founding. Harper made no equivocation about that: ". . . it is proposed in this institution to make the work of investigation primary, the work of giving instruction secondary."[91]

The seminar method, imported from the German universities, became the standard method of training young scholars in the new graduate schools. Charles Kendall Adams is generally credited with its introduction into America with his seminar in history at the University of Michigan begun in 1871. Adams did not have all the elements of what emerged as the American form, but did demand increased use of the library in fulfilling the requirements of the course.[92] The American seminar was highly influenced by the laboratory methods of the sciences. By the 1880s, the method was well enough developed that it deserved treatment as a distinct pedagogical technique calling for manipulation of the apparatus of knowledge to an end. Frank Hugh Foster, describing the process as applied to history, drew the inevitable comparison:

> As the student who has merely read descriptions of chemical reagents and their effects upon one another, does not understand them as does he who has also seen them, and putting them into new combinations, has watched them developing new properties, so the historical student needs to see the simple, unco-ordinated facts of history, and himself seek in their combination of some

mysterious event, before he can fully understand the labors of other men.[93]

It was a place where the fledging scholar learned the art of research in the humanities and the social sciences in preparation for the task of performing real research in the real world.

The seminar as it came to be developed in its ideal form was a largely self-contained enterprise that demanded highly original minds applied to a controlled set of problems and tools. It was designed as an intense community experience. Foster described the optimal facilities of the seminar demanding that rooms for the exclusive use of the group be set aside because the students of a seminar needed them "just as a family needs a house." Every student should have his own key to the rooms and a drawer that could be locked for his materials; carrels were to be provided for the advanced students. Ample table space and light were mandated. If possible, Foster also desired a "dressing-room, where the dusty student, just returned from a long walk, can wash and refresh himself, and so with the least possible delay can sit down undisturbed and pursue his labor till his time for study is exhausted."[94] It was a method of immersion that replaced the synthesis of the classical college, in which every student studied the same object, with a diversity of intellectual pursuits, but with a new synthesis of aspirations and propinquity.

The earned doctorate, of course, became the object of these developments, and by the beginning of the twentieth century, the PhD was regarded as the standard recommendation of academic fitness. From the first earned PhD awarded by Yale until 1925, 16,673 earned doctorates were given by seventy-five institutions in America.[95] By 1900, the requirements for the degree had been highly standardized in America's graduate schools. With a few local variants; a bachelor's degree from a reputable college was required for admission to a program; a reading knowledge of French and German was necessary; three years of study—more rarely two—with the last year in residence were required; concentration of work in one major and two minor areas of study was specified; an original research project in the form of a thesis was to be completed; and the candidate must pass an examination set by the faculty in all areas of study pursued. It was understood that the degree was to be awarded only for a high level of attainment in a special branch of learning.[96]

Even before Hopkins, the PhD was gaining a value that it could not have enjoyed in the classical college. Milton Wylie Humphreys returned to Washington and Lee after taking his PhD at Leipzig in 1874. He may have justly exaggerated his welcome in his unpublished autobiography:

> Many students, even students whom I did not know procured my photograph and brought it to me for my signature, and were uniformly disappointed because I would not add "Ph.D." to my name. So rare was the degree in those days in America. Puffs, more or less true, of the "brilliancy" of my achievement appeared in many papers, among them the New York Tribune. . . . one of the "Courants," I think it was the "Yale Courant," at the close of the season, collected a list of the doctorates . . . and the one *genuine* doctorate was—mine.[97]

This account may have been overdrawn, but it is evident that the attitudes of American educators toward the doctorate and toward specialized research were changing radically after the Civil War.

The American version of the PhD gradually came to be preferred by Americans who appreciated its particular advantages over the German course of study. When Nicholas Murray Butler graduated from Columbia in 1882, he was advised by Professor Archibald Alexander to continue his study toward the PhD at Columbia rather than go directly to Germany as he planned. Alexander pointed out that the requirements in Germany were so highly specialized and technical that they were a waste of time for an American student. Butler followed this advice and when he finally got to Germany was happy to have been relieved of the technical requirements for the degree and left free to pursue what he found most beneficial.[98]

By 1901, American graduate schools had evolved so far that an American student in Berlin could view the great German universities without the compulsion to eulogize. David Kinley, who had been a Hopkins graduate student, wrote Herbert Baxter Adams from Berlin on February 16, 1901, that he had become quickly disillusioned with the German university. He granted that except in the areas in which the material of research could be found only in Germany, the universities "had nothing to offer that our students cannot get better in our own country."[99] American graduate study had come of age and American graduate schools had assumed international respectability.

The PhD with its emphasis on intense specialization, was not universally admired. Humanist Irving Babbitt thought the examinations given candidates a trivialization of scholarship. He complained of hearing of examinations for the PhD where the student, trying to prepare himself to teach modern literature, was questioned entirely on obscure points of medieval history and linguistics.[100] William James, in a celebrated article, deplored the insistence on the PhD as a basic requirement for college teaching. It was, according to James, a bauble and a senseless bit of vanity. Even such a man as David Starr Jordan failed to see the values of degrees, pointing to a number of able college teachers who had never taken a degree.[101]

Jordan could point to such men as George Lyman Kitteridge and Francis James Child of the Harvard faculty. Child's study at Göttingen was interrupted by an outburst of productive scholarship that foiled his attempts at answering the technical requirements for a degree. It was Child whose scientific exactitude established the study of folklore as a major academic discipline. Though Child did not complete his dissertation at Göttingen, he was awarded its PhD in 1854 on an honorary basis. Kitteridge, of course, was an object of undergraduate myth at Harvard. One of the recurring tales about him was his answer to the question of why he did not have a PhD. "Who," Kitteridge was said to have replied, "would examine me?" On several occasions, he claimed the story to be untrue.[102]

Significantly, Child and Kitteridge, though both held a variety of honorary doctorates, declined to be addressed as "Dr." No such qualms assailed Francis Snow who, as a scientist at the University of Kansas, was awarded an honorary PhD by his alma mater, Williams College, in 1881. Afterward, he was known to the citizens of Lawrence as "Dr. Snow."[103]

The practice of decorating the faculty with honorary doctorates was not uncommon as the PhD became an academic commodity. Though the PhD as an honorary degree accounted for less than 10 percent of the honorary degrees granted, it became a point of contention between the rising universities that claimed sole rights to grant the degree for substantial learning and the smaller colleges that granted the degree for little or no actual work.[104]

The degree was viewed as a symbol of academic respectability and the practice of institutions' trading honorary degrees for their faculty developed rapidly. Men like John H. Harris, president of Bucknell, found it a source of pleasure when, in 1881, he secured an honorary doctorate from a neighboring institution for a deserving member of his faculty who lacked this embellishment. The title "doctor" identified a fully accepted member of the academic community and became a much sought honor. But the sham of the honorary degree could not withstand the growing sense that a degree must represent real achievement. Opposition to such practices as the mass granting of honorary degrees to celebrate important collegiate events from groups with an interest in the recognition of the earned doctorate grew quickly. By 1897, through the efforts of the United States Bureau of Education, the Federation of Graduate Clubs, the Association of American Universities, and various other educational agencies, the honorary doctorate was in disrepute. By 1910, it was considered bad taste to award the PhD, or any other degree that would normally be awarded for actual academic programs, *honoris causa*.[105]

Productive research in the form of publication became the ideal of the emerging American university. The PhD was only the training ground of researchers who would become teachers in the new era of American higher education. Graduate education's new focus on research had a direct effect on the undergraduate levels of higher education. The laboratory system, utilized in the graduate schools, whereby language, literature, and the arts were treated with the same intellectual precision as chemistry and physics had spread to undergraduate education by the time Louis Franklin Snow wrote his criticism of the American college curriculum in 1907.[106]

Abraham Flexner, with ample justification, attributed the spread of the seminar and research methods into the lower levels of the colleges to an inherent uncertainty in the undergraduate curriculum in conflict with a sense of purpose at the graduate level. Graduate work and methods under such a situation prevailed. Flexner associated the practice of loosing holders of freshly coined PhDs on the youth of the colleges with what he perceived to be a failure of college education. He felt that much undergraduate instruction was too specialized to be of any value to its audience. This, he attributed directly to the employment of newly ordained PhDs to teach undergraduate students. With their "personal fortune and interest" lying in other areas, they are given control of classes and "in the name of academic freedom" given license to follow their own notions of what is appropriate.[107] Flexner was not alone in his perception of the widespread use of the methods of graduate work at the undergraduate level. At least one early textbook on college teaching that deplored the condition, affirmed that by 1920 it had become commonplace to use seminar methods at the undergraduate level in which each student prepared a paper using references on a specific topic and delivered it to a class.[108]

There was a natural antipathy between the old-style college professors and the new researchers. Humanist Henry Seidel Canby of Yale was sometimes shocked at their attitudes toward undergraduate students:

> The hard-boiled school I respected, yet something in their tenets made me stubbornly rebellious. There was a Cambridge graduate on our faculty, an Englishman older than myself, with whom I argued over many a stein of beer. We have the stuff, he would say, let the little lambs come and get it if they wish. If they are goats who won't eat good food, that is their affair. I can give them good mathematics, and if they want mathematics I will work with them. If they don't, why should I coddle them![109]

The new education, with its emphasis on research, was antithetical to the classical college's mission of maturing young men. For it assumed social maturity and a sense of intellectual purpose among students. But as the methodology of the seminar filtered down into the colleges, so did the attitude of common purpose. The harsh monastic discipline of the classical college was, to a degree, replaced by a spirit of a cooperative venture directing the energies of the faculty outward toward the pursuit of knowledge rather than downward toward the maintenance of order among the undergraduates.

Harvard was an early leader in the movement toward treating students as part of the educational community. When Eliot was elected to the presidency, the college rules for undergraduate students were published in a booklet of nearly forty pages. By 1877, these rules had been replaced by a set of broad statements that required fewer than five pages. Eliot's attitude toward students stemmed from his experiences at the Massachusetts Institute of Technology where students were treated as mature adults. The removal of rules and the need for the faculty to enforce them made the traditional antagonism between faculty and students at Harvard a thing of the past. At Cornell, White felt that the unruliness of students derived from a lack of any real interest in the classical curriculum. Rather than have the faculty dissipate its energies, White took "the ground that, as far as possible, students should be treated as responsible citizens." As citizens, they were left to the civil authorities.[110]

The development of close relationships between professors and students that were necessary for the new forms of learning and research did much to diminish the necessity for close faculty supervision of student conduct. Michigan State University had the normal discipline problems expected from a group of exuberant students from the farms. The close working relationship between faculty and students was such, though, that an eastern college president visiting the campus in the 1880s felt compelled to comment on the absence of the traditional feeling of two hostile camps.[111]

The emerging American university valued men above all other resources. The emphasis on research and scholarship above buildings, religion, and traditions meant that researchers of the highest caliber were demanded. Gilman set the tone for the new era in his inaugural address at the Hopkins when he announced that, in hiring professors, "We shall not ask from what college, or what State, or what church they come; but what do they know, and what they can do, and what do they want to find out." Johns Hopkins, Clark, and the University of Chicago had the advantage of opening with a philosophy that placed the quality of the faculty above all else. Their success in the early development of graduate education is directly attributable to this.[112]

The assembly of a group of proven scholars on a faculty frequently was too great a temptation for presidents who tried to assemble their own faculties; the practice of one institution raiding another for its faculty—or at least the best men on the faculty—became common. William Rainey Harper's attempt to build a faculty for the University of Chicago provided a blatant example of unorthodox faculty-building.

By the end of the second year of Clark University's existence, it was becoming increasingly evident that financial difficulties lay ahead, and the faculty became anxious about the future. G. Stanley Hall, president of Clark, was not frank about Jonas Gilman Clark's intentions regarding the future of the university. During the third year, the Board of Trustees was faced with having to cut either salaries or the faculty by half. The horns of this dilemma were ultimately avoided, as a majority of the faculty tendered their resignations before the board could act.

While Hall attempted to keep his university operating by persuading the faculty to return at reduced salaries, William Rainey Harper arrived in Massachusetts. Because of Standard Oil's taint on the new University of Chicago, he had had difficulties recruiting a faculty. When he heard of the problems and dissatisfaction at Clark in 1892, Harper, without informing Hall, hired away a majority of the faculty that Hall had painstakingly collected. He almost doubled their salaries at Chicago and even took the instructors and students. Hall was furious and threatened to go to the public attacking Rockefeller who was then unpopular because of the oil trust and his methods of business. Harper relented somewhat and returned a few of the minor men to Hall, but informed them that the cancellation of their Chicago contracts was directly due to Hall's interference.[113]

Gilman, when trying to assemble a faculty for Johns Hopkins, often tried to hire professors away from Harvard. Harvard's inability to develop a graduate program kept many of the best scholars in the country at a low level of instructing and grading the efforts of undergraduate students. But Harvard was regarded as a "plum" in the groves of academe because of the high salaries paid and the diverse curriculum established by Eliot. In the end, Gilman got no Harvard men for the Hopkins, but the Hopkins did produce scholars that were well received as members of the Harvard faculty.[114]

Especially in the early years of the land grant colleges, there was intense demand for men of proven ability to form their faculties. Michigan State University was a pioneer in the field of agricultural education. It had managed to develop and maintain a successful curriculum for a number of years until the state legislature forced a cut of faculty salaries in 1879 and the school immediately lost the best of its faculty to schools that could pay more. The college had recovered and prospered again when the Hatch Act and the second Morrill Act provided money to many new and struggling agricultural colleges that, belatedly realizing their need for agricultural scientists, could afford the money and facilities necessary to lure away Michigan State's faculty.[115]

Demand for competent men was such that labors of devotion to a particular institution, the binding force of the classical colleges, could no longer be relied upon to make faculty members place the welfare of the college above their own aspirations. In the 1870s, William A. Anthony, Professor of Physics at Iowa State University, had planned a period of study in the East during the winter vacation. The trustees, however, vetoed this and required him to remain on campus to superintend the installation of the plumbing in some of the buildings under construction. Because skilled workers were scarce, Anthony was forced to perform most of the physical labor himself. Shortly after this, Anthony accepted a position at Cornell where his talents were better utilized.[116]

Even Oberlin, a college of long established traditions, had difficulty in securing men of quality for the faculty. Oberlin graduates, qualified to be fit teachers, were as enamored as the rest of the scholarly world of the Muses of research. The college preferred to hire its own graduates after appropriate training and experience. But its attempts to secure the best men were thwarted by insistence on a Christian faculty of the highest moral character. One economist, an Oberlin graduate that the college was particularly eager to hire away from Yale, declined because Oberlin disapproved of smoking. Robert A. Millikan, Oberlin, 1891, refused an appointment there as professor of physics in 1896, preferring a position as assistant to Michelson at Chicago at half the salary offered by Oberlin.[117]

Competent scholars, the kind in demand for the faculties of America's new universities and revived colleges, increasingly were demanding facilities and freedom rather than tradition and status in their choices of positions. In a letter of November 13, 1890, William P. Trent, a graduate student at Johns Hopkins who was teaching at the University of the South, asked advice of Herbert Baxter Adams. Trent had been approached about accepting a position at the University of Georgia as professor of history and political science and wanted Adams's opinion of the offer. His overriding consideration was the institution: "I would rather," he wrote, "get a subordinate place in a large university with a *library* and the chance to make a scholar of myself than to be *full professor* at a very unfledged university."[118]

Increasing academic mobility alarmed many university administrators. With no idea of who would be teaching from year to year—or in some cases from day to day—they felt that they were losing control of their own institutions. Marion Burton, president of the University of Minnesota, made a curious proposal before the National Association of State Universities of the United States of America in 1919. With an impassioned cry of "The hunting season should close sometime!" he proposed that the group agree not to make raids upon each other after July 31 of each year. His reasons were purely administrative. Burton first sought to stabilize the organization by eliminating the uncertainty accompanying such a situation. Finding and procuring new faculty members at short notice was a difficult administrative problem that Burton felt his proposal would eliminate.[119] By the 1920s, faculty members were more intensely aware of their identities as chemists, economists, and anthropologists than as college teachers. Their audience was not college students, but their peers, and was reached not through the classroom, but through journals, books, and the platforms of learned societies.[120]

To be sure, the picture was not totally one of a bright and harmonious cooperative search for knowledge. Students were frequently ill-prepared, particularly at the land grant colleges and state-supported institutions. Probably 50 percent of the students enrolled in America's state universities in 1870 were doing work that the early twentieth century might consider preparatory. Over 90 percent of the students at West Virginia University were enrolled in the preparatory department. The lack of adequate secondary schools hampered attempts at collegiate level instruction. When Oklahoma State University was organized in 1891, no students capable of college work could be found. Not until 1913 did a majority of the land grant colleges require a full high school education of their entering students.[121]

Standards and requirements for admission to the new institutions became a major problem in the developing national system of American higher education, and the mechanisms that served the classical colleges soon proved inadequate. Institutional diversity in admission requirements increasingly became impossible to justify. The situation described by Augustus Frederick Nightingale in 1879[122] demonstrated the diversity of standards for measuring students' preparation. Because of the widely varying entrance requirements in America's undergraduate institutions, a preparatory academy or high school had to commit itself to preparing its students for admission to one, or at best, a small number of contemporary colleges.

The University of Michigan took the first step toward defining the quality of the students admitted by their previous education rather than by examination in specific topics. Michigan, in 1871, agreed to accept graduates from its own state's high schools on a limited basis without examination. By 1873, Indiana and Illinois were also doing so.[123]

But laying the task of certifying preparatory schools on the individual colleges and universities ultimately failed to establish a wide enough base of standardization to remove the institutions totally from the task of examining prospective students. The next major move occurred in 1884, when members of the Massachusetts Classical and High School Teachers Association approached Charles W. Eliot about the problem. As a result, the New England Association of Colleges and Secondary Schools, was formed in 1885 for the purpose of accrediting preparatory schools.[124] Eliot had been working with a more informal association of New England colleges for several years on the problem of standardizing admissions requirements. On March 9, 1880, he had written to Daniel Coit Gilman about the difficulties he had as chairman of a committee dealing with the subject with the Yale faculty whose "manners and customs . . . are those of a porcupine on the defensive."[125]

The success of New England encouraged other groups to work in the same direction. In 1895, the Michigan Schoolmaster's Club approached James Burrill Angell with a similar idea, and a meeting at Northwestern University led to the organization of the North Central Association of Colleges and Secondary Schools. The Middle States Association of Colleges and Secondary Schools, formed in 1889, was an organization led by the colleges; it grew directly from the College Association of Pennsylvania which was formed in 1887 to promote legislative funding for higher education. The Southern Association of Colleges and Secondary Schools was formed under the direction of Chancellor James H. Kirkland, of Vanderbilt at the same time as the North Central Association, but it was forced to rely on the North Central Association for guidance because of the general disarray of education in the South.

These associations began listing schools that had been inspected and approved in 1905. The North Central Association produced a list of accredited colleges in 1913 using standards derived from those of the United States Bureau of Education and the Carnegie Foundation. Other associations followed, with the Southern Association accrediting its higher education members in 1919, the Middle States Association in 1921, and the Northwest Association in the early 1920s. But the Western Association, though it had existed informally since 1921, did not vote to accredit colleges until 1948, and the conservative New England Association did not accept accreditation until 1952.[126]

Lack of a strong central accrediting agency did not entail total chaos in New England. The College Entrance Examination Board, the brainchild of Nicholas Murray Butler, was authorized by the Middle States Association to offer standardized admission examinations. In July, 1901, the first of these was held in sixty-seven centers in the United States and two in Europe. Only Columbia, Barnard, and New York University utilized the examinations as their sole entrance requirement; thirty-seven allowed them as an alternative to their own examinations. In the first examination, 758 of the 973 prospective students were seeking admission to Columbia and Barnard. But by 1910, most New England colleges accepted the board's examinations either without, or in lieu of, their own.[127]

While the institutions were standardizing admission requirements, faculty members rebelled against what they came to view as a major shortcoming in the developing American university. The freedom that they had found in European universities was lacking at many of the American institutions. To be sure, the German universities were never as free as Americans thought them. The position of professors as civil servants and employees of the state limited freedom of teaching to the confines of the universities. In their public pronouncements, the German professors expected to be loyal to their employers. Until the 1890s, *academic freedom* was a concept principally confined to student freedoms in America and especially to the elective system. During that decade, though, it increasingly was applied to protect professors from arbitrary dismissal by governing boards for expressing unpopular views.[128]

At times, the confused role of a founder interfered with perceived professorial rights and duties. In 1900, Edward A. Ross, a Hopkins PhD, was fired from Stanford. Ross came to Stanford in 1893 as professor of economics and finance. He was a stimulating lecturer who was disliked by many of the rest of the faculty for his unorthodox style. He took a large part in Bryan's 1896 campaign for the presidency and made numerous speeches and public pronouncements for free silver and free trade and against Chinese immigration. Mrs. Leland Stanford took opposing views. Ross's behavior during the election scandalized Mrs. Stanford who regarded Ross as a personal employee. She demanded that President David Starr Jordan dismiss him. Jordan tried unsuccessfully to appease her, but to no avail. Ross's firing aroused great concern nationwide. Public opinion was for Ross and held Mrs. Stanford responsible, but academic circles felt the fault was Jordan's. Later, Ross affirmed the obligation of every scholar to speak out on public issues in his competency and the necessity of every scholar to assert this right.[129]

But it was not only in the private schools that there were problems. When Herbert Baxter Adams was offered the presidency of Ohio State University in 1894, he wrote to ask the ex-president, Walter Quincy Scott, about the situation there. Scott answered Adams on June 13, 1894, and told a sordid tale of his summary dismissal by trustees intent on placing control of the university under the Campbellites. This was only the culmination of a long-standing feud between Scott and the trustees. He had earlier opposed the probably corrupt sale of university lands, refused to overrule the faculty when it expelled the son of the president of the trustees for his academic failings, and refused to hire the son-in-law of the secretary of the trustees, a man who had not completed high school, as an assistant professor of Latin.[130]

In 1897, Dr. Jerome H. Raymond, who held a University of Chicago PhD, was appointed president of West Virginia University. At the age of twenty-eight, Raymond was bright, energetic, committed to the university movement, and tactless. He earned the enmity of the older members of the faculty by his suggestion that they take leaves of absence to do graduate work and his insistence on hiring young holders of the doctorate. Raymond attempted too much for West Virginia to assimilate without adequately preparing the way for the new learning. When he was asked and refused to award a fellowship to a protégé of Governor George W. Atkinson in 1899 on the ground that the man was not adequately prepared, the governor assumed the refusal was on political grounds and rebuked the president: "I hope you will not allow the regents to name all those fellowships for their personal friends only!" By 1901, Raymond had so alienated the legislature and most of the newspapers in West Virginia by his insistence on the values of scholarship that he was forced out of office. The legislature reversed many of the reforms he had instituted to turn the college into a university, but Raymond had permanently forced the school out of the collegiate rut into the modern university movement.[131]

Isolated incidents of interference and manipulation could not impede the growth of a movement that was assuming national aspects. Scholarship, fractured by the development of highly specialized areas of study, ceased to be united by institutional

ties and sought a new unity in disciplines. By 1909, in commem-
oration of the founding of the American Historical Association,
it could be written:

> The last twenty-five or thirty years have witnessed the growth of
> many such societies, so that for each of the departments of study
> recognized in a modern American university there exists a society
> national in scope and in the extent of its membership, which links
> together the scattered devotees of the particular specialty, brings
> them into mutual acquaintance, friendship and regard, effaces
> local jealousies and chauvinistic zeal for individual universities,
> and increases devotion to the scientific ends pursued in
> common.[132]

The historian at Yale had more in common with his counterpart
at Cornell or California than with his colleagues in Yale's
physics department.

The Association of American Universities was the first permanent formal national group concerned with the promotion of
graduate education in general in the United States. The call for
the first conference was jointly issued by the presidents of Harvard, Columbia, Johns Hopkins, the University of Chicago, and
the University of California. The first conference was held at
the University of Chicago, February 27–28, 1900. The problems
considered at this meeting indicate strong concern for the standardization of American graduate education so that the difficulties of students moving from one university to another
would be eased, for raising international respect for the American doctorate, and for raising the standards of weak American
graduate schools.[133]

The Association of American Universities, with such groups
as the Association of Land Grant Colleges and State Universities, founded in 1887, the National Association of State Universities (1895), the Federation of Graduate Clubs (1896), [134] the
American Association of Collegiate Registrars (1910), the Association of American Colleges (1915), and the Association of
Governing Boards of State Universities and Allied Institutions
(1924), indicate growing concern for, and interest in, the national aspects of American higher education as a profession
itself. Not only had scholars developed a national consciousness, higher education itself had.

Perhaps the most significant manifestation of an emerging consciousness that American higher education was national in scope and purpose and that there was a higher academic loyalty than that given the individual institution was the formation in 1915 of the American Association of University Professors (AAUP). As originally organized, it was an elite group of recognized scholars and researchers who had held positions in colleges and universities for at least ten years. By 1920, the experience requirement was reduced to three years, but not until 1929 was provision made for nonvoting attendance at meetings by graduate students. Though it was organized as an elite group, membership was not universally considered to be a great honor. At the 1916 meeting, historian Charles A. Beard was elected to membership. Somehow, he was never informed about this. When the association dunned him for his dues two years later, he refused to pay, writing, "I regarded it as a futile enterprise when it was begun, and the results have confirmed my suspicions."[135]

Before the formation of the AAUP, some steps had been taken by outside professional organizations to investigate infringements of academic freedom. The American Economic Association's committee to investigate and report on the Ross case at Stanford in 1901 was an early noteworthy instance. Later, the American Psychological Association and the American Philosophical Association appointed a joint committee that investigated the firing of John M. Mecklin from Lafayette College. The AAUP itself grew out of awareness that concerted action was necessary among various disciplines whose members were threatened by infringements of their academic freedom. Accordingly, the American Economic Association, the American Sociological Society, and the American Political Science Association jointly appointed a committee to consider the relation of the individual institutions to the teaching profession. A call to form a more comprehensive organization than the individual societies, the AAUP, was the result.[136]

The AAUP represented, in a real sense, a "closing of ranks" among faculty members and the growth of a national awareness that they were a distinct group with a specific function in society.

Through the early decades of the twentieth century, faculty members of America's institutions of higher education felt themselves besieged on several fronts. The change in the composition of boards of trustees of the various institutions brought a new set of values to the new universities. Higher education had come to be dominated by business. By 1930, the view had emerged among faculty members that the privilege enjoyed by professors in the age of the classical college had been eroded by trustees who approached their responsibilities in much the same way as they did their business enterprises. Court decisions and acts of trustees that defined the relationship between the faculty and the governing boards as an employer/employee relationship and asserted the employer's right to control the activities of the employees did much to create, in the minds of the faculty, a sense of entrenchment against the wrongful intrusion of outside power into the realm of faculty autonomy.[137]

John Ervin Kirkpatrick expressed the views and fears of many academics of the change in governance that accompanied the emergence of a secularized higher education in America. The process of appointing men of commerce and industry "puts into position of great power a class not fitted by temperament or experience for the task given them." The skills and knowledge necessary for the administration of as intricate a mechanism as a university could not be learned in the counting house. The practice of inviting a "successful man of affairs," who, many years earlier, had spent his time and acquired his degree to direct the affairs of the college was detrimental to the higher purposes of the institutions. The idea that such a man "returning for an hour or two from his city office as a chief director of his alma mater" would be a better administrator than his old classmate who had traveled a different road through graduate study and spent the same time intimately involved in education and educational administration was in Kirkpatrick's view "one of those curious conceits which survive and give grounds for the pessimist's faith in the general stupidity of humanity."[138]

Thorstein Veblen had earlier railed against the same phenomenon. Veblen vengefully attacked the intrusion of business ethics and principles into the academic enterprise. He deplored what he perceived to be the growing view "that learning is a merchantable commodity, to be produced on a piece-rate plan, rated, bought and sold by standard units, measured, counted and reduced to staple equivalence by impersonal, mechanical tests." This attitude, in Veblen's view, contradicted the essential creative purposes of the university—teaching and research. The evolution of a bureaucratic structure of American higher education led to a standardization and control that was intolerable. It established standards and measures by which production was judged that countered the needs of "scholarly and scientific thought." The imposition of standards of accounting and the habits of mind of the business world "must unavoidably weaken and vitiate the work of instruction, in just the degree in which the imposed system is effective."[139]

At the same time that American professors felt themselves being forced into the mold of the business world from above, the changing nature of the institutions in which they labored was forcing them to welcome the very bureaucratization that they instinctively rebelled against. Competition for academic jobs through the first decades of the new century had become vigorous. From the 1890s to the 1920s, the supply of new PhDs graduated in America increased almost beyond the capacity of the institutions to absorb them. Only 136 PhD degrees were awarded in the 1890–91 academic year, but by 1928, 1447 were granted. From 1900 on, employment possibilities, at least at the more prestigious universities, were increasingly constricted, and as more young holders of the doctorate approached the colleges and universities, the people already holding positions felt less secure. Academic tenure became, under such a circumstance, an important concern of faculty members. The essential purpose of the AAUP from its founding was the protection of college and university teachers from arbitrary dismissal. But not until 1940 did this group and the Association of American Colleges reach any real and substantial agreement on the principles and procedures of securing tenure. The fight for tenure mandated a regularization and codification of the rights and responsibilities of faculty members. Attempting to gain security through tenure forced many teachers into the awkward situation of opposing the bureaucratization process being forced upon them by boards of trustees while supporting the definitions, uniformity, and standardization necessary for an objective and equitable form of promotion and tenure.[140]

Another issue of growing concern to faculty members was the realization by some that the PhD programs by which they had been trained inadequately prepared them to assume their duties as teachers. In addition to their autonomy being threatened from above by trustees who would have them operate education and research like a business, college teachers were also pressured by educationists who would intrude teacher training as an essential part of a doctoral program in any subject. After finding state boards of education amenable to the requirements for teacher training in the developing public school systems of the nineteenth century, departments of education in colleges and universities looked to the problem of education at the higher levels and made frequent attempts to push their specialties into the graduate programs of other disciplines. In the 1920s, several programs offered by educationists were roundly refused by departments which reserved the PhD as an evidence of research and scholarly accomplishment.[141]

Faculty members had long found the claims of educationists distasteful. The promotion of form without content struck many scholars as a perversion of the purposes of education. Committee Q of the AAUP was established in 1929 to investigate the extent of the "excessive requirements in the professional training of secondary teachers." The concern of this committee was with the movement "to extend such requirements to college and university teaching." In 1933, a published survey established that education preparation for teachers had been firmly established on a national scale. But the committee did not approve. It concluded that the amount of professional training given teachers at the lower levels "should be as restricted as possible" and limited to "only those things that are not obvious and that cannot be left to the judgement of a person reasonably endowed with intelligence and the power of observation." The committee condemned the courses offered for teacher training by the educationists as unworthy of a student of talent: "the practical part of the professional courses consists for a large part of facts that are obvious, or so simple that they can be acquired with a small amount of formal instruction."[142]

A few years later, the Committee of College and University Teaching of the AAUP reported on the state of the art and flatly rejected any attempt to require special training for the college teacher. This committee was disturbed by the increasing tendency it saw to require teacher training for employment at the junior college level: "when one bears in mind the ease with which this requirement of courses in education was extended from the high schools to the junior colleges in some states, its extension from these institutions to the lower divisions of the state university would seem to be by no means an unthinkable contingency." From there, the infection could logically be expected to spread to the upper levels of college instruction and into the graduate schools. The committee readily recognized that even though there was much opposition by the practitioners of the academic disciplines to the notion that educationists should have a part in the training of college teachers, the idea had some merit. One of the principal duties of a faculty member was teaching, and it was something that should at some point be addressed in the doctoral programs. But the committee found no real value to the offerings of departments of education preferring, rather, this should be a function of the academic departments. Courses in methods of instruction in the various disciplines and the active participation of a member of the department "who is especially interested in the problem of teaching" were the appropriate solutions to the problem. The intervention of education departments and schools was rejected.[143]

* * * * * *

By the end of the first decade of the twentieth century, the structure that would support the American university was complete. Undergraduate education had expanded from the strict, highly circumscribed set of courses that formed the classical curriculum into a maze of elective major subject areas bolstered by related minor areas in a diversity of academic disciplines and vocational preparations.

The rise of new forms of scholarship and research transformed the moribund classical college. It was no longer possible for a good—or even a great—teacher to acquire the academic respect commanded by a competent, productive scholar.

American colleges and universities had essentially abandoned the religious purposes of the antebellum college and the emphasis was on knowledge rather than piety.

A new scientific spirit in the land and a new sense of American consciousness coagulated many forces that were latent in the antebellum dissatisfaction with the colleges. Adding required course after course to the eighteenth-century curriculum proved impossible after a critical mass had been attained. The burgeoning clumps of accumulating scientific facts, the application of scientific methodologies to literature, history, and the arts, and the concurrent breakdown of what had been taught as "moral philosophy" into a wide spectrum of distinct academic disciplines—economics, political science, education, history, anthropology, and certain branches of philosophy among others —fractured the realm of knowledge. As Darwin's hypothesis forced the natural sciences out of courses in "Evidences of Christianity," the emerging social sciences taught that man could study himself with profit.

Business and industry found that new developments in the sciences were useful for economic exploitation. The need for well-trained technicians, scientists, and researchers into new uses for natural resources led directly to research into new markets through which a profit might be made. Industrialists increasingly looked to American colleges to supply the basic training that would enable them to capitalize on highly trained men to exploit new discoveries and, in a small way, returned that boon by financing facilities in the developing universities.

The Morrill Acts had proved that diverse vocational education could be practical. After groping for a new form as an alternative to the classical curriculum, the colleges chartered under the act and those benefiting from it shared some concepts with the classical college: they assumed a body of knowledge—ability to write coherent English, the basics of American history, and the essential physical facts of the world—that should be known by any graduate. Onto this, they grafted a set of increasingly specialized courses that would produce persons capable of functioning and producing meaningful work in an industrial society.

The necessity for basic research at the colleges benefiting from the Morrill Acts became immediately evident to the ministers of scientific bent that were employed as professors and in-structors at the new colleges. They devised numerous ways to teach that which was known only to the initiates. Systemati-cally recorded knowledge about weather, soils, and crops had to be extrapolated from research in the sciences and from personal observation.

The halting and faltering steps made by the New England col-leges toward developing programs beyond the undergraduate curriculum had been focused by Daniel Coit Gilman and Johns Hopkins University on the model of the German university. Em-phasis on rigorous, specialized training, the demand for research, and the insistence on productive scholarship became the ideals of the university movement in America. Through the influence of graduates of the Hopkins, of Clark, and of the University of Chicago, with the 10,000 men and women who had studied in the universities of Germany, graduate study became requisite for aspiring teachers in America's colleges and universities.

These new teachers and researchers sought and found their identities in a broader arena than the classical college could offer. The classical curriculum fractured under the impact of a multitude of specialized areas of study. The unique character possessed by each of the classical colleges was threatened and finally overwhelmed by growing awareness that what truly counted in the final tally was not morality or orthodoxy, but knowledge and productive scholarship. It was no longer possible for identity to be defined by association with a particular institu-tion. Rather than being a professor or student at Union, Har-vard, or Knox, one became a mathematician, botanist, or historian, or at least a nascent one. National societies arose in distinct specialties where adherents found a commonality of in-terest and work that had ceased to exist at their respective institutions.

Competent scholars became the primary need at the emerging universities. Men of proven scholarship were in demand. If men of proven scholarship could not be had—and frequently they could not—men of potential productivity were substituted. The PhD as a sign of potential productive scholarship, became the identifying mark of a successful college teacher.

Many members of these faculties felt themselves powerless in the new universities. The same phenomenon that was responsible for the revitalization of American higher education and the value placed on research was, to many minds, responsible for a subversion of the role and authority of faculty members. The secularization of America's colleges introduced a new ruling interest to higher education that affirmed the values of organizational efficiency and production over piety. In addition, the dual duties of teaching and research resulted in an internal conflict that resisted resolution. The new academic culture affirmed the value of research over teaching but recognized that teaching was an important duty that had been neglected in the development of graduate education in America. But this realization was not strong enough to persuade scholars of the value of teacher training programs proposed by colleges of education.

Notes to Chapter 2

1.   U.S. Department of Commerce, *Statistical Abstract of the United States, 1925*, no. 48 (Washington, D.C.: Government Printing Office, 1926), pp. 39, 372, 373.

2.   Howard Mumford Jones, *The Age of Energy: Varieties of American Experience, 1865-1915* (New York: Viking Press, 1971), pp. 104-106.

3.   Henry Adams, *The Education of Henry Adams*, ed. Ernest Samuels (Boston: Houghton Mifflin Company, 1974), p. 380.

4.   J. C. Furnas, *The Americans: A Social History of the United States, 1587-1914* (New York: G. P. Putnam's Sons, 1969), p. 636.

5.   U.S. Department of Commerce, p. 745; see, for example, any of the dozens of subscription books appearing after the Spanish-American War, such as José de Olivares, *Our Islands and Their People as Seen Through Camera and Pencil*, 2 vols. (St. Louis: n.d., Thompson Publishing Co., 1899).

6.   Furnas, pp. 598-602.

7.   Richard Hofstadter, *Social Darwinism in American Thought* (New York: George Braziller, Inc., 1959), p. 30; Walter P. Metzger, *Academic Freedom in the Age of the University* (New York: Columbia University Press, 1964), pp. 49-50.

8.   Furnas, pp. 881-82.

9.   Henry Steele Commager, *The American Mind: An Interpretation of American Thought and Character Since the 1880's* (New Haven: Yale University Press, 1950) pp. 82-87.

10. Hofstadter, *Social Darwinism*, p. 31; Commager, pp. 89, 91-107, 203.

11. George E. Peterson, *The New England College in the Age of the University* (Amherst, Mass.: Amherst College Press, 1964), pp. 16–17.

12. Francis Wayland, *Thoughts on the Present Collegiate System in the United States (Boston: Gould, Kendall and Lincoln, 1852), p. 154.*

13. J. W. Hoyt, "An American University," in U.S. Commissioner of Education, *Report 1870* (Washington, D.C.: Government Printing Office, 1870), p. 418.

14. Henry P. Tappan, *University Education* (New York: George P. Putnam, 1851), p. 48.

15. J. Leo Wolf, "On the Organization of a University," *Journal of the Proceedings of a Convention of Literary and Scientific Gentlemen, Held in the Common Council Chamber of the City of New York, October 1830* (New York: J. Leavitt and G. and C. and H. Carvill, 1831), pp. 247–48.

16. *Journal of the Proceedings of a Convention of Literary and Scientific Gentlemen, Held in the Common Council Chamber of the City of New York, October, 1830* (New York: J. Leavitt and G. and C. and H. Carvill, 1831), p. 141.

17. Theodore Francis Jones, ed., *New York University, 1832–1932* (New York: New York University Press, 1933), p. 214.

18. Richard J. Storr, *The Beginnings of Graduate Education in America* (Chicago: University of Chicago Press, 1953), pp. 118–24.

19. Earle D. Ross, *Democracy's College: The Land-Grant Movement in the Formative Stage* (Ames, Iowa: Iowa State College Press, 1942), pp. 22–27.

20. Andrew Ten Brook, *American State Universities, Their Origin and Progress; a History of Congressional University Land-Grants, a Particular Account of the Rise and Development of the University of Michigan, and Hints Toward the Future of the American University System* (Cincinnati: Robert Clarke and Company, 1875), pp. 91–103.

21. David Madsen, *The National University: Enduring Dream of the U.S.A.* (Detroit: Wayne State University Press, 1966), pp. 16–18; 22–28; John S. Brubacher and Willis Rudy, *Higher Education in Transition: A History of American Colleges and Universities, 1636–1956*, 3d ed. (New York: Harper & Row, 1976), p. 220.

22. Alexander Dallas Bache, "A National University," *American Journal of Education* 1 (May 1856): 478.

23. Edmund Jones James, "The National University in View of Present Conditions," *Transactions and Proceedings of the National Association of State Universities in the United States of America*, vol. 16 (Lexington, Ky.: Transylvania Printing Company, 1918), p. 31; Madsen, p. 10; George N. Rainsford, *Congress and Higher Education in the Nineteenth Century* (Knoxville: The University of Tennessee Press, 1972), pp. 24–25.

24. Herbert Baxter Adams, *Thomas Jefferson and the University of Virginia*, U.S. Bureau of Education, Circular of Information no. 1, 1888 (Washington, D.C.: Government Printing Office, 1888), p. 127.

25. *Ibid.*, p. 111.

26. Philip Alexander Bruce, *History of the University of Virginia, 1819-1919: The Lengthened Shadow of One Man* (New York: The Macmillan Company, 1921), 3: 73-76.

27. Storr, pp. 48-51; Charles William Eliot, "The New Education: Its Organization," *Atlantic Monthly* 23 (February 1869): 206-207.

28. Mary Vernace Bean, *Development of the Ph.D. Program in [sic] United States in the Nineteenth Century*, unpublished doctoral dissertation, Ohio State University, 1958), pp. 79-80.

29. Robert P. Newman, "A Patron Saint for General Education," *AAUP Bulletin* 39 (Summer 1953): 274; Henry James, *Charles W. Eliot, President of Harvard University, 1869-1909*, 2 vols. (Boston: Houghton Mifflin Company, 1930), 2:11; Charles William Eliot, "Inaugural Address of Dr. Eliot," in Charles William Eliot, *Charles W. Eliot the Man and His Beliefs*, ed., with a biographical study, William Alan Neilson, vol. 1 (New York: Harper and Brothers, Publishers, 1926), p. 1.

30. *Ibid.*, p. 13-14.

31. Charles William Eliot, *University Administration* (Boston: Houghton Mifflin, 1908), pp. 132-33.

32. Henry James, *Charles W. Eliot*, 1:245, 247; George Paul Schmidt, *The Liberal Arts College: a Chapter in American Cultural History* (New Brunswick, N.J.: Rutgers University Press, 1957), p. 172.

33. Peterson, *New England College*, p. 56.

34. D. E. Phillips, "The Elective System in American Education," *Pedagogical Seminary* 8 (June 1901): 212.

35. George Wilson Pierson, *Yale College, an Educational History, 1871-1921* (New Haven: Yale University Press, 1952), pp. 80-82.

36. David Starr Jordan, *The Days of a Man, Being Memories of a Naturalist, Teacher and Minor Prophet of Democracy*, 2 vols. (Yonkers, N.Y.: World Book Company, 1922), 1:293-94; Edith R. Mirrielees, *Stanford, the Story of a University* (New York: G. P. Putnam's Sons, 1959), pp. 75-76.

37. Richard Hofstadter and C. DeWitt Hardy, *The Development and Scope of Higher Education in the United States* (New York: Columbia University Press, 1952), published for the Commission on Financing Higher Education, pp. 51-52; Eliot, "Inaugural Address," 1, 26.

38. Hofstadter, *Development*, p. 3.

39. Daniel Coit Gilman, *The Launching of a University and Other Papers* (New York: Dodd, Mead & Company, 1906), p. 22.

40. Metzger, *Academic Freedom*, pp. 64-65.

41. Clyde Kenneth Hyder, *Snow of Kansas: The Life of Francis Huntington Snow with Extracts from His Journals and Letters* (Lawrence: University of Kansas Press, 1953), pp. 230-41.

42. Jordan, *Days*, 1:114.

43. Metzger, *Academic Freedom*, pp. 56-57.

44. Andrew Dickson White, *A History of the Warfare of Science With Theology in Christendom*, 2 vols. (New York: D. Appleton and Company, 1903), 1:vii.

45. Peterson, *New England College*, pp. 138-39; Hofstadter, *Development*, p. 33; Metzger, *Academic Freedom*, p. 185.

46. Earl James McGrath, "The Control of Higher Education in America," *Educational Record* 17 (April 1936): 262, 266.

47. Charles Franklin Thwing, *The American and the German University* (New York: Macmillan, 1925), p. 40.

48. Gilman, *Launching*, pp. 8-9.

49. Richard Harrison Shryock, "The Academic Profession in the United States," *AAUP Bulletin* 38 (Spring 1952): 40.

50. John W. Burgess, *Reminiscences of an American Scholar: The Beginnings of Columbia University* (New York: Columbia University Press, 1934), pp. 139-40.

51. Daniel Coit Gilman, *University Problems in the United States* (New York: The Century Co., 1898), p. 13.

52. Peterson, *New England College*, p. 23.

53. Jones, *Age of Energy*, p. 175; Metzger, *Academic Freedom*, pp. 139-41.

54. Merle Eugene Curti and Roderick Nash, *Philanthropy in the Shaping of American Higher Education* (New Brunswick, N.J.: Rutgers University Press, 1965), pp. 152-56.

55. Murray G. Ross, *The University: The Anatomy of Academe* (New York: McGraw-Hill Book Company, 1976), p. 48.

56. Ross, *Democracy's College*, pp. 50-51; Edward Danforth Eddy, Jr., *Colleges for Our Land and Time: The Land Grant Idea in American Education* (New York: Harper & Brothers, 1957), p. 21; "An Act Denoting Public Lands to the Several States and Territories Which May Provide Colleges for the Benefit of Agriculture and the Mechanics Arts," U.S. Office of Education, *Report of the Commissioner of Education for the Year 1890-1891*, 2 vols. (Washington, D.C.: Government Printing Office, 1894), 1:582-83; Rainsford, p. 96; "Receipts and Disbursements Under the Act of August 30, 1892," U.S. Office of Education, *Report of the Commissioner of Education for the Year 1890-1891*, 1:594-95.

57. *Register of Debates*, 20th Cong. 2d sess., HR; 1829, pt. 7:163.

58. Paul A. Varg, "The Land Grant Philosophy and Liberal Education," *Centennial Review* 6 (Fall 1962): 435-37.

59. *Ibid.*, p. 441.

60. Ross, *Democracy's College*, pp. 70-72.

61. Andrew Dickson White, *Autobiography of Andrew Dickson White*, 2 vols. (New York: The Century Company, 1905), 1:300-301, 309.

62. Frederick Rudolph, *The American College and University: A History* (New York: Alfred A. Knopf, Inc., 1962), pp. 255-57.

63. Ross, *Democracy's College*, pp. 105-106.

64. White, *Autobiography*, 1:287-92.

65. *Ibid.*, p. 300.

66. *Ibid.*, p. 373.

67. *Ibid.*, p. 395.
68. *Ibid.*, p. 362.
69. Eddy, pp. 70–71; Ross, *Democracy's College*, pp. 102–103, 86–95, 121.
70. Varg, p. 439; Ross, p. 158, 155; Jones, *Age of Energy*, p. 170.
71. Eddy, p. 87.
72. Isaac Phillips Roberts, *Autobiography of a Farm Boy* (Ithaca, N.Y.: Cornell University Press, 1946), pp. 97–98.
73. Eddy, p. 87, 97–98, 102; Rainsford, pp. 122–25.
74. Commager, p. 227; Gladys Bryson, "The Emergence of Social Sciences from Moral Philosophy," *Ethics* 42 (April 1932): 315–23.
75. Morris Hadley, *Arthur Twining Hadley* (New Haven: Yale University Press, 1948), pp. 160–63, 225.
76. James, *Eliot*, 1:251.
77. Eliot, "Inaugural Address," p. 11.
78. James, *Eliot*, 2:19–20.
79. Abraham Flexner, *Daniel Coit Gilman, Creator of the American Type of University* (New York: Harcourt, Brace & Co., Inc.), pp. 38–48.
80. "Notes," *The Nation* 20 (Jan. 28, 1875): 60.
81. Gilman, *University Problems*, p. 167; Francesco Cordasco, *The Shaping of American Graduate Education: Daniel Coit Gilman and the Protean Ph.D.* (Totowa, N.J.: Rowman and Littlefield, 1973), pp. 55, 96–101; Hugh Hawkins, *Pioneer: A History of the Johns Hopkins University, 1874–1889* (Ithaca, N.Y.: Cornell University Press, 1960), pp. 99–100.
82. Gilman, *University Problems*, p. 55.
83. W. Carson Ryan, *Studies in Early Graduate Education*, Carnegie Foundation for the Advancement of Teaching, Bulletin no. 30 (New York: The Carnegie Foundation for the Advancement of Teaching, 1939), p. 24.
84. James, *Eliot*, 2:22.
85. Hawkins, pp. 308–309.
86. Edward Alsworth Ross, *Seventy Years of It: An Autobiography* (New York: Appleton Century Company, 1936), p. 40.
87. Cordasco, p. 74; Ryan, p. 32.
88. Herbert Baxter Adams, *Historical Scholarship in the United States, 1876–1901: As Revealed in the Correspondence of Herbert B. Adams*, ed. W. Stull Holt, the Johns Hopkins University Studies in Historical and Political Science, ser. 56, no. 4 (Baltimore: Johns Hopkins Press, 1938), p. 66.
89. Thomas Wakefield Goodspeed, *The Story of the University of Chicago* (Chicago: University of Chicago Press, 1925), pp. 9–16; 37–48.
90. Edgar F. Goodspeed, *As I Remember* (New York: Harper & Brothers, 1953), pp. 86–87.
91. Harper's incomplete report as given in Goodspeed, *The Story of the University of Chicago*, p. 61.
92. John Cushman Abbott, *Raymond Cazallis Davis and the University of*

Michigan General Library 1877-1905, unpublished doctoral dissertation, University of Michigan, 1957), pp. 91-93.

93. Frank Hugh Foster, *The Seminary Method of Original Study in the Historical Sciences* (New York: Charles Scribner's Sons, 1888), p. 15.

94. *Ibid.*, p. 18.

95. Henry Alfred Todd, "The Functions of the Doctor's Degree in the Study of Modern Languages," Modern Language Association of America, *Proceedings of the Twenty-Fourth Annual Meeting* (Baltimore: Modern Language Association of America, 1907), p. xlix; "Earned Doctorates in American Universities and Colleges, 1861-1966, by Institution, Year and Sex of Recipient," *American Universities and Colleges*, 10th ed.; ed. Otis A. Singletary and Jane P. Newman (Washington, D.C.: American Council on Education, 1968), pp. 1695-98.

96. U.S. Commissioner of Education, *Report of the Commissioner of Education for the Year 1898-1899*, 2 vols. (Washington, D.C.: Government Printing Office, 1900): 2:1565-66.

97. Quoted in Ollinger Cranshaw and William W. Pusey III, "An American Classical Scholar in Germany, 1874," *American-German Review* 22 (August-September 1956): 33.

98. Nicholas Murray Butler, *Across the Busy Years: Recollections and Reflections* 2 vols. (New York: Charles Scribner's Sons 1939-1940): 1: 92-93, 104.

99. Adams, *Historical Scholarship*, p. 229.

100. Irving Babbitt, *Literature and the American College, Essays in Defense of the Humanities* (Boston: Houghton, Mifflin and Company, 1908), p. 123.

101. William James, "The Ph.D. Octopus," *William James, Memories and Studies*, ed. Henry James, Jr. (London: Longman's , Green & Company, 1911), pp. 329-47; David Starr Jordan, "The Evolution of the College Curriculum," in David Starr Jordan, *The Care and Culture of Men: a Series of Addresses on the Higher Education* (San Francisco: The Whitaker & Ray Co., 1896), p. 50.

102. George Lyman Kitteridge, "Francis James Child," in Francis James Child, *The English and Scottish Popular Ballads*, vol. 1, 1882-98. Reprint. (New York: Dover Publication, 1965), pp. xxv; xxxix-xxxx; Clyde Kenneth Hyder, *George Lyman Kitteridge, Teacher and Scholar* (Lawrence: University of Kansas Press, 1962), p. 185.

103. Idem, *Snow*, p. 191.

104. Brubacher, p. 192.

105. John Howard Harris, *Thirty Years as President of Bucknell With Baccalaureate and Other Addresses*, compiled and arranged by Mary B. Harris (privately printed, 1926), p. 49; Rudolph, *American College and University*, p. 397; Stephen Edward Epler, *Honorary Degrees/A Survey of Their Use and Abuse* (Washington, D.C.: American Council on Public Affairs, 1943), pp. 61-69.

106. Louis Franklin Snow, *The College Curriculum in the United States* (New York: Teachers College, Columbia University, 1907), pp. 171-72.

107.   Abraham Flexner, *The American College, a Criticism*, 1908. Reprint. (New York: Arno Press and the *New York Times*, 1969), pp. 189-90.

108.   Paul Klapper, ed., *College Teaching: Studies in Methods of Teaching in the Colleges* (Yonkers, N.Y.: World Book Company, 1920), pp. 76-77.

109.   Henry Seidel Canby, *Alma Mater: the Gothic Age of the American College* (New York: Farrar & Rinehart, 1936), p. 109.

110.   James, *Eliot*, 1:242-244; White, *Autobiography*, 1:348.

111.   Madison Kuhn, *Michigan State: The First Hundred Years* (East Lansing: Michigan State University Press, 1955), pp. 93-94.

112.   Gilman, *University Problems*, p. 28; Ryan, p. 141.

113.   Granville Stanley Hall, *Life and Confessions of a Psychologist* (New York: D. Appleton and Company, 1923), pp. 293-97.

114.   James, *Eliot*, 2:13-14.

115.   Kuhn, pp. 87-170.

116.   Roberts, p. 102.

117.   John Barnard, *From Evangelism to Progressivism at Oberlin College, 1866-1917* (Columbus: Ohio State University Press, 1969), p. 82.

118.   Adams, *Historical Scholarship*, p. 143.

119.   Marion L. Burton, "Cooperation Between Universities," in *Transactions and Proceedings of the National Association of State Universities in the United States of America*, ed. Frank L. McVey 17 (1919): 46.

120.   Harry Woodburn Chase, "Making a University Faculty," Association of American Universities, *Journal of Proceedings and Addresses of the Twenty-sixth Annual Conference* ([Chicago]: Published by the Association [n.d.]), p. 66.

121.   Joseph Lindsey Henderson, *Admission to College by Certificate*, Columbia University Contributions to Education, no. 50 (New York: Teachers College, Columbia University, 1912), p. 24; Eddy, pp. 84-85.

122.   Augustus Frederick Nightingale, *A Handbook of Requirements for Admission to the Colleges of the United States with Miscellaneous Addenda, for the Use of High Schools, Academies, and Other College-Preparatory Institutions* (New York: D. Appleton, 1879).

123.   Henderson, pp. 50-55.

124.   William K. Selden, *Accreditation: A Struggle over Standards in Higher Education* (New York: Harper & Brothers, 1960), p. 30.

125.   James, *Eliot*, 2:30.

126.   Selden, pp. 30-32, 37-38.

127.   Claude M. Fuess, *The College Board, Its First Fifty Years* (New York: College Entrance Examination Board, 1967), pp. 37-42; 52-53.

128.   Metzger, *Academic Freedom*, pp. 109-115, 123.

129.   Mirrieless, pp. 98-100; Ross, *Seventy Years*, p. 86.

130.   Adams, *Historical Scholarship*, pp. 230-34.

131. Robert Ferguson Munn, *West Virginia University Library, 1867-1917*, unpublished doctoral dissertation, University of Michigan, 1961, pp. 64–69.
132. John Franklin Jameson, "The American Historical Association, 1884-1909," *American Historical Review* 15 (October 1909): 1.
133. Association of American Universities, *Journal of Proceedings and Addresses of the First and Second Annual Conferences Held at Chicago, Illinois February 27-28, 1900 and February 26-28, 1901* (Chicago: Association of American Universities, 1901), p. 11.
134. The date the name first appeared on *The Graduate Handbook*.
135. Metzger, *Academic Freedom*, p. 203.
136. Brubacher, p. 319.
137. William Harold Cowley, *Presidents, Professors, and Trustees* (San Francisco: Jossey-Bass, Inc., Publishers 1980); pp. 202–204; John Ervin Kirkpatrick, *Academic Organization and Control* (Yellow Springs, Ohio: The Antioch Press, Publishers, 1931) pp. 189–201.
138. John Ervin Kirkpatrick, *The American College and Its Rulers* (New York: New Republic, Inc., 1926), pp. 100–101.
139. Thorstein Veblen. *The Higher Learning in America: A Memorandum on the Control of Universities by Business Men* (New York: B. W. Huebsch, 1923), pp. 221–22, 99.
140. United States Office of Education, *Report of the Commissioner of Education for the Year 1890-91*, 2 vols. (Washington, D.C.: Government Printing Office, 1894), 2:830; United States Office of Education, *Biennial Survey of Education 1926-1928*, Bulletin, 1930, no. 16 (Washington, D.C.: United States Government Printing Office, 1930), p. 699; Walter P. Metzger, "Academic Tenure in America: A Historical Essay" in Commission on Academic Tenure in Higher Education, *Faculty Tenure* (San Francisco: Jossey-Bass, Inc., Publishers, 1973), pp. 135; 151–53; Metzger, *Academic Freedom*, p. 180.
141. Michael Chiapetta, *A History of the Relationship Between Collegiate Objectives and the Professional Preparation of Arts College Teachers in the United States*, unpublished doctoral dissertation, University of Michigan, 1950, pp. 34–36.
142. American Association of University Professors, Committee Q, "Required Courses in Education" *AAUP Bulletin* 19 (March 1933): 173, 189, 194.
143. American Association of University Professors, Committee on College and University Teaching, *Report of the Committee on College and University Teaching.* (Washington, D.C.: The Association, 1933), pp. 61, 68–69.

three

The Scholar and the Librarian

The transformation in American scholarship and learning that occurred from the close of the Civil War to the end of the first quarter of the twentieth century directly affected the libraries that served American colleges and universities. The insistence that scholarship must produce published results led directly to the development of means by which research could be made public. Scholarly monographs and specialized learned journals proliferated. The numbers of young scholars and faculty members needed to teach and guide student research increased almost exponentially. Demands for both primary and secondary research materials to support emerging American scholarship resulted in an almost jubilant amassing of published and unpublished materials at those institutions that could afford to support such collections, and grim despair at those that could not.

Publication became the yardstick by which scholars and researchers in America's revitalized colleges and universities were measured. It was not enough merely to conduct research. Research was not complete until it was made available to the world at large. When Herbert Baxter Adams was appointed at the Hopkins, there were few outlets for productive research in America. Adams instituted the first historical monographs series, *The Johns Hopkins University Studies in Historical and Political Science* in 1881 expressly to publish his own and his students' research.[1] Adams insisted that the prestige of the school where one did graduate work, or even the amount of graduate work taken, was unimportant. Recognition of the quality of the work through published results was central to the ideal of the new scholarship. He wrote Gilman on July 3, 1882, expressing his aspirations for his students: "I want to see each candidate for the Ph.D. in History obtain some corporate recognition of his work, some local reputation which will help him on in his career."[2] It was through publication that academic reputations and careers were established.

Gilman, of course, took an active interest in the publications of his faculty at the Hopkins. Within a week of the appearance of a new book by a faculty member, Gilman could congratulate him and display some knowledge of its contents. He may not have read past the table of contents, but at least he retained enough for the proper gesture of encouragement. Even Eliot, whose sympathies for research were far overshadowed by his concern for undergraduate education, eventually partook of the fervor for publication—at least to the extent of knowing the publisher, if nothing else about a young faculty member's efforts.

The increasing emphasis on production combined with other impulses in American society to effect a dramatic increase in publishing activity in the United States. From 1890 to 1916, production of books in the United States rose from 4559 titles to 10,445 titles and these represented for the most part, new titles rather than reissues. Significantly, for the same period, the yearly number of fiction titles decreased from 1118 to 932, so nonfiction titles were basically responsible for these increases.[4]

The new universities took their role in the production and dissemination of knowledge seriously. By 1919, thirty-eight university presses had been founded in the United States, beginning with that at Cornell in 1869. These presses were established expressly to give outlet to the research of graduate students and the faculty, but soon broadened their perspective to present a forum for a broad spectrum of scholarly and semischolarly writing.[5] The University of Chicago Press, for example, published Oscar Triggs's edition of Lygate's *The Assembly of God* in 1895, Edward Capps's *The Introduction of the Comedy into the City of Dyonisia* in 1903, and David

McCulloch's *Early Days of Peoria and Chicago* in 1904. The presses had earlier been established to disseminate works of scholarship, but they found that local history, definitive editions of classics, and works of broad popular appeal were remunerative and fit into their charge to serve scholarship.

There was great interest in the publication of original source materials to make them more easily accessible. Edward P. Cheyney, of the History Department of the University of Pennsylvania, approached Herbert Baxter Adams in 1893 for his opinion of a plan to publish translations of source documents in European history. Cheyney thought putting "something in the way of available original sources . . . in the hands of even undergraduate students" would be a generally well-received idea in the academic world. Even if it was not considered a financially rewarding effort, "it might be missionary work to try and encourage a rather higher kind of teaching."[6] Although this particular scheme seems not to have gone much further, efforts of groups like The Early English Text Society and individual efforts like those of Walter L. Fleming, editor of the *Documentary History of Reconstruction, Political, Military, Social, Religious, Educational and Industrial, 1865 to the Present Time*,[7] and Geoffrey Scott's edition of the *Private Papers of James Boswell from Malahide Castle*,[8] did much to promote the use of original sources in research by making them widely available.

Journals also became a major instrument of the new scholarship. The Hopkins alone contributed *The American Journal of Mathematics* (1878), *The American Chemical Journal* (1879), *The American Journal of Philology* (1880), and *Modern Language Notes* (1886) to the growing list of serials, as well as being instrumental in the success of *Contributions to Logic* and the *Journal of Physiology*.[9] At Chicago, Harper's feeling that publication of learned journals was an essential function of a true university led to the establishment of *The Journal of Political Economy, The Journal of Geology, Biblical World, The American Journal of Semitic Languages and Literature*, and *University Extension World* in the first years of the new university. These were followed by the *Astrophysical Journal* and *The American Journal of Sociology* (1895), *The Botanical Gazette* and *The School Review* (1896), *The American Journal of*

Theology (1897), and acquisition of *The Elementary School Journal* (1901), *Modern Philology* (1903), *Classical Philology* (1906), and *The International Journal of Ethics* (1923).

Periodical publication followed the same patterns of growth as did the publication of books. In 1850, there were, at best estimate, approximately 600 periodicals published in the United States. By 1905, some 6000 were published.[10] Many of these were, of course, considered ephemeral and unimportant to scholarship, but many were crucial to the dissemination of research.

To support the kind of research being conducted at the new universities, it was not enough for the library to acquire only the results of research in the form of monographs and period- icals. Primary material became recognized as a major necessity for academic research. It was the age of the great manuscript hunt, and Americans like George Lincoln Burr, Andrew D. White's private librarian, scoured Europe for the raw materials of scholarship. In 1884 White sent Burr to earn his PhD at Leip- zig and to procure books and manuscripts for White's private library which was eventually to be donated to Cornell. He rescued many valuable treasures, including "a pile of MSS. about *six feet high.*" These were the financial records of Charles X of France and his grandson the Duc de Bordeaux covering the period from 1772 to after 1850. Burr was so excited about his find that he paid the fr. 250 asked by the bookseller before hav- ing cleared the transaction with White.[11] On November 11, 1895, he wrote White:

> I am impatient to make a thorough search through the pre- Revolutionary documents for the files with Marat's name as physician to the stables, and his receipts for his pay—if they are still there. But I have been a little unwell for a day or two, and the handling of the papers makes me so wild that I haven't dared to touch them. Even their presence by my bed (some 12 cubic feet already collected) is not an anodyne. There is editing for our seminary students for a quarter-century to come.[12]

Though Burr never completed his degree, his contribution to the world of scholarship through his collecting activities was great.

Particularly after World War I, when the type of biography known as "Lives and Letters" became a significant form of literary research, manuscript material became a primary concern of scholars and, through them, academic libraries. It became a commonplace that everything had real or potential value to the thorough researcher. Gilman, at the dedication of the Sage Library at Cornell in 1891, asserted that "It is not safe for a librarian to destroy any book, lest it should be presently in demand." He pointed out that what today is rare and valuable is that precisely because it was once considered worthless, and the value of a book could not be determined for all time by any criteria.[13] Justin Winsor, at Harvard, codified this idea in "two canons" of faith for librarians:

> *First.* Nothing that is printed no matter how trivial at the time, but may be some day in demand, and, viewed in some relations, helpful to significant results. Therefore, if his storehouse and treasury admit of the keeping and caring for, the librarian feels the necessity of preserving all he can.
>
> *Second.* Let him amass all he will, he knows some investigation will find gaps that he has not filled.[14]

Winsor, to the despair of Charles W. Eliot, followed his faith.

Students as well as scholars at the colleges and universities recognized the need for the expanded facilities of the new learning. As early as 1868, students at Amherst petitioned the authorities for improvement of their college library: "The first need of our library is Books; the second, Books; the third, Books." An editorial in the Bucknell student newspaper, the *University Mirror*, on June 8, 1889, complained that the library was totally inadequate for the kind of teaching methods the university was using. The editorial pointed out that there were only four books on ethics and five on psychology in the library. And the student editor of the *Western Maryland College Monthly* petitioned the authorities for $100 a year for a student reading room in 1893. But it was not only books that were needed. Research built on all forms of information and communication. Primary sources were of utmost necessity if true research was to be successful. A library composed of secondary sources was recognized to be inadequate for graduate work and research.[15]

Everything became important in the scholars' search for new truths. Frank Hugh Foster, trying to define the types of important materials for historical research in the 1880s, ran out of categories before he ran out of materials:

> By original sources of history we mean the testimony of the
> original witnesses to the facts. For political history they are stat-
> utes, treaties, reports of departments of government, correspon-
> dence of eminent diplomatic characters, commercial statistics,
> etc. In church history they are the writings of the Fathers, as con-
> tained, for example in the "Patrologia of Migne"; the acts and
> decrees of councils, as contained in "Marisi"; the original deposi-
> tories of church doctrine, as the "Loci of Melancthon", or the
> "System of Hopkins." Decrees, reports, minutes, letters, monu-
> ments, works of Christian act, churches, etc., may be added.[16]

Acquisition of all types of material became crucial if the library
was properly to serve research.

Acquisition became, especially at the larger universities like
Harvard, almost a frenetic activity. Archibald Cary Coolidge, in
his first report to the corporation as chairman of the Library
Council in 1910, made clear his priorities for the Harvard
Library. Though difficulties of cataloging and access were for-
midable, they "should never make us lose sight of the necessity
of continuing to build up our collections by every possible
means." Coolidge cited rapidly rising prices of old and rare
books and the quick disappearance from the market of "complete sets of publications of academies and learned societies, of
archives, monuments, and other things of the sort, which the
Harvard Library ought to possess in as-great numbers as possible" as compelling reasons for the immediate necessity to acquire. If the Harvard Library was to retain its place as the
preeminent academic library in America, it had to act quickly
and forget about the niceties of library economy in favor of obtaining the materials.[17]

The quality of the library came to be defined almost exclu-
sively in terms of its holdings by university administrators. At
the fifteenth annual conference of the Association of American
Universities held in 1915, W. Dawson Johnston, librarian of
Columbia, delivered a paper in which he considered the library's
function in the university. The discussion that ensued quickly
turned from the topic of the paper, the value of the librarian, to
the more crucial questions in the minds of the university
presidents—the problems of acquiring books.[18]

Mounting desire to secure men of productive scholarship for
the faculties of the emerging universities underscored the im-

portance of expanded resources for research. When David Starr
Jordan of Stanford attempted to hire Cornell's George Lincoln
Burr, professor of history and keeper of White's private library
in 1891, he was unsuccessful. Burr answered that at Cornell he
had the facilities to continue his planned research and writing.
Though Cornell's library was meager, it was still better than
that of Stanford in Burr's field of interest—European history.
And, Cornell was comparatively close to the resources of
Boston, New York, and Philadelphia, whereas Palo Alto was not
within reach of anything.[19]

Guy Stanton Ford, of the University of Minnesota, addressed
the problem at the 1913 convention of the Association of
American Universities. Ford viewed the library as "the one central all-important institution making possible or impossible by
its strength or its weakness real university work by students and
instructors alike." He asserted that every dean and instructor
had watched their students leave for universities with better and
more complete libraries than they could offer. Every university
president had gained or lost in the strength of his faculty
because of the presence or lack of an outstanding library needed
by productive scholars.[20] Clearly, the strength of the library as
defined by its holdings was central to the university movement
as it developed in America.

Even the weaker institutions realized the utility of the library
and its resources in attracting men of quality. In 1916, the University of Southern California sought to strengthen its faculty
in philosophy. The faculty committee in charge of hiring determined that Ralph Tyler Flewelling was the man for the job.
President George F. Bovard wrote Flewelling on October 11,
1916, informing him of the decision. Bovard, however, was candid about the situation. He informed Flewelling that the committee in charge of hiring for the position thought him the person for the job and that he had the qualifications that would
"make a name for the university." But the position was not all
that it could be for a competent scholar. The library was not
very large and the appropriations for acquisitions were meager.
Though the university was willing to allow money for books
necessary for the courses offered, the president was quite
honest about further possibilities: "It is not our plan to buy

books which are not used by students taking courses." The university promised to acquire the materials necessary for the students, but refused to commit itself to support the work of the professors.[21] Flewelling accepted the offer and built what is perhaps the finest collection in philosophy in the United States for the University of Southern California.

Aside from Harvard, no academic library in the country claimed holdings of more than 100,000 volumes in 1876. By 1920, that mark had been surpassed by many. The nine university libraries in the table below could muster barely one-half million volumes in their main libraries in the mid-1870s. By 1920, they boasted almost 6.5 million, an increase of 1367 percent. These numbers of course, must be approached with caution. The 1876 Report credited La Fayette College of Easton, Pennsylvania, with 20,000 volumes. The library actually held only about 6000 volumes and those uncataloged. The librarian of Baylor optimistically reported holdings of 39,216 volumes in 1914. An inventory taken by her replacement in October, 1914, found only 30,616.[22]

GROWTH IN HOLDINGS OF ACADEMIC LIBRARIES, 1876–1920

Institution	No. Volumes, 1876	No. Volumes, 1920
Yale	78,000	1,157,000
Northwestern	30,000	192,000
Harvard	154,000	2,101,200
Univ. of Michigan	23,000	444,000
Univ. of Penn.	20,000	494,000
Princeton	29,500	444,000
Columbia	19,000	761,000
Cornell	39,000	631,000
Brown	45,000	258,000

Undeniably, growth in resources was the major trend in both college and research libraries. In addition to holdings of books, subscriptions to periodicals increased. George Works found dramatic increases in subscription lists in the first quarter of the twentieth century. Of the sixteen institutions surveyed, only Cornell showed a decrease in subscriptions, but Cornell also had established a high level of subscriptions at an earlier date than most of the others.

GROWTH OF PERIODICAL SUBSCRIPTIONS OF
ACADEMIC LIBRARIES, 1900–1925

Institution	1900	1925	Percent Growth
Iowa State	200	1,414	607
Univ. Cal.	7,000 (1913)	11,179	59
Univ. Cinn.	351 (1902)	1,063	202.8
Cornell	2,334 (1916)	2,288	−2
Univ. Ill.	414	9,943 (1924)	1,401.7
Univ. Iowa	213	1,176	452.1
Univ. Mich.	775	3,361	333.7
Univ. Minn.	321 (1906)	1,715	534.3
Univ. N.C.	200 (1907)	1,700	750
Oberlin	73 (1902)	451	517.8
Univ. Oregon	158 (1909)	778	392.4
Rutgers	520 (1915)	665	25.7
Stanford	334	1,255	275.7
Tulane	79	228	188.6
Vassar	457 (1923)	542	18.6
Yale	8,899 (1920)	11,548	29.8

A dramatic change in the financial situation of American higher education enabled institutions to meet the demand for increasingly available library materials. In 1875, the total income for higher education in America was $7,960,569. By 1925–26, receipts were $479,777,664. Some of this money went toward buying library materials. The combined book budgets of the universities of California, Illinois, Michigan, Minnesota was $456,000 in 1900. By 1920, it was $4,837,000. Even Southern universities—the University of Alabama, Georgia, Mississippi, North and South Carolina, Tennessee, Virginia, and Louisiana State—though slow in their development, demonstrated concern with the growth of the libraries. From 1900 to 1920, these institutions increased their combined book budgets from $63,000 to over $441,000.[23]

The development of substantial funding for acquisitions was responsible for much of the growth. The culls from Mr. Sibley's butter-firkin could not support research and the haphazard appropriation of a few hundred or a few thousand dollars here and there for new books could not keep pace with the rapid developments in research. Sustained funding was necessary if academic libraries were to support the work of their faculties and students. The following table indicates the substantial growth in annual acquisitions and the relatively high level of support that academic libraries had achieved by the 1925–26 academic year. These institutions responded to the challenge of the university movement by offering the most meaningful commitment they could make to research and their libraries—money.

Gifts continued to be an important source of collection development until the turn of the century. The decline of student literary societies in the northeast between the end of the Civil War and 1876 because of the development of a liberalized curriculum, athletics programs, fraternities, and student activities programs, and the emergence of a student body uninterested in the discipline of debate usually culminated in the donation of the society libraries, some of which were significant collections, to the college library. In the South, this event lagged somewhat behind Northern schools, but by the beginning of the new century, college and university libraries across the country were swollen by these collections.[25]

In some cases, this was not a simple process. Students at Amherst donated the books of two literary societies, the Athenian and the Alexandrian, to the college library in 1867, with the condition that a new library building be erected. The college administration declined. The students again petitioned for a new building to house the merged collections in 1873. In 1875, the condition was accepted, but not until 1883 was a new addition to the old building completed and the collections merged.[26]

Gifts from professors were also important sources of material. Many besides White collected with the idea that eventually their personal libraries would go to their colleges. James Russell Lowell, a compulsive bibliophile on the Harvard faculty, wrote Charles Eliot Norton on April 15, 1878, complaining of the lack of good booksellers in Spain. "I buy," he wrote, "mainly with a view to the College Library, wither they will go when I am in Mount Auburn."[27] The library of Johns Hopkins, for many years after its founding, was added to primarily through gifts.

GROWTH AND EXPENDITURES FOR
MATERIALS, 1925-1926[24]

Institution	Volumes Added	Expenditures for Materials ($)
Brown	19,906	36,460
Bryn Mawr	4,397	12,966
Univ. California*	28,624	78,304
Univ. Chicago	23,105	70,750
Univ. Colorado	9,765	25,200
Columbia	30,773	101,240
Cornell	18,270	52,420
Dartmouth	9,780	31,154
Duke (1928-29)	28,860	95,406
Harvard	81,459	179,807
Univ. Illinois	49,325	114,076
Indiana University	8,825	20,367
Iowa State (1927-28)	13,303	50,400
Univ. Iowa	19,381	57,439
Johns Hopkins	9,715	37,566
Univ. Kansas	8,517	20,000
Univ. Michigan	23,331	90,055
Univ. Minnesota	24,786	84,187
Univ. Missouri	9,825	16,600
Univ. Nebraska	9,572	41,000
Univ. North Carolina	11,259	23,957
Univ. North Dakota	3,248	9,232
Northwestern University (Evanston & Chicago)	14,561	42,827
Oberlin	13,314	15,500
Ohio State	13,429	63,030
Univ. Oregon	12,136	26,186
Univ. Pennsylvania	18,106	53,670
Princeton	23,910	60,020
Univ. Rochester	8,900	53,212
Smith College	11,509	15,090
Stanford	14,119	45,859
Univ. Texas	13,585	32,863
Vassar	5,089	14,900
Univ. Virginia	4,220	4,966
Univ. Washington	12,464	47,453
Washington University	16,301	69,550
Wellesley College	3,367	12,077
Univ. Wisconsin	17,817	54,236
Yale	66,935	112,031

*Exclusive of departmental libraries

But these were not the random collections of sermons donated by retiring clergymen that had characterized the collections of the classical colleges. Such collections as the private library of Johann Kaspar Bluntschli, Heidelberg Professor of Law, which was purchased by a group of Baltimore citizens in 1883 and formed the basis of the history and political science seminar, and the bequest of John W. McCoy's library of 8000 volumes of Americana, travel, and fine arts, were the gifts that Hopkins sought.[28]

The preference of money to buy books over the donation of books themselves asserted itself as a healthy sentiment that what really mattered was the gift itself. Both Archibald Cary Coolidge, director of the library at Harvard from 1910 to 1926, and Louis Round Wilson, librarian at the University of North Carolina from 1899 to 1926, cultivated men of means who were willing to contribute to the purchase of special collections and items as they came onto the market.[29]

The desire to lure appropriate gifts sometimes resulted in "seeding" the collection. John Buell Munn (Harvard PhD 1917) was professor of English at New York University. He was also a frequent contributor to the Harvard library. In 1925, he purchased the notebooks of Joseph Conrad to give to the Harvard library. Though he thought it "another fool thing" to have made the purchase when he wrote to Coolidge on September 18, he did it from a wish to "start up an interest in the modern field." He noted that there were many collectors of modern literature among Harvard graduates and he wanted them to be aware of Harvard's interest in the area: "I'm against mss. as much as you are, but by this we may swing a fine Conrad library in the near future."[30]

Exchanges also became a major source of materials for academic libraries. The growth of university presses and scholarly publications of various departments of the universities gave libraries a source of wealth unassociated with budgets. By 1923–24, exchanges were a major library activity at the larger universities. In that year, the University of California received some 30,000 individual pieces and distributed 50,000. The University of Michigan received 4990 and sent out 5312. The University of Minnesota was sent 3171 books and 5100 pamphlets and distributed 213 books and 1718 pamphlets. Yale received 9252 individual pieces and sent 4203. These were individual issues of journals, catalogs, books from the university presses, proceedings of societies located on the campus, and official university publications. But they represented a real and concrete supplement to the library's materials budgets. It was widely recognized that this represented an exchange of value for value rather than an attempt to give university publications the widest dissemination possible. In most libraries, records were kept in parallel columns so that what was sent out could be easily matched against what was received.[31]

The rapid growth of resources in the form of books, manuscripts, and periodicals through purchase, gifts, and exchanges was only one aspect of the effect of the university movement on the American academic library. The demands for resources and their accompanying growth led early to problems of access and logistic difficulty in handling the bibliographical mass. The notion that the library was a valuable collegiate resource that must be protected gradually lost ground to recognition that the library was a laboratory and the materials tools which could wear out in the course of use.[32]

Much of the pressure to liberalize access to the college and university libraries came directly from the faculty. In 1875, Henry Adams petitioned the Harvard Corporation to turn the library from an exhibit hall into a working collection. Adams pointed out that as assistant professor of history, he required his students to "use to the utmost possible extent the resources of the College Library." The arrangement of Gore Hall, however, thwarted this educational plan: "The students require room, especially table-room, which is not given them." Adams pointed to the waste of needed room which was "occupied by show-cases, stands or other fixtures, which do not necessarily belong there and which add nothing to the proper usefulness of the institution." He requested that these fixtures be removed and "that a long table may, so soon as the Honorable Corporation think proper, be substituted." The table was granted.[33]

One of the more significant manifestations of liberalization was an increase in hours of opening. The universities studied by George Works in his survey of university libraries demonstrated that the academic library of 1925 had increased its hours of service dramatically over the opening hours of the classical college. By the end of the 1924–25 academic year, sixteen of the libraries surveyed by Works were open an average of eighty-nine hours per week.

The liberalization of hours of opening was due directly to the demands for books and materials of research and the view of most institutions that the library was for reference. Consequently, the books had to be on the shelves if the library was to perform its proper function. As a result of this attitude, many universities severely limited the use of books outside of the library while liberalizing hours of opening.

In many cases, this was found to be a difficult policy to enforce. Joseph Cummings Rowell, librarian of the University of California, opposed the library rules adopted in 1876 by the faculty library committee. In 1886, he reaffirmed his opposition to the policies he was forced to work under. The 1876 rules called for circulation of books to students only on the written authorization of a teacher in charge of a department for the specific books to be released. Soon after the 1876 rules were adopted, Rowell modified them by interpreting them to mean that he himself as librarian was the head of a department and could authorize lending books to students. Rowell was driven to this by the rigid lending policies that required students to procure written permission to take a book out of the library overnight and the policy of allowing students access to the shelves. The students, rather than troubling themselves or their professors, would merely secrete the books on their persons and leave the library. Rowell felt that this was morally degrading to the students and ultimately injurious to the library.

After Rowell announced to the president the plan by which he had thwarted the intent of the 1876 rules for ten years, a new set of rules was adopted in 1887 whereby all students were allowed to remove up to three books at one time from the library. These could be taken out after 4 PM and were due back before 10 AM the following morning. On Friday, they were due on Monday morning. The only exceptions to this were made with the written permission of the university president who could allow the books to remain out longer than one night. Both graduate and undergraduate students were subject to this ruling which required a $5 deposit of all students wishing to make use of the privilege.[35]

The University of Missouri followed a similar pattern. Until 1873 books circulated freely to faculty and to students who had paid a deposit. In 1873 all circulation was stopped, but the next year professors were allowed as many as six books for up to two weeks. When the students petitioned for the same privilege, they were denied. The Board of Curators affirmed that Missouri was to have a reference and not a circulating library. But, by 1892, that had proved an impossible regulation and a system of cash deposits for circulation privileges was in force.[36]

It was not only the threat of book losses that forced liberalization in circulation policies. In 1856, the University of Michigan ceased allowing students to use books outside the library building. But by 1906, massive congestion around the desk where students requested books from the closed stacks for use in the reading room forced the library to allow them to withdraw books for use outside the library, put shelving for a 6000 volume browsing collection in the reading room, and turn the faculty reading room into a periodical room.[37]

One common device of reconciliation between access and preservation lay in the development of browsing and circulating collections housed in the various reading rooms. As late as 1905, conservative Princeton allowed a few people with guides into the stack tower for the view only on commencement day or when an important football game was being played. But the library did maintain a browsing collection of 40,000 volumes in the reading room. The Library Council of Ohio State broadened its policies in allowing books to circulate for four days with the possibility of two days' renewal. Provision was made so that the Library Council could designate certain classes of books as "circulating" that would not require the signature of an instructor for the student to withdraw them.[38]

Circulation of books had, by the mid-1920s, become a major activity in American academic libraries. For the academic year 1925–26, the University of Chicago reported a total circulation of 482,910 volumes; the University of Cincinnati, 209,085; Northwestern University, 159,178; and the University of Southern California, 176,247.[39]

The library, in the rhetoric of college administrators, had

become a major instrument through which the ideals of research and scholarship were realized in the university movement. By the turn of the century, the image of the library as the "heart" of the modern academic institution was firmly established in the oratory of commencement days and building drives. The interdependence between productive scholarship and the raw materials of research had become generally recognized. Charles F. Thwing, addressing the problems of administering academic institutions, defined the university as "a unique combination of the library and of the scholar." Without scholars, the library "is a pile of bricks without an architect." Without a library, the scholar "is an architect without bricks." The edifice of the university was firmly constructed on the imagination and talents of the scholar utilizing the building materials of the library.[40]

Through the half century from 1875 to 1925, increased demands for materials were satisfied with vastly increased holdings. Demands for greater access were accorded extended hours of opening. As students and faculty members increased and the new forms of teaching and scholarship spread through the country, circulation of books became a major function of the college libraries. Academic librarians' use of the old tools of ledger books for circulation records, book catalogs, or the librarian's memory for finding tools, and a fixed place in each alcove for storage in order to control the college treasury of books became increasingly difficult to apply to the new expanded role of the library in the academic institution.

The increased demands placed on the library resulted directly in the position of the librarian becoming a full-time occupation in American higher education. Institution after institution across the country found that the part-time faculty member, with perhaps the aid of a few indigent students, was inadequate for the task of maintaining what was quickly becoming a major facility of the expanded university. A few schools like Brown and Harvard had early felt the necessity for a person whose time was totally dedicated to the work of the library; as the century drew to a close, more and more colleges and universities found that the demands of the library were such as to command the attention of competent, dedicated men and women. Earl

McGrath's study of the administrative evolution of American higher education found that of thirty-two institutions, twenty-one listed the position of librarian combined with other duties in their catalogs before 1900. He found only eight such combinations after the turn of the century, and three of the eight were combinations of librarian and head of a library school.[41]

The evolution of the position of librarian from a part-time adjunct duty of a professor, college president, or janitor to a distinct academic specialization was slow. But a general recognition that the importance of the function and the complexities of the tasks mandated more than the desultory efforts of someone whose major energies were drained by various other teaching and administrative assignments did develop among administrators and faculty members so that they began to view the position as deserving the attention of a full-time person.

When President James McCosh came to Princeton in 1868, he found an ill-equipped library opened only one hour a week. He ordered it opened every day and hired Frederick Vinton away from the Library of Congress in 1873 to serve as librarian with no additional duties. Berkeley hired Joseph Cummings Rowell in 1875 to replace the series of part-time faculty members and students that had maintained the library since the beginning in 1869. The University of Missouri promoted a part-time assistant to full-time librarian in 1877 when the professor in charge of the library resigned because of bad health. The University of Alabama appointed a retired general in 1879 who was succeeded upon his death by his wife. Ohio Wesleyan appointed the first full-time librarian in 1877, but he was under the general supervision of the titular librarian, Professor of Latin, Dr. William Francis Whitlock, who was required to pay one-third of the librarian's salary out of his own pocket. Miss Julia H. Wilcos was appointed in 1883 full time at the University of Mississippi after the book budget had increased enough so that the Board of Trustees felt the position justified. Mrs. Mary J. C. Merrill accepted the position at Michigan State in 1883. Miss Carrie Watson, assistant to a professor-librarian, became full-time librarian at the University of Kansas upon his resignation in 1887. The same year, the University of Georgia hired Miss Sarah A. Frierson, "an Athens lady of middle age," to serve as the first full-time librarian. In 1887, Mrs. Zella Dixson was hired to catalog the collection of Dennison. The next year, she was appointed full-time librarian. Miss Margaret Morrow was hired at West Virginia University in 1889 because President Eli Marsh Turner, convinced the regents that a full-time librarian was necessary to deal with the increasingly complex problems of library operations. Edwin Wiley, a University of Tennessee graduate of 1891, was hired in 1892 as librarian of his *alma mater*. Olive Branch Jones, who had served as a student assistant to the library at Ohio State, was given the permanent post of librarian in 1893. The University of Illinois found its man in Percy Bicknell in 1894.[42]

Emma O. Rider became the first full-time librarian at Hiram College in Hiram, Ohio, in 1895. Bucknell hired Miss Mary E. Brown expressly to catalog the collection in 1889, though the library remained under the direction of Professor of Logic and Anthropology, W. E. Martin, until his death in 1922. Benjamin Wyche was hired at the University of Texas in 1897 after the president of the university expressed a desire for a full-time librarian. In 1898, Joseph Penn Breedlove was hired by Trinity (later Duke) to care for the library on a full-time basis, and the next year the need had been felt by the Oregon State University administrators who offered their job to Arthur Stimpson.[43]

Antioch hired its first full-time assistant in 1900. Louisiana State also hired a full-time assistant in 1901 who moved up to the librarian's position with the resignation of the professor who had been in charge of the library. Baylor's small library began an immediate expansion when James J. Carroll was hired as a full-time librarian in 1901. Otterbein College appointed Miss Tirza Barnes, who had served as an assistant under various professors, to the post on a full-time basis. After a number of years of agitation by students and pressure from the president, the Board of Trustees of Wake Forest capitulated and approved a position of full-time librarian in 1908. North Central College in Naperville, Illinois, hired one of its own graduates, Ethel B. Gibson, in 1910 as the first full-time librarian. Trinity University of San Antonio, Texas, appointed Theresa Roberts Sims, wife of a professor, to the full-time post of librarian in 1919.[44]

While smaller colleges managed with only one full-time staff member and perhaps the part-time help of a few assistants, larger universities began to develop substantial staffs. By the 1925–26 academic year, Brown University's library staff numbered twenty-three full-time positions. The University of California counted forty-three employees at the main library and the University of Chicago added their student assistants to claim 103. Columbia reported ninety and Cornell, thirty-three. The University of Illinois claimed sixty-two and Indiana eleven, though it increased to twenty the next year. Johns Hopkins reported twenty-four and Dartmouth nineteen. The University of Kansas, like Chicago, counted the students and reported twenty-two. The Universities of Missouri and Nebraska reported twenty-one and thirty. The University of North Carolina had seventeen. The Evanston and Chicago campuses of Northwestern employed twenty-five full-time people and the University of Oregon probably excluded the clerical staff when it reported eighteen. The University of Rochester had sixteen; Stanford, thirty-two. Princeton reported sixty; but the University of Virginia had only seven. The University of Texas reported thirty; the University of Wisconsin claimed thirty-four.[45]

These new full-time library positions were made necessary by the increasingly complex problems of maintaining America's academic libraries. The men and women filling these positions used new tools of cataloging and classification devised by Dewey, Cutter, and Hanson to solve the library problems they inherited from the professors who had devised their own independent and haphazard systems of bibliographic control. They also evolved a variety of methods to deal flexibly with circulation of materials to replace the ledger books of the classical college libraries.[46] The new tools of librarianship brought with them an increasing body of technical knowledge that forced academic librarians to begin to recognize themselves as a distinctly specialized group. The formation of a national professional association in 1876, the American Library Association (ALA), gave focus to the development of professional distinctions among academic librarians. True, college librarians were neither a large nor important membership of the ALA until well into the twentieth century, the influence of men like Justin Winsor, librarian of Harvard from 1877 to 1897 and president of the ALA from 1876 to 1885, and the missionary zeal of Melvil Dewey who, in addressing the 1891 meeting of the Middle States Association of Colleges and Secondary Schools, compared the library to "the college well, open to the students whenever they are in the mood to use it,"[47] incorporated a philosophy of service into the professional awareness of academic librarians.

The emerging awareness that academic librarianship was a distinct activity was complicated by the public library movement. By the 1890s, it had become a maxim that *all* libraries should be *working* libraries. The habit of thought conditioned by the public library movement as institutionalized by the ALA insisted on service over accumulation in its definition of the purpose of libraries. Edith E. Clarke of the Newberry addressing the Library School in 1889, deplored the conditions of the Columbia University Library: "Some of the books in Columbia Library belong to the museum department. . . . They are of no earthly use, but are objects of antediluvian interest." If a library is to be a working library, it "should be kept as free from lumber as possible."[48]

Some academic librarians began to go so far as to extend their activities outside their immediate institutional concerns and approached an imitation of what might legitimately be considered the functions of the public library. By the turn of the century, Louis Round Wilson, librarian of the University of North Carolina, had established policies of lending books to former students, public school teachers, and members of women's clubs throughout the state.[49] Mary G. Lacey, reference librarian of the United States Department of Agriculture, seriously attempted to interest the librarians of agricultural colleges in developing their own extension services. Since most farmers' children did not even finish high school, she proposed that librarians should tour the common schools with miniature card catalogs and offer lectures on finding information. The children or their parents would know then to write to the librarian for information. The librarian would either send the appropriate agriculture department bulletin on the particular topic or refer the question to the proper local specialist. She realized that this was usurping the functions of the agricultural stations, but felt the beneficial results would be worth the efforts of librarians: "if the librarian or someone representing him appears before the children once a year and explains the working of the experimental station and the system by which anything published by any of them can be instantly laid hold upon a personal bond is established which adds to the efficiency of the information received."[50] The missionary spirit of the library movement expanded through the period to include all libraries in its fervor.

The functions of academic libraries came to be defined in terms of the services they could render to their constituency. By 1930, a survey of land grant colleges prepared by the United States Office of Education could assert that "the efficiency of a library is measured by the service that it renders to faculty and students."[51] The logistic problems of maintaining great masses of materials in the collections, however, made librarians fear that service might suffer in the face of the mounting necessity to prepare books for use. In 1914, Azariah Smith Root of Oberlin predicted that by 1940 there would be a fourfold increase in the holdings of the larger research libraries. As the mass of material grew, and instructors became more and more specialized, there would be increasing demands on the librarians to aid in the use of materials. But even in 1914 Root perceived that librarians "fall far short of the service we ought to be rendering." Librarians even then expended too much effort readying books for the shelves to be able to devote time to their proper task of "increasing the efficient use of the book." Root called for more study in reducing the costs of processing to make more resources available for readers' services.[52]

Otis Robinson, librarian of the University of Rochester, clarified the relationship of the academic library to the general public. During the summer of 1877, the library moved to a new building, Sibley Hall. Robinson, in announcing the move to the library world through the *Library Journal*, proclaimed that henceforth the University of Rochester Library was to be a semipublic library, open to the local community without requiring a fee. Robinson felt that the new policy was "strictly in harmony with the general scope and purpose of a university." He proclaimed the true university to be "a center of educational influence." Its professors, researchers, and scholars were not paid simply to train students but to promote learning. If the professor "does his work well, he becomes the guide within that field of all within the realm of his influence." The professor has a great obligation to the general public and is not merely the servant of his immediate employer: "Whoever comes to him with a real question to be solved, or theory to be tested, or application to be made, has a claim upon him." As the professor has a public obligation, so has the university library to open its facility to the general advancement and dissemination of knowledge.

The force of Robinson's commitment is subject to some suspicion. After his display of concern for the public obligations of the university, he admitted that as a condition of the gift of Hiram Sibley, who paid for the new building, the library had to be opened to the public. But that this gift was accepted with this condition, and that the librarian could find rational philosophical reasons compatible with both the university movement and the public library movement to justify the expanded services of the library, points to a major development in the emergence of American academic librarianship.[53]

The philosophy of service that developed with the library movement emphasized use above all else. It held that a working library was the most desirable and the techniques of librarianship were subordinate to the ultimate object of enabling readers to find books. In a macabre image, Dewey elaborated on this theme when he explained the advantages of his relative classification over the fixed location of books:

> If soldiers ar ded and in the cemetary they ar as eazily found by fixt as by relativ location. But if the army is alive and militant, as every library or private working colection o't to be, its resources shud be *findable* whether in camp, on march, or in action.[54]

Academic librarians, as they adopted the techniques of the library movement, accepted a philosophy that placed use and service over custodianship and protection.

Justin Winsor emerged as probably the single most influential man in the developing field of academic librarianship in the late nineteenth century. The evident inadequacy of Sibley forced Harvard to look for a man of competent scholarship and library experience in 1877. They found him at the Boston Public Library. Winsor, while at Boston Public, was much more concerned with service to readers than with the bibliographical integrity of the collection. He instituted the policy of binding pamphlets in various groups designed to offer access through a variety of means. Copies of the same pamphlet could, for example, be found bound with others on the same subject, with others by the same author, and with others issued by the same agency. At Boston, he abolished the practice of closing in August for the annual inventory and established the first public library branch system in the United States.[55]

He brought his ideas to Harvard in 1877. His sympathy with the new forms of education and research that were developing there led immediately to the expansion of the reserve book system until it had grown beyond Gore Hall's capacity. This ultimately resulted in the establishment of small classroom libraries that Winsor accepted, feeling that the principle of use far outweighed the principle of control. He insisted only that these collections be always considered as part of the central library.[56] In a preliminary report to the Harvard Corporation written shortly after he had assumed the office of librarian, he enunciated his vision of the library. A mere guarded accumulation of books could be called a library but the real purpose of a library is to "help and spur men on in their daily work." It is only when this happens that "the library becomes a vital influence; the prison is turned into a workshop."[57] He felt that books themselves could even improve through use. In 1894 he recalled with approval having seen a number of books in a separate collection that had been lent to Thomas Carlyle by the London Library at St. James Square. They were kept as a special collection "because when he read them he had entered his pungent exclamations and pithy comments on the margins." The librarian, realizing the value of such marginalia, had habitually sent Carlyle anything that might interest him "because he was sure to scatter his distain on the blank spaces."[58]

When Winsor arrived at Harvard, he began a system that he referred to as *notes and queries*. A row of hooks was installed in the delivery room of Gore Hall and slips of paper with holes punched at the top were supplied to readers. Anyone with questions simply wrote them on the paper and hung it on the hook. Anyone with the inclination and the knowledge supplied the answer. Winsor reported that as many as forty or fifty slips would be skewered on the hooks at one time and he occasionally referred questions to various professors who would supply answers. Many were answered by Winsor himself or other members of the library staff. Winsor preferred to refer to books for the answers rather than directly answering questions from his own knowledge because he had "long known how much books of reference fail of all the good which they might accomplish, simply from ignorance of them, or inability to use them intelligently, and . . . looked to inculcating the habits of consulting such as not the least good to come from the plan."[59]

Winsor's view of service was far less mechanistic than his row of hooks might indicate. He disapproved of the growing tendency to develop annotated catalogs to guide readers and preferred employing reference librarians. The printed guides, he felt, were only "a poor substitute for a good encyclopedic adviser in the flesh, ever ready, alluring in manner, and with an enthusiasm for his work which will prove contagious."[60]

The scope of aid that Winsor offered to the Harvard faculty and students was great. In a letter dated September 27, 1881, Henry Adams, who was away from Cambridge at the time, addressed a few modest requests to the Harvard librarian:

> I return today the box of newspapers for a new load. It is astonishing how very little information is to be found in them. I want to learn all I can about the social and economical condition of the country in 1800. Can you send me a few books on the subject in the return box with the newspaper volumes? I want the Memoirs of Lindley Murray by himself. New York. 1827. John Fitch's Biography by Wescott, Phil. 1867. Colden's Life of Fulton, 1817. There is, I believe, a History or Memoir about the Middlesex Canal which I want to see; and I want to find out how much banking capital there was in the U. S. in 1800, and how it was managed. I want a strictly accurate account of the state of education and the practise [sic] of medicine. I want a good sermon of that date, if such a thing existed, for I cannot find one which seems to me even tolerable, from a literary or logical point of view. If you in your historical work have come across any facts or authorities which would aid me, I should like to beg them from you, especially if they tend to correct me. Thus far my impression is that America in

1800 was not far from the condition of England under Alfred the Great; that the conservative spirit was intensely strong in the respectable classes, and that there was not only indifference but actual aggressive repression toward innovation; the mental attitude of good society looks to me surprisingly mediaeval. I should wish to correct this impression. Did Harvard or Yale show anything to the contrary *before* 1800? I can see that Philadelphia was reasonably liberal and active-minded; was any other part of the country equally so? Was there a steam-engine in the United States?[61]

Adams, of course, was not reticent about asking aid and the nature of his requests demonstrates that he did not expect Winsor to be reluctant about granting it in the pursuit of scholarship.

Reference service emerged in the first decade of the twentieth century as a distinct, established function of the academic library. But before World War I, it focused entirely on assisting undergraduate students in using the machinery of the library. The absence of actual departmental status for reference work in academic libraries did not however, decrease its impact on the thought that defined the emerging specialty of academic librarianship. As noted earlier, the vigor of the public library movement directly affected the development of librarianship in academic institutions. Walter B. Briggs, reference librarian at the Brooklyn Public Library, addressed the College and Reference Section of the 1907 Ashville Conference of the ALA on the nature of reference work in academic and public libraries. He pointed to information bureaus in large newspaper offices that did high-quality work in supplying information with few resources. In a modern-sounding simile, he compared the reference department to "a telephone switchboard, the center which receives questions and makes connection between the inquirer and the source of information, whether it be a book or a person." Briggs went on from Brooklyn to head the reference and circulation department at Harvard that was organized in 1915. Louis Round Wilson of the University of North Carolina developed this same theme in a paper delivered to a convention of the Georgia Library Association in April, 1911. It is not enough, Wilson asserted, for librarians merely to know the tools of reference work. They must also be attuned to the life and thought of the campus to give effective service.[62]

Academic reference work, by the turn of the century, could be defined as a specific set of activities. Isadore Gilbert Mudge in her 1901–1902 report on the reference department of the University of Illinois identified four major components in reference work. She understood the necessity for a well-developed reference collection. Mudge specified that these works should be in English, but only because work at the University of Illinois used few foreign resources. She recognized the necessity for access and recommended that the reference collection be placed "where it can be most easily and conveniently consulted by the students." Printed guides and directions, notes in the tools themselves, and indexes, "such as the new Poole periodicals," were indispensable. Giving "personal help in the use of the library whenever possible, and in giving such help to endeavor always to help the student to independent and intelligent use of the library resources for himself" was acknowledged as a major element of the proper reference function of the library.[63]

By the end of the 1920s, the function and scope of reference work in academic libraries had been generally recognized to such an extent that the American Library Association's Committee on the Classification of Library Personnel could issue a report on college librarians that provided what amounted to a description of the job of a head of an academic library reference department. The typical tasks of such a person were:

> To list material published on underlying causes of farmer's political movements since Civil War; find material on traces of Marlowe in Shakespeare's Richard II and Richard III; ascertain European literature in all languages on methods used to limit progress of the corn borer; list discussion of slavery in the French literature of the 18th century.[64]

Unlike Henry Adams, the committee did not insist that the librarian attack such a diversity of problems concurrently.

Another manifestation of the intrusion of the new "library spirit" into the realm of academic librarians was the gradual development of interlibrary loan agreements. Joseph Cummings Rowell of the University of California has been credited as the first academic librarian regularly to allow his charges to leave his protective care in this fashion.[65] Rowell had advocated and practiced the lending of books among libraries as early as 1886. In 1894, he addressed a specific proposal to the university's library committee asking permission to establish reciprocal borrowing arrangements with the California State Library. The committee approved, and the arrangement was so satisfactory that in 1898 Rowell proposed a similar plan to various other libraries around the country. Forty libraries both in the East and West accepted the proposal; by 1899, the University of California had borrowed from the University of Michigan, the University of Chicago, Columbia, Harvard, and the Boston Public Library. California had lent books to the San Diego Public Library, the University of Chicago, the University of Illinois, the Los Angeles Normal School, and the Santa Rosa Public Library. Interlibrary borrowing was not frequent in the early years because of the high cost of shipping and, of course, the difficulties of locating copies of individual titles in remote libraries. But after 1900, interlibrary loan developed greater importance. The idea spread and by 1899, Harvard, Cornell, and Indiana universities among others, were involved in various agreements to lend books to other libraries. By the mid-1920s, interlibrary loan was a solidly established function of American academic libraries.[66]

The attitude toward service and concomitant feeling that the academic library and the librarian had a significant role to play in the academic community derived directly from realization that research and scholarship were the important aspects of the university movement in America. Edwin H. Woodruff, librarian of Cornell, addressed the relation of the new learning to the library at the Milwaukee Conference of the ALA in 1886. He observed that the seminar methods by which students pursued their investigations under the direction of a professor and the "topical" method, by which students used the library to prepare themselves on various subjects and reported to classes on their research in the library were increasingly used in undergraduate education. Woodruff concluded that this technique functionally turned every professor into a librarian for his department inasmuch as use was involved. Further, he asserted that *"The missing aid, distinct personal assistance, would be found in the professor."*[67]

Melvil Dewey was less sanguine about the possibilities of the individual professor's abilities to act as "librarian." In an inspirational piece appearing in the first volume of *Library Notes*, he made similar observations about the new learning and the academic library—but came to different conclusions. Dewey pointed out that "the colleges are waking up to the fact that the work of every professor and every department is necessarily based on the library." The task of students in the new order was not to master the text but "to investigate for themselves and to *use* the books." Dewey felt that it was not the professors' province to teach the use of this primarily learning tool, but the librarian's: "With the reference librarians to counsel and guide readers; with the greatly improved catalogues and indexes, cross-references, notes and printed guides, it is quite possible to make a great university of a great library without professors."[68]

The expanded role of the library in American higher education and the new sense of professional awareness fostered by the ALA and nurtured by the desire of academic librarians to create for themselves a sense of place in the academic community led directly to a general feeling that the librarian played a prominent role in the teaching process. Most academic librarians would not have gone as far as Dewey in asserting that higher education could function perfectly well without professors provided that the library were good enough, but they took the maxim that "the library is the heart of the university" seriously. Samuel S. Green's paper, "Desirableness of Establishing Personal Intercourse and Relations between Librarians and Readers in Public Libraries," read at the founding conference of the ALA in 1876, was warmly received by academic librarians. Otis Robinson, in his comments on the paper, reported that he had previously asked Green to include college librarians in his consideration. Robinson felt, "The relation which Mr. Green has presented ought especially to be established between a college librarian and his student readers." In Robinson's opinion, the position of the college librarian was a special one both in higher education and in librarianship, and "no librarian is fit for his place unless he holds himself to some degree responsible for the library education of the students."

Robinson viewed the techniques of research as the particular knowledge the librarian had to pass on to students. Factual information was there, but only as the means to develop the method. The importance of a formal college education did not reside in what was taught the students, but how they were trained in the methods of research: "All that is taught in college amounts to very little; but if we can send students out self-reliant in their investigations, we have accomplished very much."[69]

Robinson elaborated on this theme throughout his career. In the 1876 report, he proposed a formalization of the role of the librarian. The random knowledge of books received by students from various faculty members was obviously inadequate. The librarian, with his knowledge of "the reading habits of students," was in a much better position to formally educate students in bibliographical matters. He proposed a "brief course of lectures on books; how to get them, how to keep them, and how to use them" to "come from a scholarly librarian in a systematic way."[70]

Many schools instituted some sort of systematic means through which the librarian formally participated in the process of general education. The procedure described by Ada North in 1885 at Iowa State is probably typical: "The librarian gives to the Freshman class upon entering, a familiar talk upon the use of catalogues, reference books, and other library appliances." After this introduction, "one or more addresses upon books and reading, urging upon them especially a systematic plan of work and a definite purpose" are offered. These were supplemented by "a series of Monday morning talks" given by the president of the university on library-related topics "and throughout the year special aid and counsel is given by the librarian to individual students whenever the opportunity offers."[71]

But the feeling was current that the librarian had a much more diffuse and generalized teaching function than a few formal lectures on "library appliances." The Reverend T. K. Davis, librarian of the University of Wooster, speaking before the College Association of Ohio at Springfield on December 30, 1884, found an almost cosmic role for the librarian to play in higher education. The librarian with the faculty, was "responsible for the healthy moral and intellectual growth of the students."

Librarians who properly understood and realized their role in the college introduced "into the youthful mind of to-day a current reading and thinking which will silently but powerfully help to shape the Christian civilization of the future."[72] In the secularized emerging American university, however, most academic librarians did not see a religious purpose, but focused on the abandonment of general culture by the specialization of academic disciplines.

Alfred Clanghorn Potter, assistant in charge of the Order Department of the Harvard Library, read a paper before the College and Reference Library Work Section of the ALA at the 1897 Philadelphia Conference. He maintained that simply providing books for collateral reading and research was insufficient if the library was to realize its commitment to the goals of higher education. Giving the students "general culture" is the highest purpose of the college and the library could play a major part in that cultural transfer. Even though they may not be treated within the curriculum, the library must provide on its shelves the standard monuments of civilization. Further, the librarian had a duty to introduce students to them. By assuming this role, "the library can aid the college in sending out on commencement day men who are more than mere scholars, who are well read, who know the world of books and how to use it, who, in short, have attained not only scholarship but culture."[73]

Isadore Gilbert Mudge echoed this sentiment in 1906 when she pointed out the evils of the overly specialized undergraduate curriculum. The elective system had so constricted the range of subjects available to individual undergraduates that they could be well read in a few areas and totally illiterate in all others. Colleges and universities were failing to produce "the cultivated man or woman who is heir to the world's civilization." She also felt that it was the duty of the college library to rectify the situation by encouraging well-rounded reading among the students.[74]

But it was not only in the contact between librarian and student that academic librarians found their professional purpose. Ernest Cushing Richardson, librarian of Princeton, pointed out in 1915 that the acts of organization engaged in by librarians produce in themselves teaching tools. The catalogs, both author and subject, constructed by librarians were the principal form of teaching. The subject catalog was especially important. It "is a series of little bibliographical lectures, which, theoretically at least, every professor prefixes to every course." Richardson perceived no difference between the bibliographical lectures of classroom professors and the subject analysis performed by the catalogers on the library staff.[75]

The activities of the academic librarian through readers' service, the promotion of general reading, and the production of subject access through the catalogs and indexes of the library, were generally directed toward assisting the undergraduate student to cope with the burgeoning masses of materials being collected by the emerging academic libraries. The creation of special library facilities for the use of undergraduates was proposed by Harry Lyman Koopman, librarian of Brown, at the 1894 ALA Lake Placid Conference. Koopman asserted that a decline in book ownership by families had deprived students entering colleges of the cultural influence of living with books. The emerging university libraries, because of their complexity and size, were inappropriate for introducing young minds to the world of books: "while we furnish opportunity for special research to the graduate or university student in the modern sense, if we provide no corresponding privilege for the undergraduate or college student, we are discriminating harshly against the college." Koopman suggested a collection limited to 10,000 well-selected volumes separated from the research collections of the institution that would have a "professor of books" to guide the student in his reading. He also proposed a catalog that would give information about the individual book and its place in the literature of the subject. Joseph F. Daniels, librarian of the State Agricultural College of Colorado at Fort Collins read a curious paper before the College and Reference Section of the 1907 ALA conference in which he put the number of critical volumes much higher. Among other statements including urging college libraries to enter the bookselling business because they had so much in common with publishers, he observed, "There are not 50,000 books worth a place in any one main college library today."[76]

But, whether the optimum was 50,000 or 10,000 volumes, the

view that there was a limitation based on usability and value prevailed. Though men like William Warner Bishop could legitimately plead for more materials, concluding that no matter how much there were, scholarship would benefit, the preponderance of academic librarians recognized the logical necessity to limit size in order to improve services. The desire "to have the freshest and best books that can be procured, and also to secure an intelligent and vigorous administration of the library,"[77] held the day against the indiscriminate collectors.

The demands of administering the new vitalized academic libraries required more than the efforts of the librarians of the classical colleges. The complexities of mass, the intricacies of the mechanisms devised to deal with the mass, and the growth of a service orientation demanded librarians of high intellectual caliber. The library was no longer a simple financial asset of the college, but a major facility in the new forms of education and research that had developed. James Hulme Canfield, librarian of Columbia, asserted in 1906 that "the college library has become, by the very force of circumstances, a department of as much independence and dignity and value as any other department in the institution."[78] University of Colorado librarian C. E. Lowrey gave the library—and the librarian—an even larger place in the academic community, comparing the range of the varied duties of the academic librarian to that of the university president.[79] Perhaps under the sway of Dewey, President Frederick Augustus Porter Barnard argued in his annual report for 1883 that instruction in the use of books by the librarian was at least as important as the work of professors in other areas. Librarian Joseph F. Daniels of the Colorado State Agricultural College in 1907 looked to the future and saw the academic library "destined to be greater than any department of instruction." The librarian of the future "fifty years hence will be the most important member of a faculty—the dean, as we say."[80]

Academic librarians across the country began to find a purpose in their function greater than the limited vision of custodianship. They surveyed the realm of American higher education, and found the library emerging as the center of activity for both members of the faculty and students. As directors of the major facility of learning, many academic librarians at the turn of the century envisioned their administrative and teaching roles as transcending the somewhat limited and specialized tasks of the individual faculty member.

There were two aspects to the new professional awareness that developed. The administrative importance of the office vied with its scholarly significance. The daily control of the complexities of the modern academic librarian made administrative ability necessary. William Isaac Fletcher, librarian of Amherst from 1883 to 1911, described the "new-fashioned librarian" as "above all else an administrator." His daily tasks were concerned with the mechanism of the library: "He organizes, classifies, catalogs (in several different ways), introduced 'systems'—charging systems, two-book systems, delivery systems, and so on." This, with the training, evaluation, and supervision of assistants made the librarian close to the businessman in function and activity. But even Fletcher was forced to conclude that scholarship "is *sine qua non*, the one thing needful of librarianship."[81]

Rowell at Berkeley also felt that the librarian should be "possessed of all such qualities as best bestead the shrewd merchant and salesman." But, he also insisted on broad general scholarship as the primary characteristic of the academic librarian. Justin Winsor defined the type and tasks of scholarship as they related to librarianship in more specific terms. Cataloging, the major technical function of the new academic librarians was, to Winsor, not a mechanical application of a set of rules to a problem but a creative scholarly activity. A library cataloger performed "no rough work of the auctioneer's kind, but scholarly and faithful inquiry embodied in a fixed comprehensive method." The task of the cataloger was not a routine clerical operation of assigning categories to a few similar items, but a constant challenge to intellect: "Every book must be questioned persistently as to its author, its kind, its scope, its relations to all knowledge."[82]

The administrative functions of the librarian came to be regarded as a special province having the same degree of autonomy as the various specialization of the faculty. The academic library in its ongoing operations assumed, at least to librarians, an aspect of autonomy that roughly paralleled that of the other academic departments and demanded academic freedom as a criteria for full enrollment in the university movement. Louis Round Wilson addressed the problems of the librarian in the academic community in 1911 with a plea for understanding of the requirements of the situation:

> In all matters of administration of a purely business nature, such as the keeping of library accounts, placing orders, of employing assistants, of caring for the building, of classifying and cataloging books, of performing all those technical administrative duties which inhere to the position, the word of the librarian should be final. If he is to be anything more than a clerk, if his spirit of initiative is to result in the betterment of the office over which he presides, if he is to develop and grow to the full requirements of his position, he must feel the weight of the responsibility on his own shoulders, and must experience the joy which comes not from sharing in the rewards of another's toil, but in the joy of his own.[83]

But it was not in the joy of the toil that academic librarians ultimately attempted to define their academic existence. It was in the nature of that work and the part it played in the ongoing academic enterprise.

In the thinking of librarians and administrators alike, the nature of the academic library demanded that the librarian share the essential concerns of the academic community. Daniel Coit Gilman, at the ceremonies dedicating Cornell's Sage library in 1891, affirmed that a library dedicated to the service of scholars must be headed by a scholar. A "man of wide knowledge" who "should at least command Greek and Latin, French and German" and be as at home with the sciences as with literature, was needed for the demanding position as head of a scholarly library. Gilman's vision of the scholarly librarian called for a man of much broader talent than the specialist: "He should survey with an eagle's eye the vast fields of human activity and discern with prophetic instinct what books will soon be wanted."[84]

William Warner Bishop, librarian of the University of Michigan also deplored the emphasis on administrative detail over scholarship. In 1919, he looked back to "the old-fashioned librarian" who "was preëminently scholarly in his tastes and habits." Bishop abhorred the phrase—and the substance—of what he occasionally had heard called the "library business" and felt that "one of our greatest perils is the exaltation of executive ability over scholarly attainment."[85]

Academic librarians felt their way to a sense of professional dignity through defining their activities as teaching and their work as essentially scholarly in nature. W. Dawson Johnston, librarian of Columbia, addressed the fifteenth annual conference of the Association of American Universities in 1913 attempting "to make it clear that the administrative problems of the library staff are problems of instruction primarily, rather than problems of clerical attendance and mechanical dexterity."[86]

The standing of the librarian in the academic hierarchy became a crucial question for academic librarians attempting to justify the intellectual aspirations of their new professionalism. Raymond Cazallis Davis, librarian of the University of Michigan from 1877 to 1905, was so concerned about the problem that, though he was unable to attend the 1890 ALA Fabyan House Conference, he wrote a letter to be read before the College and Reference Library Section. He opened by asserting a basic assumption in American academic librarianship: "It is agreed, I think, that the college librarian should be on an equality with the members of the faculty—in all particulars that make up the standing of a professor." He does not seem to have been contradicted to any great extent at the conference. Melvil Dewey, trying to recruit students for his new school at Columbia, spread the idea by telling a group of women college graduates: "library work offers you two fields analogous to the work of the public school [public librarianship] and the college professor [academic librarianship]."[87] Clearly, the position of librarian was considered to be, at least to some degree, analogous to that of the faculty in its importance in American higher education. Some form of equality of recognition with the teachers in the expanded academic enterprise was felt mandated by the increased importance of the libraries in the work of America's colleges and universities.

William Elmer Henry of the University of Washington elaborated a rationale for faculty status for academic librarians at the Pasadena Conference of the ALA in 1911. Henry maintained that the rank of a faculty member of a college or university in no way depended on his abilities, but was determined by his education and his part in educating others. Since the college professor usually has no training for his teaching duties, his rank depends upon his degrees with no indication "that he can do any particular kind or grade of service." Henry asserted that librarians measured well against the requirements for faculty rank. Assistants in a college library, in Henry's view, could not offer themselves for employment "on any other basis than one of general scholarship." As a rule, the library would expect some form of special training for the work "either in a library training school or valuable experience in a well-managed library." Henry demanded a bachelor's degree for a position on any academic library staff and preferred a library school degree or at least experience in library work. Given these qualifications which he claimed equaled the professional preparation of members of the teaching faculty, he recommended that the director of the library be awarded the rank of professor. If there were assistant librarians, they should rank as associate professors. Other librarians of the staff should be ranked as assistant professors or instructors as their duties and preparation indicated.

The College and Reference Library Section was impressed by Henry's vision. Its members voted immediately to have the paper published as a pamphlet and sent out to all the college and university libraries in the United States. The paper, or at least the ideas behind it, had a great influence on the thinking of academic librarians. In 1927, the Bureau of Public Personnel Administration published its *Proposed Classification and Compensation Plans for Library Positions*. It was the final revision of two earlier reports prepared in 1925 on the duties and classification of library personnel for the ALA Committee on the Classification of Library Personnel and was an attempt "to formulate the personnel standards and ideals of the library profession in such a manner as to make them available for the use of individuals." The bureau assumed that details of job descriptions would vary with the local conditions, size, and type of library. They found, however, that the variations from library to library were "greater than necessary or desirable with regard to many operations exactly the same that have to be repeated over and over in nearly every library." Consequently, the classification scheme devised was based entirely upon the "size and character" of the library staff.[88]

The academic librarians of the committee reacted to the classification scheme and appointed a subcommittee composed of Charles H. Brown, librarian of Iowa State, Harold L. Leupp, librarian of the University of California, and George A. Works, of Cornell University's Divison of Education, when they received the report. The committee published, in January, 1929, its own report that replaced those parts of the bureau's 1927 report concerning academic libraries to which it objected. The specifications developed by the committee were essentially prescriptive rather than descriptive as was the bureau report.[89]

There were major differences between the two views of library work presented in these reports. On the whole, the bureau's report demanded fewer educational qualifications for the several levels of service than did the committee's. An examination of corresponding positions reveals some interesting divergences in their views. For example, the head of cataloging of a "class nine" college or university library described by the committee's report is roughly equivalent to a "grade three" cataloging head of the bureau's report, at least in salary level and the number of assistants supervised. The duties of both seem essentially the same, except that the committee's report mandates "sufficient contact with faculty in order that the cataloging and classification may be such as to tender utmost service."[90]

The committee's report strongly recommended a higher level of assistant in the catalog department. The bureau demanded for the job that two of the eight to twelve assistants in the cataloging department be of professional grade whereas the committee required at least six. Both reports stressed academic qualifications, but the committee's feeling was that "scholastic preparation equivalent to the standards maintained by the institution for the assistant professorship" that included at least a year of formal library training was equivalent to a bachelor's degree, a year at a library school, and five years' experience in a library of over 50,000 volumes. Either form of training qualified the head of a cataloging department for the official rank of assistant professor in the university.[91] The bureau's requirement allowed the bachelor's degree, the experience, and the formal library training, but permitted no alternative of academic qualifications. The bureau also did not specify an academic rank for such a person.[92]

The cataloging positions described in both reports were essentially the same. Indeed, there were only a few minor differences between the reports in all positions described. The discrepancy between them derived directly from the firmly held beliefs of the academic librarians formulating the classifications and the broader population of librarians who, through the ALA, approved the position. The unresolved differences between the two views demonstrates that by the end of the third decade of the twentieth century, academic librarians firmly felt they deserved a higher position in the hierarchy of American higher education than the general group of librarians would allow. This position should be officially recognized through the mechanism of ranked titles identical to those of other faculty members of America's colleges and universities.

* * * * * *

By the 1920s, the forms of education and research developed by the university movement had a profound effect on the libraries serving American institutions of higher education. Research and publication had become requisite for anyone aspiring to a position on a university faculty. In all areas of study, the necessity for publication of research in monographs and in the newly founded scholarly and scientific periodicals led directly to the establishment of university presses and journals connected with universities.

To keep scholars in the forefront of new knowledge, it became imperative that colleges and universities collect the new publications in their libraries. In addition, demand by researchers for manuscripts, laws, numerous editions of the same published text, and any other form of recorded information that would provide the raw materials for scholarship became endemic at America's colleges and universities, and academic libraries became increasingly important in the struggle of institutions adopting the philosophy of the university movement to attract and retain competent graduate students and faculty. In the rhetoric of commencement days, the library became the "heart" of the institution.

Institutions responded to their commitment to support the kinds of learning and research mandated by the university movement by greatly enlarging the support given to their libraries. Collections and facilities expanded at enormous rates and America's academic libraries became a major facility of the revitalized institutions. Vastly increased annual budgets for materials, the systematic search for appropriate gifts to develop areas of specialized research, the centralization, either in physical location or through cataloging control, of departmental and seminar collections, and the absorption of the old student literary society libraries, were the principal means through which the central libraries expanded the resources they could offer to productive scholarship.

In the new order, the bucolic practice of opening the library doors to the academic community for a few hours a week became increasingly inappropriate. Access to the collection was demanded by the researchers and nascent scholars that crowded the American academic landscape in growing numbers. By the 1920s, it was widely realized that the materials collected by the libraries, to be truly useful, must be available when demanded and opening hours of eighty hours or more a week were common. Administrators, faculty members, and librarians attempted to maintain their facilities as reference libraries. But, eventually, they had to concede to the demands for circulation privileges. They responded in a variety of ways, and the dominant one came to be virtually unlimited circulation to the senior members of the academic community—the faculty, and to a lesser extent, the graduate students—and the establishment of smaller collections directly available to undergraduates for browsing and circulation.

The expanded functions of the library demanded much of the professors, presidents, and students who had served the classical colleges as librarians. They soon found the jobs too much for their time and energies. The position of librarian at the new revitalized academic institutions became established as the university movement was entrenched in the thinking of American academics as a full-time position in American higher education. Institution after institution hired men and women who could dedicate their time and energies to making the libraries of the most possible use to the academic community. Many were placed directly in the position of the librarian and some were hired to assist the professor who held titular control of the library. By the 1920s, academic librarianship was generally recognized as being a full-time occupation at America's institution of higher education and men and women were hired in increasing numbers to fill the function. Some of the colleges and universities had employed substantial staffs.

The public library movement became established in America concurrently with the emergence of academic librarianship as a full-time occupation. Through the ALA, the association of librarians most to influence the new developments in the field, academic librarians began to absorb and be absorbed by the new ideas of service developing from librarians. Men like Justin Winsor, who firmly embraced the views of Samuel Swett Green of the relations between librarian and reader, and Melvil Dewey, who saw the profession as an integral whole and made no distinctions among the myriad forms that it could take, influenced the emerging full-time occupation of academic librarianship.

A full-time occupation seeks a form and a philosophy to distinguish itself from other occupations. Academic librarians found theirs in the ideals of the ALA and sought a purpose and meaning for the activities of librarians in the field of readers' services. Though they formed no great proportion of the ALA membership at the time, the ideals of utility and service became maxims by which academic librarians lived and sought professional identity. Through lectures in bibliographic and research methods, informal help through reference work, and the production of teaching tools to enable the novice researcher to achieve his goals by consulting the catalogs of the librarians and the guides they prepared, the emerging academic librarians sought a teaching role in American higher education.

Formalized lectures and development of tools to reach the materials collected by academic libraries were only a minor part of the emerging role of the academic librarian in the university movement. The feeling that the emphasis on intense specialization that developed first in graduate study and slowly filtered into the undergraduate curriculum countered many librarians' vision of the purpose and scope of undergraduate education.

The generalized cultural benefits of collegiate education was op-posed by the emphasis on exact and highly specialized knowl-edge. Librarians developed an awareness that the library, with its ability to provide a diversity of materials with a number of radically divergent views and theories, provided a capacity to balance the skewed vision of the world offered by the intensely specialized researcher who had become a college or university professor. The public library movement and the development of academic librarianship as a full-time occupation coalesced to in-fect the university movement with the spirit of the library movement.

Helping students to cope with the masses of materials ac-cumulated by academic libraries, offering lectures on bibliog-raphy and research methods, and generally attempting to sup-plement the activities of the faculty in encouraging under-graduate students to broaden their education through reading, became the functions that academic librarians came to identify as their functions in American higher education. Librarians assumed a role that was applauded in the rhetoric of adminis-trators in the direction and encouragement of undergraduates in the mysteries of research and learning in higher education.

By the late 1920s, academic librarians held sufficient sense of place and their function in the academic community that they could strongly question a conception that categorized them with other librarians. The distinctions that could be made be-tween libraries of comparable size as opposed to what should be similar functions in the same kind of library were abandoned in favor of a system that conceived of academic librarians as distinct from other types of librarians. Academic librarians strongly felt their qualifications and functions entitled them to a recognized place in the hierarchy of American higher educa-tion on the same basis as other ranked faculty members of the institutions.

Notes to Chapter 3

1. Howard Mumford Jones, *The Age of Energy: Varieties of American Experience, 1865-1915* (New York: The Viking Press, 1971), p. 167.

2. Herbert Baxter Adams, *Historical Scholarship in the United States, 1876-1901: As Revealed in the Correspondence of Herbert B. Adams,* ed. W. Stull Holt, the Johns Hopkins University Studies in Historical and Political Science, ser. 61, no. 4 (Baltimore: The Johns Hopkins Press, 1938), pp. 54-55.

3. Henry James, *Charles W. Eliot President of Harvard University, 1869-1909,* 2 vols. (Boston: Houghton Mifflin Company, 1930), 2:16-17.

4. Fred E. Woodward, *A Graphic Survey of Book Publication, 1890-1916,* U.S. Bureau of Education, Bulletin, 1917, no. 14 (Washington, D.C.: Government Printing Office, 1917), pp. 7, 21.

5. John William Tebbel, *A History of Book Publishing in the United States,* 3 vols. (New York: R. R. Bowker Company, 1972-78), 2:535-36; 3:279-85.

6. Adams, *Historical Scholarship,* p. 208.

7. 2 vols. (Cleveland: A. H. Clark, 1906-1907).

8. 18 vols. (Mount Vernon, N.Y.: Rudge, 1928-34).

9. Carson Ryan, *Studies in Early Graduate Education,* Carnegie Foundation for the Advancement of Teaching, Bulletin no. 30 (New York: The Carnegie Foundation for the Advancement of Teaching, 1939), p. 44.

10. Frank Luther Mott, *A History of American Magazines, 1741-1850* (Cambridge, Mass.: The Belknap Press of Harvard University Press, 1957), p. 342; *idem, A History of American Magazines, 1885-1905* (Cambridge, Massachusetts: The Belknap Press of Harvard University Press, 1957), p. 11.

11. Burr to White, November 7, 1885, in Roland H. Bainton, *George Lincoln Burr, His Life: Selections from His Writings,* ed. Lois O. Gibbons (Ithaca, N.Y.: Cornell University Press, 1952), pp. 31-32.

12. Bainton, p. 33.

13. Daniel Coit Gilman, "Historical Address," in Cornell University, *Exercises at the Opening of the Library Building ... October 7, 1891* (Ithaca, N.Y.: Cornell University, 1891), p. 47.

14. Justin Winsor, "College and Other Higher Libraries," *Library Journal* 4 (November 1879): 400.

15. Donald B. Engley, "The Emergence of the Amherst College Library, 1821-1911," Master's thesis, University of Chicago, 1947, p. 67; Orin Oliphant, *The Library of Bucknell University* (Lewisburg, Pa.: Bucknell University Press, 1962), p. 78; Alethea Hoff, "A History of the Library of Western Maryland College," Master's thesis, Drexel Institute of Technology, 1954, pp. 16-17; Frank Strong, "The Minimum Conditions, Environmental, etc., That Should be Considered Favorable to Graduate Work," *Transactions and Proceedings of the National Association of State Universities in the United States of America* (1905), p. 40.

16. Frank Hugh Foster, *The Seminary Method of Original Study in the Historical Sciences* (New York: Charles Scribner's Sons, 1888), p. 16.

17. William Bentinck-Smith, *Building a Great Library: the Coolidge Years at Harvard* (Cambridge, Mass.: Harvard University Press, 1976), pp. 104–105.

18. W. Dawson Johnston, "The Library as a University Factor," Association of American Universities *Journal of Proceedings and Addresses of the Fifteenth Annual Conference* (Published by the Association, 1913), pp. 46–48.

19. Bainton, p. 66.

20. Guy Stanton Ford, "The Library and the Graduate School," Association of American Universities, *Journal of Proceedings and Addresses of the Fifteenth Annual Conference* (Chicago: published by the Association, 1913), p. 40.

21. Wallace Nethery, *Dr. Flewelling and the Hoose Library: Life and Letters of a Man and an Institution* (Los Angeles: University of Southern California Press, 1976), p. 13.

22. Princeton University, Library, *College and University Library Statistics, 1919/20 to 1943/44* (Princeton, N.J.: Princeton University Library, 1947), *passim*; Frederick Vinton, "College Libraries," U.S. Department of the Interior, Bureau of Education, *Public Libraries in the United States of America: Their History, Condition and Management*, part 1 (Washington: Government Printing Office, 1876), pp. 60–126; Lloyd F. Wagner, "A Descriptive History of the Library Facilities of Lafayette College, Easton, Pennsylvania, 1824–1941," Master's thesis, Catholic University of America, 1951, pp. 20–21; Roscoe Rouse, Jr., *A History of the Baylor University Library, 1845–1919*, unpublished doctoral dissertation, University of Michigan, 1962, p. 320.

23. George Alan Works, *College and University Library Problems, A Study of Selected Group of Institutions Prepared for the Association of American Universities* (Chicago: American Library Association, 1927), pp. 124a; U.S. Bureau of Education, *Biennial Survey of Education, 1924–1926*, Bulletin, 1928, no. 25 (Washington: U.S. Government Printing Office, 1928), p. 804; Benjamin Edward Powell, *The Development of Libraries in Southern Universities to 1920*, unpublished doctoral dissertation, University of Chicago, 1946, pp. 190–91.

24. Princeton University, Library, *passim*.

25. Thomas S. Harding, *College Literary Societies: Their Contribution to Higher Education in the United States, 1815–1876* (New York: Pageant Press International, 1971), pp. 313–15.

26. Engley, pp. 57, 84.

27. James Russell Lowell, *Letters of James Russell Lowell*, ed. Charles Eliot Norton, 2 vols. (New York: Harper & Brothers, Publishers, 1894), 2:215.

28. Arthur D. Young, "Daniel Coit Gilman in the Formative Period of American Librarianship," *Library Quarterly* 45 (April 1975): 130.

29. Bentinck-Smith, pp. 106–107; Maurice Falcolm Tauber, *Louis Round Wilson, Librarian and Administrator* (New York: Columbia University Press, 1967), pp. 60–61.

30.   Bentinck-Smith, p. 132.

31.   American Library Association, *A Survey of Libraries in the United States*, 4 vols. (Chicago: American Library Association, 1926), 1:252.

32.   *ALA Survey*, 4:163-64.

33.   Robert W. Lovett, "The Undergraduate and the Harvard Library, 1877-1937," *Harvard Library Bulletin* 1 (Spring 1947): 223.

34.   *Works*, pp. 48-49; the libraries were Iowa State, Columbia, Cornell, Oberlin, Rutgers, Stanford, Tulane, Vassar, Yale, and the universities of California, Cincinnati, Illinois, Iowa, Michigan, Minnesota, North Carolina, and Oregon.

35.   Dora Smith, "History of the University of California Library to 1900," Master's thesis, University of California, 1930, pp. 70-75.

36.   Henry Ormal Severance, *History of the Library University of Missouri* (Columbia: University of Missouri, 1928), p. 32.

37.   Theodore Wesley Koch, "Student Circulation in a University Library," *Library Journal* 31 (November 1906): 758-61.

38.   John Rogers Williams, *The Handbook of Princeton* (New York: The Grafton Press, 1905), pp. 57, 59; Skipper, pp. 260-71.

39.   Carl Milton White, "Trends in the Use of University Libraries," American Library Association, *College and University Library Service; Trends Standards, Appraisal, Problems: Papers Presented at the 1937 Midwinter Meeting* (Chicago: American Library Association, 1938), table I: "A Summary of Recorded Use for Twenty-Three Libraries."

40.   Kenneth J. Brough, *Scholar's Workshop: Evolving Conceptions of Library Service*, Illinois Contributions to Librarianship, no. 5 (Urbana: University of Illinois Press, 1958), pp. 23-25; Charles Franklin Thwing, *College Administration* (New York: The Century Company, 1900), p. 191.

41.   Earl James McGrath, *The Evolution of Administrative Offices in Institutions of Higher Education in the United States from 1860 to 1933*, unpublished doctoral dissertation, University of Chicago, 1938, p. 148.

42.   The Princeton Alumni Weekly, *The Harvey S. Firestone Memorial Library* (Princeton: 1949), p. 6; Smith, pp. 156-57; Severance, p. 28; Powell, p. 133; Irwin, p. 153; Mary Elizabeth Nichols, "Early Development of the University of Mississippi Library," Master's thesis, University of Mississippi, 1959, pp. 25-26; Madison Kuhn, *Michigan State: The First Hundred Years* (East Lansing: Michigan State University Press, 1955), p. 95; Clyde Kenneth Hyder, *Snow of Kansas: The Life of Francis Huntington Snow with Extracts from His Journals and Letters* (Lawrence: University of Kansas Press, 1953), p. 201; Elizabeth La Boone, "History of the University of Georgia Library," Master's thesis, University of Georgia, 1954, p. 95; G. Wallace Chessman, *Denison: The Story of an Ohio College* (Granville, Ohio: Denison University, 1957), p. 109; Robert Ferguson Munn, *West Virginia University Library, 1867-1917*, unpublished doctoral dissertation, University of Michigan, 1961, p. 136; Powell, p. 135; Skipper, p. 35; Yenawine, p. 48.

43.   John H. Stein, "The Development of the Hiram College Library from the Literary Societies Which Formed its Nucleus," Master's thesis,

Kent State University, 1950, p. 75; Oliphant, pp. 87–88; Louis G. Moloney, *A History of the University Library at the University of Texas, 1883–1934*, unpublished doctoral dissertation, Columbia, 1970, p. 89; Joseph Penn Breedlove, *Duke University Library, 1840–1940: A Brief Account with Reminiscences* (Durham, N.C.: Friends of Duke University Library, 1955), p. 69; William Hugh Carlson, *The Library of Oregon State University: Its Origins, Management, and Growth, a Centennial History* (Corvallis, Ore.: 1966), p. 11.

44.   Judith K. Meyers, " A History of the Antioch College Library, 1850 to 1929," Master's thesis, Kent State University, 1963, p. 107; Powell, p. 137; Rouse, p. 196; Nancy C. (Vermilya) Baughman, "A History of the Otterbein College Library," Master's thesis, Western Reserve University, 1955, p. 23; James M. Nicholson, Jr., "A History of the Wake Forest College Library, 1876–1946," Master's thesis, University of North Carolina, 1954, p. 49; Clarence N. Roberts, *North Central College: A Century of Liberal Education 1861-1961* (Naperville, Ill.: North Central College, 1960), p. 132; Jay B. Clark, "The Odyssey of a University Library, 1869–1968," *Journal of Library History* 5 (April 1970): 122.

45.   Princeton University, Library, *passim.*

46.   *ALA Survey*, 2:173–76.

47.   Charles E. Hale, *The Origins and Development of the Association of College and Research Libraries, 1899-1960*, unpublished doctoral dissertation, Indiana University, 1976, p. 2; Melvil Dewey, "Relation of the Colleges to the Modern Library Movement," Association of Colleges and Preparatory Schools of the Middle States and Maryland, *Proceedings, 1891*, vol. 4 (Globe Printing House, 1891), p. 80.

48.   Edith E. Clarke, "Departmental Arrangement of College Libraries," *Library Journal* 14 (August 1889): 341.

49.   Tauber, p. 64.

50.   Mary G. Lacey, "The Opportunity of the Agricultural College Library," *South Atlantic Quarterly* 9 (January 1910): 79–80.

51.   Charles Harvey Brown, "The Library," in Arthur J. Klein, *Survey of Land-Grant Colleges and Universities*, United States Office of Education, Bulletin 1930, No. 9, 2 vols. (Washington: United States Government Printing Office, 1930), 1:618.

52.   Azariah Smith Root, "Future Development of College and University Libraries," *Library Journal* 39 (November 1915): 812.

53.   Otis H. Robinson, "College Libraries as Semi-Public Libraries: The Rochester University Library," *Library Journal* 2 (October 1877): 57–60.

54.   Melvil Dewey, "Melvil Dewey's Introduction," Dewey, *Dewey Decimal Classification and Relative Index*, 17th edn. vol. 1. (Lake Placid Club, New York: Forest Press, Inc., Lake Placid Club Educational Foundation, 1965), p. 78.

55.   Joseph Alfred Borome, *The Life and Letters of Justin Winsor*, unpublished doctoral dissertation, Columbia University, 1950, pp. 94–95, 101–106.

56. *Ibid.*, pp. 330–35.

57. *Ibid.*, p. 295.

58. Justin Winsor, "The Development of the Library, Address at the Dedication of the Orringer Lunt Library, Northwestern University, Evanston, Ill." *Library Journal* 19 (November 1894): 373.

59. Winsor, "Library Questions and Answers," *Library Journal* 3 (June 1878): 159.

60. Winsor, "Library Lectures and Other Helps," *Library Journal* 3 (May 1878): 120.

61. Henry Adams, *Letters of Henry Adams (1858–1891)*, ed. Worthington Chauncey Ford (Boston: Houghton Mifflin Company, 1930), pp. 329–30.

62. Samuel Rothstein, *The Development of Reference Services Through Academic Traditions, Public Library Practice and Special Librarianship*, ACRL Monographs no. 14 (Chicago: Association of College and Reference Libraries, 1955), pp. 36, 45; Walter B. Briggs, "Reference Work in Public and College Libraries: A Comparison and a Contrast," *Library Journal* 32 (November 1907): 493; Louis Round Wilson, "Organization and Administration of the College Library," *Library Journal* 36 (November 1911): 564.

63. Quoted in John Neal Waddell, *The Career of Isadore G. Mudge: A Chapter in the History of Reference Librarianship*, unpublished doctoral dissertation, Columbia University, 1973, p. 88.

64. American Library Association, Committee on the Classification of Library Personnel, *Budgets, Classification and Compensation Plans for University Libraries: Report of the Committee on Classification of Library Personnel of the American Library Association, December, 1928* (Chicago: American Library Association, 1929), p. 53.

65. Benjamin Putnam Kurtz, *Joseph Cummings Rowell, 1853–1938* (Berkeley: University of California Press, 1940), pp. 34–35.

66. Smith, "History of the University of California Library," pp. 145–49; Ernest Cushing Richardson, "Co-operation in Lending Among College and Reference Libraries," *Library Journal* 24 (July 1899): 156; ALA, *Survey*, 2:220–23.

67. Edwin H. Woodruff, "University Libraries and Seminary Methods of Instruction," *Library Journal* 11 (August–September 1886): 223–24.

68. Melvil Dewey, "Libraries the True Universities for Scholars as Well as People," *Library Notes* 1 (June 1887): 49–50.

69. Samuel Swett Green, "Personal Relations Between Librarians and Readers," *Library Journal* 1 (November 30, 1876): 124.

70. Otis H. Robinson, "College Library Administration," U.S. Office of Education, *Public Libraries in the United States of America: Their History, Condition and Management*, part 1 (Washington: Government Printing Office, 1876), pp. 505–525.

71. Ada North, " A Western University Library," *Library Journal* 10 (June 1885): 124.

72. T. K. Davis, "College Library and the College," *Library Journal* 10 (May 1885): 101.

73. Alfred Clanghorn Potter, "The Selection of Books for College Libraries," *Papers and Proceedings of the Nineteenth General Meeting of the American Library Association* (American Library Association, 1897), p. 39.

74. Isadore Gilbert Mudge, "Stimulation of General Reading in the College Library," *Library Journal* 31 (November 1906): 764.

75. Ernest Cushing Richardson, "Place of the Library in the University," *ALA Bulletin* 10 (January 1916): 9.

76. Harry Lyman Koopman, "The Functions of a University Library," *Library Journal* 19 (December 1894): 27–29; Joseph F. Daniels, "Indeterminate Functions of a College Library," *Library Journal* 32 (November 1907): 489–90.

77. William Warner Bishop, "Our College and University Libraries—A Survey and a Program," *School and Society* 7 (September 18, 1920): 210; Davis, "College Library and the College," p. 101.

78. James H. Canfield, "The Modern College Library," *Education* 27 (November 1906): 131.

79. C. E. Lowrey, "University Library: Its Larger Recognition in Higher Education," *Library Journal* 19 (August 1894): 266.

80. Rothstein, p. 14; Daniels, pp. 488–89.

81. William Isaac Fletcher, "Modern Librarianship," *New Hampshire Library Commission Bulletin* 3 (December 1902): 185, 187.

82. Joseph Cummings Rowell, "Standards of Success," *Library Journal* 21 (March 1896): 110; Winsor, "The College Library," p. 14.

83. Wilson, p. 561.

84. Daniel Coit Gilman, *University Problems in the United States* (New York: The Century Co., 1898), pp. 254–55.

85. William Warner Bishop, "Changing Ideals in Librarianship," *Library Journal* 44 (January 1919): 6.

86. Johnston, p. 31.

87. Raymond Cazallis Davis, "The Relation of the Librarian to the Faculty," *Library Journal* 15 (December 1890): 140; Melvil Dewey, *Librarianship as a Profession for College-Bred Women* (Boston: Library Bureau, 1886), p. 18.

88. William Elmer Henry, "The Academic Standing of College Library Assistants and Their Relation to the Carnegie Foundation," *Papers and Proceedings of the Thirty-third Annual Meeting of the American Library Association Held at Pasadena, California, May 18–24, 1911* 33 (Chicago: American Library Association, 1911): 259–62; Bureau of Public Personnel Administration, *Proposed Classification and Compensation Plans for Library Positions: Report of the Bureau of Public Personnel Administration to the Committee on the Classification of Library Personnel of the American Library Association* (Washington, D.C.: Bureau of Public Personnel Administration, 1927), pp. 6–7, 37.

89.   ALA, Committee on Classification, p. 4; Bureau of Public Personnel Administration, p. 34.

90.   *Ibid.*, p. 121; ALA, Committee on Classification, p. 51.

91.   Bureau of Public Personnel Administration, p. 122; ALA, Committee on Classification, p. 51–52.

92.   Bureau of Public Personnel Administration, p. 122.

four

The Professionalization of Academic Librarianship

Attempts of academic librarians to find a form and dignity for their occupation by developing a strong role in the academic enterprise were not very successful. Librarians developed philosophies that called for strong and active participation in the educational and research efforts of the universities; members of the faculty and administrators looked at the library and saw an educational and research utility. Their demands were conditioned by the increasing necessity for resources to support the new forms of American academic life. The first tentative steps of America's colleges and universities toward providing increased access to their libraries' resources were stumbling ones. Merely keeping the library doors open longer hours did not prove to be an effective answer to the needs of students and faculty members who expected more of the person in charge of the library than the mere maintenance of order. Low salaries and the prevailing view of the universities that the most obvious problem of access, opening hours, was the only problem, led to the employment of people with few intellectual qualifications and small commitment to serving the academic community.

The myopic view of the functions of the library by the new full-time caretakers and their intellectual limitations did little to establish an aura of respect for the librarian's position in the institutions. "Two-Week" was the soubriquet students gave

Oregon State University librarian R. J. Nichols. Students offending his sense of decorum in the library would be expelled with the cry of "Two weeks for you!" During his tenure from 1902 until he retired to farming in 1908, the two-week expulsion was a standard punishment.[1] Sarah A. Frierson had a more difficult time at the University of Georgia. She became the first full-time librarian in 1887 when the trustees determined that hiring a local Athens lady would be the best they could do with the money they had available. Her job was to maintain order and to check out books. She was not totally satisfied with these limited functions and filled much of her time brightening the library by growing flowers in the room and around the building. She was known to the students as "Miss Puss." They had a continuing joke of bringing her pages from periodicals that they had torn out and complaining that someone had ruined the magazines. She consistently praised them for pointing out the mutilation.[2]

But it was in the attitude of the new librarians toward their work that the students found their greatest source of dissatisfaction. Students at Stanford preserved the name of an otherwise forgotten desk attendant in the pages of the campus newspaper around the turn of the century:

Trot, trot to Trader to try to get a book,
Trot, trot away he goes just to take a look,
Trot, trot back again to say it isn't there,
Trot, trot away again as if he didn't care.
AND I DON'T SUPPOSE HE DOES![3]

Others, like Joseph R. Dickinson, fared better with students. Dickinson, who served as assistant librarian under the titular librarian and professor of Latin, was known to the students at Ohio Wesleyan as "Joe Dick." During his term of office, 1877–98, his principal task was maintaining order in the reading room. Though bound by the rules not to allow anyone into the alcoves, students soon found that he frequently looked in another direction. Dickinson was, however, a man of considerably greater parts than most other librarians of the period. His previous experience as a bookseller enabled him to almost totally recall where each of the 25,000 volumes, arranged in alcoves by the names of their donors, was to be found.[4]

Miss Clara Hough, librarian of West Virginia University, was more typical. She was hired in 1889 to keep the library open for more than the few hours each day that a professor could devote to the task. Though the president wanted someone with high capabilities, the regents would appropriate only $300 a year for the position, and President Eli Marsh Turner was forced to settle for a person with a high school education who was capable of no more than the most routine tasks.[5]

When it became obvious that the library must necessarily be opened for more than a few hours a week, there was no corresponding awareness that any particular competency beyond ability to unlock a door and maintain order among unruly students was required. Consequently, the pattern established in the classical colleges of hiring on the basis of convenience rather than special qualifications was continued. When the president, the regents, or the faculty looked to providing adequate library access as called for by the new forms of teaching and scholarship, they turned to the first answer they could find. Doorstops that could intimidate students seemed to be the most obvious solution, and like iron anvils, these were cheaply available.

It soon became evident that this was inadequate. One faculty member at the University of Mississippi was shocked to find that Mrs. Alice B. Beynes, librarian from 1888 to 1898, kept all foreign language books on an obscure top shelf. They were "originals" and no one had ever requested them. She had no qualifications for the job and viewed the essential task of the librarian as keeping the books clean. Even when new librarians came with the intellectual background and awareness of library functions that would set them above the average, they greatly underestimated the complexities of library operations. Herbert Charles Nash served as Stanford's librarian from 1896 to 1899. He had been the private secretary of the founder, Leland Stanford, and tutor to Stanford's son. When Nash took the post, he immediately realized that a catalog of the collection was needed. With seventy-eight student volunteers he cataloged the 12,000 volumes of the library in a weekend. Nash's successor noted many inaccuracies in the card catalog.[6]

Faculty members and administrators gradually came to feel that something more than this level of ability was needed. Faculty dissatisfaction with the intellectual defects of "Miss

Puss" at the University of Georgia forced them officially to define the desirable characteristics of an academic librarian. On March 25, 1897, the faculty secretary urged the Prudential Committee of the Trustees to hire someone more capable, "competent to direct, in a measure, the reading and selection of books of those who use the library," someone with "a general and comprehensive knowledge of books and their contents." In addition to this, the faculty would have in the librarian, "a skillful bibliographer."[7] President Mark W. Harrington of the University of Washington came to a similar conclusion in his 1894-96 annual report. In addition to acquiring more good books, Harrington recognized that "an equally effective way to make a library useful is to have an active, energetic librarian who understands his business." He was less sanguine about salaries than the faculty of the University of Georgia, though, and settled for requesting only a small appropriation "with the expectation of finding some trained young man who is willing to grow up to his place."[8]

While colleges and universities searched for the appropriate qualifications for librarians, solutions were beginning to evolve. With the university movement in the last quarter of the nineteenth century, academic pursuits became only one concern of American higher education. The demands for technical competency and research in a variety of areas directly related to vocational proficiency led to the establishment of university-connected professional schools. By the turn of the century, the triumvirate of law, medicine, and theology as the learned professions had been joined by dentistry, teaching, pharmacy, architecture, accounting, and agriculture, among others. The founding of the Wharton School in 1881 formally declared even business to be a learned profession.[9] The new areas of study did not include one leading to a "Bachelors of Hemstitching" as one New York congressman was reported to have feared;[10] they did establish a precedent for more diversification. These eventually culminated at the graduate level in a wide array of conferred professional degrees with such odd titles as Master of Commerce (MC), Master of Education for the Deaf (MED), Master of International Studies (MIS), Master in Planning and Urban Design (MPUD), and Master of Library Science (MLS).

The first tentative steps toward evolving training for librarianship were almost entirely the responsibility of Melvil Dewey. Against the guarded approval of the ALA and the hostility of the trustees of Columbia, Dewey forged a program of formal training that eventually won the acceptance of librarians as a basic definition of professionalism. Much of Dewey's success in the development of library education can be attributed not to the merit of his ideas, but to the forcefulness of his personality and the amorality of his manipulations.

William Warner Bishop was often an opponent of Dewey in the forum of the ALA. But in remembering the early days of the movement, he admitted his respect for Dewey's "original and valuable contributions to librarianship"—"on the housekeeping side of library work." Indifference to Dewey, Bishop remembered, was impossible: "You were either a pro-Dewey enthusiast or a violent opponent at once." It was not only in the library world that Dewey aroused these animosities. Sydney Bancroft Mitchell of the University of California Library met a man who had been an instructor in physics at Columbia when Dewey was there. When the man found that Mitchell was a librarian, he asked him if he had ever known "a damned fool called Dewey."[11]

Dewey's move to Columbia was directly occasioned by two men who were in the pro-Dewey camp, Columbia President Frederick Augustus Porter Barnard and John Burgess. Burgess had been hired by Barnard as part of an effort to transform Columbia into a leading institution of the university movement. The Reverend Beverley Betts, who had served as Columbia's librarian since 1865 was, to them, obviously inadequate for the central role envisioned for the library. Indeed, Burgess saw Betts as an obstruction. To Burgess, Betts's argument against expanding the library—"it was a useless waste of money, since the students did not use the library already existing"—proved his incompetence to act as librarian more than "his lack of conception of the nature and purpose of a library." Burgess remembered a pupil at Amherst who, although not a particularly outstanding student of history or political science, "was of great service to me and his fellow students in making the literature of these subjects accessible to them, by his new method of subject cataloging."[12]

Burgess suggested to Barnard that Dewey be contacted

about tne problem. Barnard and Dewey were already acquainted. The president of Columbia was also president of the American Metric Association for which Dewey served as secretary. The American Library Association, the Library Bureau, and the American Metric Association maintained adjoining offices in Boston at 32 Hawley Street. In 1883, Burgess and Barnard consulted Dewey about finding a replacement for Betts. Though they may have already had Dewey in mind for the post, Dewey ostensibly went to New York to confer with the Library Committee of the trustees about recommending someone for the job. But Dewey himself took the precaution of having several leading librarians in the country write to the trustees recommending him for the position. These letters and Dewey's eloquence at expounding his views of library administration led the trustees to offer him the job.[13]

Dewey came to Columbia with his own dream of developing a formal program of training for librarians. His proposal to establish a library training school at Columbia was not a radically new idea in American librarianship. In the discussion following the presentation of the proposal to the ALA in 1883, Samuel Swett Green pointed out that it had been a much discussed topic on shipboard among those going to the 1877 London meeting. When Green returned from England he had approached Justin Winsor with the idea, and though nothing was done at Harvard, it had continued as a frequent subject of informal discussion at subsequent librarians' meetings.[14]

Dewey, however, presented his proposal in a more thoughtfully prepared and formal state than had earlier proponents of library education. Before accepting the Columbia position, Dewey had persuaded the trustees to support a formal role in educating librarians.[15] By 1883, his thinking on how best to realize this vision of professional preparation was fully developed. Dewey was aware that the dignity of librarianship could only be enhanced by association with university education. His original proposal to the Columbia trustees to establish a "Professor of Bibliography and the School of Librarianship" emphasized this:

> In asking thus earnestly this cooperation we hardly overrate the importance of the proposed undertaking to the library interests

of the entire country, in raising our work to the full rank of a regular profession, with its recognized courses of instruction, its certificates and degrees conferred by the University, and chiefly in providing for the new libraries opening almost daily, and for the old ones taking on new life, men and women trained in the best methods, and full of that potent influence which we call "the modern library spirit."[16]

Dewey convinced Barnard that the idea had the unqualified support of librarians. In his 1884 report to the trustees, Barnard noted that the proposed school at Columbia afforded "gratification" to "the members of the Association of American Librarians."[17]

In the end, the trustees were not impressed. Dewey's impatience with what he considered obstructive attitudes irritated them. His innovations at Columbia came too quickly for the more conservative members of the trustees. What one commentator called the "Barnard-Burgess-Dewey revolution" was viewed by many with outright alarm. When Whitlaw Reid asked Dewey to become the executive secretary of the State University of New York in 1888, the Columbia trustees felt only relief.[18]

At Columbia, Dewey's School of Library Economy was never firmly established as part of any real educational program. In accepting the idea, the trustees insisted that no part of the expense should be carried by the university and that the library facilities and staff bear the cost and inconvenience with what resources were already available. No room was given for classes that could not be readily spared by the library. No extra money for instructional salaries was given. Dewey established the Columbia experiment in an "academic limbo." As far as the college was concerned, it was Dewey's own operation and totally an internal library matter. Indeed, the early graduates of Columbia's program had difficulty in obtaining any official recognition for their work. Barnard had requested in his 1887 annual report to the trustees that a diploma be granted for the work of the school's students that would bear "the seal of the college and the signature of the President." This was never provided.[19]

When the school was officially moved to Albany on April 1, 1889, attempts were made to secure certificates for the students who had earned them. Although the trustees had originally agreed to some form of academic honor, none had been provided.

After much badgering by the students and by the librarian of Teachers College, the new president agreed to recognize the twenty-three students who had completed the course. Seth Low affixed his signature to a very noncommital document:

> I hereby certify that . . . . was a member of the School of Library Economy, connected with Columbia College, from the beginning of the college year 1887–88 until the close of the School, April 1, 1889, successfully pursued the prescribed course of study and passed all required examinations upon the same.

These were sent as simple letters with no adornment of seals nor guarantee of any rights or privileges.[20]

Melvil Dewey's small efforts at Columbia and at Albany could not supply the rapidly growing demand for training from those who would become librarians or from those who would hire librarians. By 1921, Charles Clarence Williamson could identify fifteen institutions advertising themselves as library schools: beside the Albany School, Pratt established a school in 1890, the Armour Institute—later moved to the University of Illinois—in 1893, the Carnegie Library at Pittsburgh in 1901; Simmons College in 1902; Western Reserve University in 1904; The Carnegie Library in Atlanta in 1905; the University of Wisconsin in 1906; New York Public Library in 1911; The University of Washington in 1912; Syracuse University and the Riverside Public Library in 1913; the Los Angeles Public Library in 1914; the St. Louis Public Library in 1917; and the University of California in 1919.[21]

These were only the better-established schools. Other colleges, universities, normal schools, and public libraries developed a wide variety of training programs to supply the need for librarians. Benjamin Wyche at the University of Texas began a library methods class in 1910 that emphasized cataloging to provide trained help for the university library. James Hulme Canfield, Dewey's successor as Columbia's librarian, began a class in formal training in library work in 1904 when he found that keeping younger assistants was impossible. He required two years of college for admission. Miss Emily Turner was a Pratt graduate hired as librarian of Antioch in 1921. She was impressed with Antioch's program that required all students to alternate periods of work and classroom study. Starting in 1923, librarianship became one of the programs. Graduates were employed in Ohio public libraries as well as at Antioch. Josephine Cushman of the University of Akron offered a single course in the spring of 1922 for a single hour of credit. It was designed for local teachers who wanted work in school libraries. Even Chautauqua entered the arena with a summer school begun in 1901 to offer six-week courses of lectures and library practice with Dewey acting as general director. The resident director, Mary E. Downey, noticed that many students were repeating this short course and, in 1918, the Chautauqua Summer School for Librarians began. The first class of four students received the BLS for four summers' work in 1920, and the school expanded through the decade.[22]

By the 1920s, a wide variety of programs, ranging from local training in small public libraries through normal schools and college courses to fully functioning library schools, was operating to produce formally trained librarians. But the form that education for librarianship would eventually assume was beginning to take shape. Three schools, by virtue of their productivity, assumed leading roles in the field. The Albany School, The University of Illinois School, and the program of the Pratt Institute together had produced 2250 of the 4664 librarians graduated from the fifteen schools surveyed by Williamson.[23]

Both Pratt and Illinois had close ties to Melvil Dewey and the Albany School. In the 1890s, the University of Illinois, under the presidency of Andrew Sloan Draper, was in a great period of expansion and development. Until 1894, it had had no full-time librarian. When Draper arrived, he appointed Percy Bicknell, an Eastern man who held the Illinois attempt at university education in contempt.[24] Draper quickly became dissatisfied with Bicknell, and the construction of a new building brought an opportunity for change.

When Draper was State Superintendent of Public Instruction of New York in 1886, he had met Melvil Dewey and been favorably impressed by his views on librarianship. This was before Draper's return to New York, and the eventual clash with Dewey. He quite naturally asked Dewey to recommend a replacement for Bicknell. Dewey did not hesitate to suggest Katharine Lucinda Sharp, then librarian and head of the

Department of Library Economy at the Armour Institute of Chicago. She was a favorite of Dewey's and had graduated from Albany in 1892. Dewey cautioned Draper that she would not consider going to Urbana unless the library school was moved also. Draper found this fit well with his own plans for expanding the curriculum and made her his offer. She began in September, 1897. The movement of Sharp and the Armour School was an extension of Dewey's earlier role in establishing library education in the West. It was Dewey that Frank Wakeley Gunsaulus turned to in 1893 when the Armour Institute was established. Gunsaulus, who was once Dewey's pastor, accepted his recommendation of Katharine Lucinda Sharp as the best person to organize a library economy department and she accepted the position in 1893.[25]

At Pratt, another Dewey disciple, Mary Wright Plummer, began a program in 1890 that differed slightly from both the Albany and the Illinois schools. She made no pretense at academic respectability and designed the curriculum and entrance requirements for students "who could not afford the longer time or the greater expense of the Library School [and] who could not, in some cases, have availed themselves of the school advantages for lack of college education." The school was dedicated to training a lower grade of library worker than either the Albany or Illinois schools.[26]

Through Dewey's influence and the active interest of the ALA, American library education developed a reasonably consistent form by the 1920s. In his survey of 1921, Williamson found that a core curriculum had been defined by all the eleven schools concerned in this part of the study. Cataloging, book selection, reference work, classification, and administration accounted for more than half of the work required of the students.[27]

The direct sustained interest of the ALA in the problems of library education was crucial to the development of library schools. When Dewey first proposed the school at Columbia, a committee of the ALA was appointed to consider the issue. By 1905, the field was so complex that the descendant of that committee, the Committee on Library Training, was forced to make the first attempt to develop a standard for library training. The committee examined and made recommendations on the three types of schools they thought most important. It distinguished library schools from summer schools and those from apprentice classes. In the last two, it exempted various subjects. It demanded a curriculum that included work in classification, cataloging, the various areas of library clerical and manual work, reference work, trade bibliography, and book selection. For the summer schools, it dropped classed cataloging—retaining the dictionary—and retained expansive classification although dropping decimal. For the apprentice classes, it even dropped the requirement that trade bibliography and book selection be studied.

Even more important for the emerging profession, the committee established standards for admission to the various courses that indicated the different purposes to be served. For the established schools, it recommended two to three years of college work. At the summer schools, the student needed only to hold a library position. For the apprentice classes, the student needed at least two years of college work, though some members of the committee were willing to accept examination. The committee seemed reluctant to address the issue of correspondence courses. Two of the six members disapproved entirely; the others agreed to them provided they were offered only to persons already holding a written promise of a position in a library.[28]

In the next year, the committee elaborated on the standards, but limited its consideration to the established schools, ignoring the apprentice classes and the correspondence courses. It asked for either three years of education beyond high school or a satisfactory examination in history, literature, languages, and economics for admission. For the summer schools, it required only that the applicant have a job in a library or the written promise of one.[29]

Until the effect of the Williamson report began to be felt at the end of the 1920s, a major factor in the development of library education was the formation of the Association of American Library Schools (AALS). The first meeting of representatives of the library schools was held in Albany on June 29–30, 1915. There, representatives of the schools adopted a constitution containing a membership policy that, in essence, was a statement of standards for those schools that would receive the recognition of the library profession. Membership was limited to schools that required high school graduation or equivalent preparation of their students. The short courses, summer courses, and other haphazard programs were eliminated by the requirement that the course take at least one full academic year of work designed to prepare the student for employment in a variety of libraries.

But, the AALS was never very effective in maintaining even these modest membership requirements. It persisted for many years in defining membership requirements by the current practice of the schools, not by any optimum definition of library education. The ALA attempted to fill the void through an evolution of committees that culminated in the Board of Education for Librarianship. The first annual report of this group was delivered at the 1925 Seattle Conference in the wake of the Williamson report and contained a set of minimum standards for library education that were largely descriptive. These standards essentially obtained until 1933 when the board revised the approach and produced standards that were prescriptive rather than descriptive and reflected the changing nature of library education brought about by the Williamson report.[30]

But standards for education set by a profession are not, of course, sufficient to insure general acceptance of any particular form of preparation for the vocation. Two elements determine the validity of a specific form of education for a profession. In lieu of legal requirements such as licensing, the necessity for training must be recognized by those who would practice the profession and by those who would utilize their services. It was first necessary to make prospective students aware of the schools in order to recruit them for the profession. Such popular publications as William Isaac Fletcher's *Public Libraries in America*, listing Pratt, Drexel, the Los Angeles Public Library, and Amherst's summer school as appropriate places to gain library training, undoubtedly had an effect in making it generally known that such training was possible. Publication of this book in a widely distributed series aided in disseminating this information. Popular magazines also contributed. The publication of an article in an early 1900s issue of *Ladies Home Journal* lured Helen Gordon Stewart to enter the New York Public Library program in 1908. She would have preferred to have attended the Albany School but did not have the college degree required for the full program there. Herbert Putnam also contributed to the spread of the gospel of library education with a 1900 article in the popular *Independent* that discussed both foreign library education and the American schools.[31]

The ALA's interest in the recruitment of librarians and in library education also had its effect. At the 1913 midwinter meeting, the Committee on Publicity for Library Schools voted to send letters to the colleges around the country explaining the functions of the schools. George Utley's list of college publications was used, and mimeographed letters were sent to over 180 college publications. A different form letter was used for men's colleges, women's colleges, and coeducational institutions. In these letters, students interested in the field of librarianship were referred to either the secretary of the American Library Association or to their own college librarians for further information. The committee did not feel that this was a highly successful effort and recommended that the approach be made through local campus groups interested in vocational education in the future.[32]

Everett Robins Perry of the Los Angeles Public Library and a 1903 recipient of the BLS from Albany suggested to Phineas Lawrence Windsor, chairman of the committee in 1913, that the approach might well be made through sending speakers to the colleges and having "graduates of the colleges now in library work write articles for their alumni publications" and to fraternity and sorority publications. Neither proposal was new. Odo Surratt, librarian of Baylor University had spent the summer of 1903 at the Albany School before she took over her duties. In the summer of 1905, she returned to Albany for more education and while there wrote back to the Baylor student newspaper with a detailed and glowing description of the school and the work there. Dewey himself addressed an 1886 meeting of the Association of Collegiate Alumni in an attempt to recruit students to the new school at Columbia.[33]

Individual academic librarians also spread the word. In 1895,

Mary Jones, librarian of the University of Nebraska, recommended to her friend, Helen F. Officer, that she go to the Armour Institute if she wished to become a librarian. Miss Officer applied to Armour, but withdrew her application in June after deciding to attend the Albany School. And Luther Day Harkness of the Oberlin College Library wrote directly to Sharp in 1894, inquiring about entrance examinations, application procedures, and housing at the Armour School for a recent Oberlin graduate.[34] Public librarians across the country were undoubtedly approached in the same way by prospective librarians.

To establish and maintain their validity, the schools had to develop some degree of acceptance by prospective employers that a person who had been educated to be a librarian was a better employee than one who had not. In Illinois, Katharine Lucinda Sharp did her share in creating a demand for trained librarians. In addition to serving as director of the Armour, and later of the University of Illinois library and library school, she was head of the Bureau of Information of the Illinois State Library Association which was widely advertised around the state. The bureau drew questions from many communities wishing to start libraries. Sharp answered them pushing home the fact that *trained* librarians were a vital necessity. The demand for her graduates has been directly attributed to her success at this.[35] Typical of the responses to her efforts was a letter from the president of McKendree College in Lebanon, Illinois: March 2, 1896, he wrote Sharp about a circular he had received; he asked for more information and warned that he "may later on have occasion to annoy the Bureau with specific questions." Admitting that his library was inadequate and disorganized, he wrote: "The thought has occurred to me that it might not be unpracticable for you to suggest someone who would be competent to take charge of it, and bring it in order—for a nominal consideration, for the present in the hope of compensation, adequate, for such service in the future."[36]

The Library Bureau assumed a major role in the placement of library school graduates. Because of the nature of its business and its contact with librarians across the country, it was natural that along with furniture, equipment, and supplies, it would be called upon to supply librarians. Perhaps because of Dewey's interest in both the Library Bureau and the Library School, the Bureau established itself officially as a placement center for the Columbia school. But it was a business arrangement, and the Bureau charged the job seeker 5 percent of the applicant's salary for the first year.

The Library Bureau did not limit its activities in this area to Dewey's school. It also contacted other schools when jobs became available and particular qualifications in an applicant were needed. In 1895, a request directed to George B. Meleney, manager of the Chicago office, prompted a query to the Armour Institute. The search was for "a young man to catalog a University library." Meleney had already written that "we could send a young woman from the Armour Institute without doubt." But, on being told that "the situation is such that a young woman could not be accommodated," turned to Katharine Lucinda Sharp.[37]

By the 1920s, librarians generally accepted the necessity for some form of professional training. Though some early leaders in the library world held firmly to the belief expressed by Justin Winsor that apprenticeship in large libraries was the only reasonable method of training librarians, the demands of the growing public library movement, coupled with the success of the early library schools, led ultimately to the acceptance of formal training. When Dewey first approached the idea of formal education, he pointed to other areas to justify the need. Normal schools were provided "by the hundred" for school teachers "where the best methods of teaching are taught." Every occupation, "Physicians, lawyers, preachers, yes even our cooks," had opportunities for specialized training. But librarians must learn their business by "experiments and experience." Dewey, of course, deplored this inconsistency and called for the development of similar forms of formal education. It was a view that others held. By 1914 the Texas Library Association could only deplore the lack of a local library school. Fearful of having newly created public libraries fall "into the hands of untrained persons," the association called for a school to be established in Texas. Those in the North were too far away to be useful.[39]

There were, of course, objections to the definition of professional librarianship in terms of education. The short-lived Library Workers Association of the early 1920s was a direct manifestation of working librarians' concern over the new emphasis. On September 23, 1920, the association adopted a constitution that explicated its concern over the relationship of education to professional status. Its announced purpose was "to promote the interest of library workers," with particular emphasis on "those who have not enjoyed the benefits of library school training." It sought to "improve the standard of library service" by establishing channels of communication to exchange experiences and information to help workers "continue their self-education," to expand the employment potential of library personnel who were not graduates of the formal programs of library education, and "to cooperate with other library organizations in stimulating in them a strong professional consciousness." The association, through Marian Catherine Manley, librarian of the Sioux City Public Library when elected secretary of the association, further explained that it was concerned with matters of personnel. In 1921, she asserted the "correlation of work in summer, extension, correspondence and library school courses"; that work, together with credit for experience, should be counted toward recognized library school degrees. When the ALA was increasingly inclining toward the position that professional integrity resided in the BLS degree and, through the development of standards, tending to regard the various short courses, correspondence courses, and other formal and informal methods as illegitimate, the Library Workers Association focused on a real concern of many librarians. But the development of the 1925 standards which were more descriptive than prescriptive and allowed alternative paths toward professional status removed the necessity for this organization and undoubtedly contributed to its demise.

One must add that though his name was not officially connected with the group, John Cotton Dana, gadfly of the ALA, was probably the guiding light of the association. Neither Catherine Van Dyne, president of the association, nor Marian Catherine Manley had higher education or formal library training. Both, however, had been trained by Dana in library methods at the Newark Public Library and the meetings of the association were held in conjunction with those of the Special Library Association. When the Library Workers Association was formed there was no thought of establishing any relationship with the ALA. Indeed, the organizers felt that the ALA would have no interest in such a group.[40]

From its first proposal by Dewey, formal library education was conceived as being basically instruction in the techniques of library economy. In his prospectus of the Columbia School, he made this clear:

> The course will include little of the antiquarian or historical except when necessary to illustrate or enforce modern methods. Its aim is entirely practical; to give the best obtainable advice, with specific suggestions on each of the hundreds of questions that rise from the time a library is decided to be desirable till it is in perfect working order including its administration.[41]

The emphasis on the practical application of technical skills obtained through the period of restructuring library education in the wake of Williamson's report.[42]

But Dewey and the ALA found another purpose for the library schools beyond the mere teaching of technical skills. The schools themselves assumed a function of promoting the "library spirit." Even Dewey—a man so concerned with detail that he masqueraded as a filing cabinet by having his suits made with pockets that would accommodate different sizes of notepaper corresponding to different subjects upon which he took notes[43]—acknowledged the importance of attitude over technical proficiency: "one full of zeal and high ideals will find a way to lern the technique; but the most skilful master of routine and bibliografical detail has litl in his knowledge to beget that almost divine inspiration, without which the best educational and filanthropic work is seldom done."[44] Dewey never intended the technical side of library work to constitute the total of library education. He made a clear distinction between the clerical and the higher functions of librarianship. Yet for Dewey, it was not the work itself that determined this distinction, but "the spirit with which it was done" that distinguished professional librarianship from a mere job in a library. He distinguished two phases of activity that he termed the *mental* and the *moral*. To the mental plane of functioning, he consigned "all thos who do the work from a personal ambition to make a reputation or gain a higher salary."

On this level were those librarians who worked "primarily for the comfort and advancement of the librarian." The professional level of librarianship was, however, on the moral plane, "where the librarian puts his heart and life into his work with as distinct a consecration as a minister or missionary and enters the profession and does the work because it is his duty or privilege." It was on this plane of mystical communion with a higher level that Dewey placed librarianship as a profession. Dewey compared the clerical and housekeeping aspects of library work to "a screen by which the best material is sifted out for the real library work."[45]

This view helps explain the peculiar character of early library education. Dewey, the school at Columbia and Albany, and the profession in general, defined *librarianship* in terms of personality as well as detailed technical competency. In giving advice to applicants to the newly founded Library School, Dewey pointed out that in lieu of a personal interview, "the Library Bureau finds it necessary to require a photograph, with note of height, weight, and color of hair and eyes, in order to give the trustees a correct impression of one's personality." It is noteworthy that Dewey's insistence on such personal information from applicants contributed to his ouster from Columbia.[46]

Dewey, with other early library educators, used the intensely practical curriculum precisely as a "screen" to eliminate unfit candidates for the profession. Dewey did not go as far as James Whitney of the Boston Public Library who advised the Cincinnati Conference of the ALA in 1882 that the librarian selecting assistants might "well go back of the candidate himself to his ancestors, to see what of intellectual as well as physical quality he has inherited from them,"[47] but there is evidence that in recommending a student for a job, the faculty at Albany "tended to favor the safe, personally preferred, man and women." At least the students felt so.[48]

But there is more concrete evidence that the ALA and the library schools consciously attempted to define *professionalism* in terms of social respectability. The public library movement in a period of massive immigration and social change in America recognized its responsibility to an older set of values and its obligation to education and acculturation. It was inevitable that when the ALA Committee on Library Training considered apprenticeship as a method of training librarians that was not under the control of the established library schools, it should be cautious about the type of person who would be acceptable to the profession. The committee directly addressed the problem in its report in 1903:

> The librarian of the small town, which is thoroughly American-ized, intelligent, and respectable, can know personally the candidates for apprenticeship and feel comparatively safe as to the kind of person, socially speaking, who is likely to present for library work. He does not need such rigid bars as the librarian of the city library, with the constant pressure for "places" of crude persons of all nationalities. [sic] coming from homes of no refine-ment, and armed with nothing but a high school diploma as with a weapon. The high school education given to a naturally intelli-gent person, of whatever nationality, is sufficient preparation, perhaps, so far as informational equipment is concerned, but it cannot make a gentlewoman, and it is gentlewomen that our large city libraries want. Hence the need for more careful sifting in the case of successive promotions.[49]

With this, the ALA gave official sanction to the notion that a quality independent of simple technical competency determined the level of professionalism in librarianship; rather, that depended on qualities that could not be taught but resided in the acculturation process over which the profession itself had no control.

The schools early demonstrated an uneasy attitude to the dual purpose of giving students technical education and incul-cating a professional attitude. The schools developed a sense of community and purpose to the mastery of the technical details that mirrored the missionary spirit of the library movement. Visitors to Dewey's school were impressed by the dedication of students and faculty to the work at hand. The intensity of the effort, according to one 1887 visitor, surpassed mere enthu-siasm and became "complete devotion to the work."[50] But the vehicle through which the schools sought to develop the library spirit in their students was highly technical and practical. Even when the schools made some real attempts at injecting theoretical aspects of librarianship into the program, they largely failed. The examinations given by the Albany School in 1910 in elementary and advanced cataloging and classification included some questions that called for a relatively high order of intellect and analysis applied to problems of bibliographic organization. But these were optional questions. The required portion called for evidence of practical ability in cataloging and classification, and a careful student could select combinations of questions that would avoid all but the most practical and basic application of the rules to the problems.[51] When Charles Clarence Williamson surveyed the library schools in 1921, he found an inordinate preoccupation with the techniques and details of library work. He attributed this to a universal conviction that the schools must teach what working librarians needed to know. The result was a profound conservatism in the curriculum that inhibited the schools from taking any large role in library development.[52]

This criticism was not startling to most librarians. Ernest Cushing Richardson had addressed the issue in 1890 when he gave a generally favorable report on the Albany School to the Fabyan House Conference but observed that it was open to the charge of "teaching methods without science, praxis before principle." Richardson attacked several of Dewey's favored hobbyhorses when he questioned what he considered the unwarranted amount of time spent on teaching the library hand and the entire hour devoted to a discussion of fountain pens. On occasion, the interests of the ALA in improving public library practice flared in open conflict with those librarians who demanded standards of intellectual acuity in ALA activities. William Coolidge Lane, librarian of Harvard, was a member of the Publication Committee. In 1910, he held up the publication of a series of tracts designed to help small public libraries, asserting that their quality was too low to bear the ALA imprint. But Reuben G. Thwaites finally persuaded him to allow their release.[53]

Williamson's most severe criticism of the library schools—that they failed to distinguish between clerical and professional functions of librarians—was widely realized. In 1910, Adam Julius Strohm of the Detroit Public Library observed that the courses demonstrated "a sense of confusion from their mixture of trifles and ponderousness." Strohm found the juxtaposition of bulletin boards dealing with paleography, classification, and typewriting, weakened the intellectual consistency of the curriculum. Williamson attributed the confusion observed by Strohm and others to the nature of library work. He found that library administrators made no distinctions among the various grades of service, and indeed, it was generally held that clerical workers could attain professional status through experience at their jobs. The schools, following this lead, made no distinctions in the courses. Rather, the emphasis on the personality of the student at the point of admission to the schools was assumed to define the characteristics of professionalism and it did not lay within the province of the schools to attempt a curricular distinction.[54]

The teaching methods in the early library schools were directed toward practice work as befitted a course of study that emphasized the practical to the almost complete exclusion of the theoretical. Mary Wright Plummer, a member of the class that entered the Library School in January, 1877, described her experience:

> We began at once on our work under the instructors appointed, applying ourselves first to the attainment of the library hand. Later we were allowed a choice between this and the printed hand, and several adopted the latter. . . . the next step was acquaintance with the accession-book, as being simplist. . . . From this we went on to gain a slight knowledge of the writing of shelf lists and condensing of titles, giving but short time to this as we were to return to it later.
>
> The writing of catalogue cards came next. For some time this was done on slips of author and subject sizes until we could be trusted to take the regular cards. Piles of books were brought up to us to be catalogued, and we took them as they came without selection. Our previous instruction on the slips had been in systematic order—biographies for a few days, then analyticals, then works in series, etc., so that we might master the writing of one kind of card before going to another.

From there the class went on to classification and ended the first term with a few weeks "spent in carding according to the dictionary system." The second term was devoted to apprenticeship, where students applied the *theory* to which they had been exposed in the preceding term. The majority of students found classification "fascinating but difficult" and chose to work at cataloging for their apprenticeship period.[55]

But the schools did not totally rely on practice as a pedagogical technique. Short courses imbedded in the formal longer terms and guest speakers were among the most common methods used by the schools to enrich their programs. Sydney Bancroft Mitchell entered the Albany School in 1903. He found a general lack of focus to the program, and though "the longer courses were competent in routines and practices," the short courses—some as short as only a few lectures—were at best haphazardly related to the others. Rather, they seemed to Mitchell to be "without integration with each other or the general objectives of the curriculum."[56]

Williamson found widespread use of guest lecturers at the library schools. The lectures were not limited to instructional areas. Many were clearly designed to inspire the students with the spirit of the public library movement as part of the schools' acculturation effort. Others fit into neither category, "but are considered to have value in introducing the students to the leading personalities of the library profession." Many lecturers were administrators whom the schools invited solely to enhance the placement prospects of the students: "Impressed with the merits of the school which urges him to become a special lecturer, the prospective employer is likely to seek no further for candidates for positions on his own staff."[57]

The substance of the early library school curriculum was directed toward technique and acculturation rather than any desire to bring thought, research, or application of basic principles to the problems of libraries. It is doubtful, though, that the majority of students could have assimilated more than the basic terminology and methods of library work as it was taught. Mary Wright Plummer, a woman of major attainments though limited formal education, reported great difficulty in mastering the substance of librarianship when she enrolled in Dewey's first class at Columbia in 1887. For the first few weeks, the class took notes on the lectures with little comprehension of what they were about "in the faith that someday we should look them over and find that practical experience had made them comprehensible." She concluded that this happened only in part. Examination of her notes and those of her classmate, May Seymour, taken in the first classes of the Columbia School, reveals that the lectures were generally at a very superficial, elementary level.[58]

Low salaries in the field, an incomplete definition of what library education meant, and the necessity for the schools to keep enrollments high at any cost in order to sustain the effort have all been cited as excuses for the quality of students library schools attracted. Though Katharine Lucinda Sharp made constant efforts to maintain entrance standards at the Armour Institute, she was besieged by prospective students—some with pathetic appeals—for admission to the program. One young woman could not understand the high requirements for admission. Though she confessed she could not meet the demands, she had perused the prospectus of the Armour curriculum and felt certain she could satisfactorily complete the course if given a chance. She begged Sharp only "for a month trial in it" and agreed that if she could not perform creditably, she "should be willing to give it up."[59]

An even more pathetic appeal was addressed to Sharp later in the same year. The writer had obviously been in correspondence about the program previously, but approached it with a more sincere degree of earnestness when she wrote on December 1, 1896, from Minneapolis:

> Since leaving Chicago I have been here, trying another treatment for my throat. Papa wrote yesterday giving me permission to begin studying again, if I wished. [sic] Has given me the choice of any College, or any other Institution of learning; but I feel that I have been out of school too long to attempt a regular course in a College or University. So [sic] have turned at once to my library work.[60]

Of course, the crux of this letter is the assumption of an inherent distinction between the work of the library school and a "regular course" in a college or university.

Through the period of developing education for librarianship until the effect of the Williamson report was fully realized in library education, the work of the library schools was rarely viewed in the context of a regular course at an academic institution. From its inception at Columbia, Dewey and many others conceived of the library school program as distinct from the work of American higher education—at least at the under-graduate level. At the opening of the Columbia school Dewey hoped to admit no students without a degree from a respectable college. But the school could not absolutely demand a college degree for admission until 1902; only 117 of the 267 students who had matriculated held college degrees though 160 had at least some college courses.[61]

Dewey himself seems to have been somewhat embarrassed by the Albany School's poor showing. He testified before the United States Congress Joint Committee on the Library of Congress in 1897 and was asked a pointed question on the number of college graduates among Albany's graduates. He hedged: "The proportion who have received a college training increases each year." He estimated that at the time 80 percent of the students were "college bred," which was Dewey's term indicating a class of society more than a sign of intellectual attainment. When pressed further, Dewey confessed that the school admitted students without "college training whom we think it unwise to shut out; but the usual rule is that candidates should receive a college education before coming to us."[62]

At the major schools, the association of professional educa-tion for librarianship with the undergraduate curriculum was early perceived to be inappropriate. Pratt, of course, never had the opportunity or the necessity for the juxtaposition. The Albany School had the legal ability to confer the appropriate advanced degrees, but had no university setting to give the endeavor the aspect of an academic effort. Of the three major schools, the University of Illinois alone attempted to implant the library school in the undergraduate program. In 1902, the University's Council of Administration approved a Bachelor of Arts in Library Science degree (BALS) for the completion of three years of general study and one year in the library school, thereby legitimizing the level of professional education at the undergraduate level. At the same meeting, the board authorized a Bachelor of Library Science degree (BLS) for one year of library school work beyond the BALS because it represented the amount of work beyond the basic requirement for any second bachelor's degree in the university. It also authorized a Master of Library Science (MLS) for a third year of work beyond the BLS.

Katharine Lucinda Sharp thought the facilities at the University of Illinois insufficient to sustain the dignity of a master's degree and never considered awarding it. By 1906, she had concluded that the BALS was inappropriate and petitioned the deans of the College of Literature and Arts and the College of Science to abolish the degree. They accepted her contention that the undergraduate diploma was not a recognized credential in the library world and that it was draining students who would attempt the BLS program. The BALS was abolished at Illinois, and the BLS was established, as at Albany, as the standard credential for trained librarians.[63]

It was not a belief that the intellectual challenges of the library schools were such as to demand such preparation that mandated the college degree for aspiring students to many library educators. Rather, the undergraduate background was considered as an integral element in the preparation of librarians. Though Mary Wright Plummer could not require much beyond high school graduation for admission to Pratt, she firmly held that sound academic preparation was a vital necessity for librarians. Addressing a meeting of the Illinois Library Association in 1903 at the University of Chicago, she granted that "there may be unending enthusiasm, a knowledge of technique, and genuine goodwill toward the cause of librarianship," but these alone were not enough. Rules and rituals applied without knowledge common to all well-educated people could not enhance the status of librarians:

> Let us take the case of a catalog card. It may be beautifully and legibly written or printed; it may have its words and sentences separated by the proper number of millimeters; its construction may be according to the A.L.A. rules or the Cutter rules or the Library School rules, and it may yet contain some blunder of ignorance that would make a librarian blush to find it in his catalog.[64]

Only librarians appreciated "the millimeters and the rules," but every educated person could tell the errors occasioned by lack of common knowledge that should be part of every librarian's equipment.

But unfortunately, few schools could require a college degree from entering students. In 1923, a survey by the ALA Temporary Library Training Board found only three schools—the University of California, the University of Illinois, and the Albany School—that required a college degree of applicants for admission. The University of Texas, the University of Washington, and Simmons awarded a bachelor's degree for completion of the library school curriculum in conjunction with the academic program of the institution. Others, like Syracuse, offered a bachelor's degree or a certificate depending on the student's course of study outside the library school.[65]

The schools that did not demand a college degree for admission or did not award a bachelor's degree for library school work as a major in a four-year program generally required an entrance examination that would equal a college education for admission. Williamson examined these tests and concluded that they were not as rigorous or comprehensive as they appeared. The questions asked followed a similar pattern from year to year and the candidate for admission could easily form a close idea of what was needed to pass. Further, the schools themselves did not seem to be concerned with reading the examinations closely or committed to any minimal level of acceptable performance. In keeping with the notion that the personality of the librarian was at least as important as intellectual attainments, the schools held to the theory "that the examiners can learn what they need to know about the candidate whether he answered the questions correctly or not."

Williamson found library schools averse to accepting standardization of the entrance examinations. Their arguments were reminiscent of those Eliot encountered in his advocacy of standardization of college admission policies. Some schools refused to deny the perfection of their own examinations. Others wished to retain the flexibility that control over grading allowed. And some schools specified that they sought "a particular type of student and for that reason could not dispense with their own examinations."[66]

At the time of the Williamson report, there was only a slight

connection between college degrees and library schools. Williamson found that only about half of the graduates of library schools
held college degrees. A large proportion of these were awarded
for some combination of course work that counted the library
school work toward graduation.[67] Another survey of 1924 conducted by the Temporary Library Training Board found that 43
percent of library school students held college degrees; 80 percent of the 621 students enrolled had at least one year of college
work upon admission to the schools.[67]

The faculties of library schools were as ill-prepared as the students by current standards. Only 52 percent of the instructors
in twelve library schools examined by Williamson were college
graduates. Eighty-one percent were library school graduates
and half of these were teaching at the same school from which
they had graduated. This lack of preparation was reflected in
the status of the faculty in the schools associated with colleges
and universities. Although the head of the school usually held
the rank of professor, all the rest of the teachers held only the
rank of instructor with a few anomalous assistant professors.[68]

The low standards of the early library schools and their insistence on personality over any objective criteria of professionalism were all aspects of an attitude that bordered on the anti-
intellectual. Standardization of technique and procedure emphasized by the schools fostered a system that relied on tradition and precedent for validation of its forms.[69] Dewey himself
studiously avoided the intellectual in favor of the practical. He
addressed the problem of library handwriting in the first
volume of his "text-book" periodical, *Library Notes:*

> More and more impressed with the importance of this subject, so
> apt to be neglected for something intellectual, we have spent
> some time in trying to find approximately what is best. These
> results have been revised item by item by about a dozen catalogers
> and librarians who discust every doubtful point, examined and
> tested samples, made individual experiments and reported at the
> next meeting, and in all ways made a business of hunting down the
> solution. These efforts lasted for an hour daily for nearly an entire
> week.[70]

Dewey felt strongly that this kind of research was vitally
necessary for librarianship. Good legible handwriting was im-

portant for librarians and the innovation of the typewriter could never obviate this.

But the antiintellectualism of the schools went beyond the lack of any attempt to evolve principles of librarianship and the curricular refuge of memorization of rules and regulations. Dewey's 1884 "Circular of Information" held out hope for the proposed school's relationship to Columbia. In it he announced that students in the new school were expected to take advantage of the opportunities for learning offered by the various departments of the college. Unfortunately, the advantages proved too much for some students. Carolyn Maria Hewins reported in a paper read by Ernest Cushing Richardson on September 10, 1890, at the Fabyan House Conference that the move to Albany was ultimately good for the students. While the school was at Columbia, "there was a constant temptation for the pupils to listen to all the lectures on subjects connected with literature or history offered them by the faculty of Columbia." They developed "mental indigestion" from this diet. She asserted that students quickly concluded that attending these lectures only complicated matters and it was better "not to attempt to listen to or make notes on lectures on subjects not in the direct line of library work while taking the school course." Albany was a far better place for the school because it was "not under the constant stimulus of metropolitan life and thought."[71]

To be sure, not all students found sufficient stimulation at the Albany School to satisfy them. Chalmers Hadley even went so far as to become the leader of an outright rebellion of the junior class in 1906.[72] But this came to nothing against the consensus of the schools, the ALA, and the working librarians that what was needed were librarians who knew the rituals of librarianship.

The low intellectual quality of early library education was evident from the beginning and the charges of the Williamson Report were not surprising to most academic librarians. Azariah Smith Root, librarian of Oberlin, was serving a brief term as head of the New York Public Library School in 1917 when he addressed the Louisville Conference on the problems of library schools. He felt that the schools were so involved in training people to fill the lower positions in libraries that they were ignoring the higher administrative positions. Root, however, did not find any real fault with the schools for this state. Rather, he felt that the solution lay in raising entrance requirements so as to admit students better able to comprehend deeper topics of library interest.[73]

Others perceived that the problem was not with the quality of the students, but with the schools themselves. Aksel G. S. Josephson observed in 1900 that entrance requirements for the schools had been steadily rising over the years while the quality of instruction had remained the same. He cautioned that unless the programs were improved to correspond to the increasing preparation of the students, "the faculties of the schools may someday be confronted with the fact that the step from the college to the library school will not be regarded as a step upward." William Warner Bishop echoed this in 1923 when he expressed the view that attempting to promote the library schools to graduate status by requiring college degrees for admission was a mistake. Many of the subjects that must be treated by library education were too elementary to be appropriate for college graduates. Bishop asserted that these elementary subjects should be treated at the undergraduate level "where they can be studied without taking undue time from cultural and disciplinary courses." He would then place the professional training on a truly graduate level "under teachers trained to handle mature students."[74] Where Bishop hoped to find such teachers is unclear. Only a few years before, he had written to Ernest Cushing Richardson complaining about his inability to find anyone qualified to conduct a "bibliographic seminary." He wanted "people who are distinctly of the grade of university instructors, and who can rank as Assistant or Associate Professors, as they work up," but these were not available.[75]

Sydney Bancroft Mitchell, perhaps, came as close as any to the essential problem of both librarians and library school instructors in the academic community. In his reaction to the Williamson Report on behalf of the University of California library school, he noted that trying to operate a library school in a university context had inherent difficulties. The university requirements for faculty members in the various departments were difficult for library school instructors to meet, "inasmuch as a mere college graduation with a year or so at a library school is not readily accepted as the equivalent of the doctor's degree at present an essential for most university instructors."[76] Yet, Mitchell was optimistic about the educational preparation of most library school faculty members. Most library school instructors teaching at schools associated with the colleges and universities at the time of the Williamson Report were not college graduates. At Illinois, only one of five had graduated; at Simmons, five of nine; at Western Reserve, five of eight; at Wisconsin, five of eleven; at Washington, four of nine.[77]

Through the period, there arose almost an antipathy between the aims and attitudes of academic librarians and the public-library-directed development of library education. The inappropriateness of library education as it developed had been apparent for decades before the Williamson Report. This derived directly from the involvement of the ALA with the development of education for librarianship and the lack of any sustained involvement of American academic librarianship with the library movement.

In the first place, the reliance on academic degrees as proof of professional competency did not exist within the public library movement. Before 1925, only the Albany School awarded a master's degree, but it had been conferred on only eleven people and represented more an honor than any recognition of real academic achievement. The first PhD awarded by a library school was not granted until 1930,[78] although academic librarians had debated the issue of appropriate credentials for their special area for many years.

Though present among ALA's members, academic librarians consistently relegated their special area to a secondary position in favor of the public library movement. Indeed, not until the 1923 Hot Springs Conference did the College and Reference Section go so far as to adopt a constitution. Thus a period that has been referred to as *sequestered professional internalization* was ended.[79]

From the beginning of formal library education when the ALA established a Committee on the Proposed Library School, academic librarians were conspicuously absent from any special consideration in planning.[80] Well into the 1920s, Dewey's view of the purpose of library education held the official sanction of the association. Dewey maintained that the purpose and value of the library schools derived directly from the public library movement. At a 1918 meeting of the American Library Institute (ALI), in which the topic of the PhD in library science was taken up, Dewey explained:

> My impres'n is strong that our librari schools [sic] shud shape their corses for the staf of the tipical public librari. The vast majoriti of their graduates wil of cors wurk ther. Hardli any librari skool is adequatli equipt to train speciali for universiti wurk. . . . I shud lyk to see one or mor of the leadin universities in our main sections, preferabl lyk Harvard, Chicago, U of Cal and the best one we cud fynd in the South ofer a 1 year graduate cors, suplementin our librari skools, and devoted definitli and entyrli to tranin for universiti libraries.[81]

But Dewey's solution tied the training of academic librarians to a system that thwarted some of the essential needs of academic librarianship. ALA endorsed history, languages, and literature as essential equipment for the library from the beginning of the consideration of Dewey's proposed school.[82] The entrance requirements to the growing number of schools reflected this basic assumption. This background, however, was unsatisfactory for the diversity of expertise needed in the academic library. Charles Harvey Brown in his chapter on libraries in the 1930 Office of Education report on land grant colleges and universities observed that these institutions were not being served by the library schools. The emphasis in the land grant universities was on the pure and applied sciences, and the library schools had few if any graduates with that background. As director of the library at Iowa State University, he inquired of several schools in 1929 and found that none had any students with undergraduate majors in the sciences.[83] Dewey's view that the academic specialization be based on a general liberal education and library school preparation countered the need for specialists in these libraries.

Aksel G. S. Josephson of the John Crerar Library formally addressed the problem in 1900 in a paper read before the Chicago Library Club. Josephson proposed a separation of the two-year library school program that was then standard. He would have the junior year devoted to preparing students for the minor professional positions in libraries and concentrate on cataloging. The lower course required high school graduation for admission. The senior course would be connected with a college or university and offer the MA and PhD degrees. To this, he would admit college graduates and, upon examination, graduates of the junior course who had completed a specified period of work in libraries. After studying classification, cataloging, library administration, bibliography, and a set of elective subjects, the student would prepare a thesis for admission to the higher degree. Josephson maintained that some form of bibliography was appropriate for this final effort.[84]

The next year he elaborated on this proposal before the ALA's Instruction on Bibliography Round Table. He reported that he had tried to interest "some university authorities" in the idea with no success. The best he could do was quote a letter from William Torrey Harris, Commissioner of Education, that was polite but noncommital to the notion of establishing an advanced school in Washington.[85]

The topic was raised in various forms over the years and emerged again in 1918 at the annual meeting of the ALI. Amy L. Reed of Vassar advocated the awarding of the PhD for two or three years' work on a course in librarianship to be offered by universities. The thesis for this doctorate was to be "a bibliography with little or no text, except the necessary annotations." She combined a series of rigorously practical work in book selection and other library subjects with work in the university library and insisted on intensive study of some special subject that would give the student "a knowledge of the true nature of research and the acquisition of scholarly method gained through intensive study of a highly specialized subject; three minors, history, English, and a third, should be taken." She demanded a final course "in the history and theory of education," to "synthesize the whole of the educational experience." This program obviously had to lead to the PhD for the aspiring academic librarian. The degree was necessary if librarians were to achieve equality with the faculty. The express purpose of the proposed program was to "supply to would-be librarians the necessary common basis of intellectual experience with his colleagues of the faculty on which to build up mutual sympathy and respect and power of intimate cooperation towards the common goal." The use of a degree already recognized as the mark of academic acceptability was crucial to her in the move "towards the more outward but equally important recognition by proper ranks, titles and salaries" for librarians.[86]

Edith Coulter reaffirmed this position before the College and Reference Section at the 1922 Detroit Conference. She felt that the library schools should take the lead in establishing the doctorate as the standard credential for academic librarians. If one or more schools offered "a higher research degree," it would eventually become recognized by academic institutions and accepted as proper preparation for academic librarians. Until this happened, though, she saw no recourse but for the aspiring academic librarian to earn the PhD in more traditional fields: "It is true that without either the higher academic or the higher professional degree he will be handicapped throughout his professional life and consequently will not perform his greatest service."[87]

It was not just in the position of head of the library that the higher degree was recommended. Frederick C. Hicks, law librarian at Columbia, expounded the notion at the 1918 ALI meeting that library directors "are not merely made, but grow and are selected by processes sometimes natural and sometimes artificial." Consequently, the establishment of any course of formal instruction leading to a specific degree was inappropriate for administrative positions. But demands placed on "the knowledge, judgement, and tact" of the reference librarian made "education equivalent to that of a doctor of philosophy" mandatory. Hicks asserted that for the work of such a person, the degree need not be actually conferred, but "it would be a distinct advantage to the library and to the reference librarian if it had formally been bestowed."[88]

The question of higher degrees for librarianship was functionally laid to rest by the academic institutions themselves in 1923. That a proposal for advanced degrees would have to obtain the approval of the Association of American Universities (AAU) was obvious to those in the American Library Association who concerned themselves with the problem. At the 1924

Saratoga Springs Conference, the Temporary Library Training Board—composed of Adam Strohm, Harrison Warwick Craver, Linda A. Eastman, Andrew Keogh, Malcolm Glen Wyer, and Sarah C.N. Boyle—presented its recommended standards for library schools. They included standards for a graduate-level program that allowed for the granting of a PhD, but observed that the question of appropriate degrees would have to be settled by the AAU.[89]

Wyer was chairman of the Committee on Degrees of the Association of American Library Schools (AALS), and had already submitted the proposal to the university authorities. In December, 1923, he had petitioned the Association of American Universities for "the opinion and, if possible, the sanction of the AAU regarding the degree program which the library schools have considered now for several years and formulated with a good deal of care." The AAU refused to accept the BLS and MLS when they considered the proposal in the fall of 1924. Rather, they preferred the designation AB or BS and MA or MS "to be recommended provisionally until work shall have been on a graduate level." They also refused to allow any higher degrees, reporting, "It is probably not desirable for the present to plan curricula and work beyond the Master's degree, at least until problems concerning Bachelor's degrees and Master's degrees have been solved." They advised anyone desiring more advanced work "to seek them in scholarly fields."[90]

It would seem, though, that the interest in advanced degrees was primarily limited to a small proportion of academic librarians at the time. At the 1919 meeting of the ALI, a report was entered into the record of a survey made by the New England Librarians' Committee on Graduate Training for College Library Assistants. A questionnaire was addressed to college librarians in New England which in part asked for reactions to a course of graduate study that might lead to the doctorate. The committee concluded from the responses "that, however desirable such a course might be, there is, in fact, at present but little actual demand for it." It found that only in the largest universities was there the possibility of "positions offering sufficient inducement to scholars, both in the matter of pay and in the promise of leisure for continued research which normally accompanies equivalent teaching positions."[91]

The idea that the doctorate in librarianship was the appropriate degree for academic librarians was formally abandoned by the ALA in 1925. In the minimum standards for library schools developed by the Board of Education for Librarianship, it is clear that the work offered at the graduate level that required a bachelor's degree and two months experience as objective criteria for admission was conceived as the appropriate level of preparation for college and university librarians.[92]

If the profession misinterpreted the nature of the doctorate in the realm of academic librarianship, it also misread the nature of research in librarianship that constituted an academically acceptable standard. Ernest Cushing Richardson, as president of the ALI, addressed the 1916 meeting at Atlantic City. In what appeared to be an attempt to form a special interest group of research librarians apart from the ALA, he pointed out the unique relationship of librarians to research:

> It is an interesting fact that many of the ordinary everyday processes of the library are strictly research work, containing all the main elements of research method. Every book cataloged which requires looking up for full name of an author or for its bibliographical history, is, for example, in a small way, an essay in research, and this work is all the time training those who do it in the method of research. It is a matter of curious observation that even the more brilliant men from our University graduate schools, who are supposed to have been trained in research, need retraining in exactness and bibliographical methods, at least, before they are suited to the modern use of a library, and what is true of the cataloging department is almost equally true of purchase and reference departments.[93]

But others less enthusiastic than Richardson recognized a primary distinction to be made between research and the work of the librarian. William Warner Bishop, then superintendent of the reading room at the Library of Congress, observed in 1915 that there was a clear difference between reference work and research. Reference work was the job of the librarian and research that of the reader. "Reference work," he emphatically concluded, "is in aid of research, but it is not research itself."[94]

Edith Coulter endorsed the same view before the College and Reference Section of the ALA at the 1922 Detroit Conference. She pointed to the low status of the assistant in the academic hierarchy, the job itself allowed little time or energy for pursuit of advanced degrees or for research. She exhorted academic librarians to engage in bibliography because it is "the parent of research." She maintained that librarians were better equipped to compile bibliographies than chemists, botanists, or economists because of their greater knowledge of "bibliographical law." She would have librarians take the field of bibliography as their special province of research and, as necessary, consult subject specialists for advice. This, she maintained, would, in conjunction with the librarian's role in bibliographic instruction, enable the librarian to gain "recogniton of equality with the faculty."[96]

Andrew Keogh recognized that an advanced library school was probably an impossibility in 1919 when he recommended graduate work in established areas with especial emphasis to be given to bibliography for research librarians. Keogh asserted that for the PhD degree, a dissertation which "not only incorporated discoveries of importance, but by sound criticism throws light on disputed literary or historical or other problems," would be acceptable. Further, he intimated that the dean of the graduate school of Yale had been receptive to the idea.[97] Keogh overestimated the kind of research possible. For the most part, the views of Granville Stanley Hall on the antithetical relationship between administration and research obtained in the academic world. Hall asserted that by its very nature, the process of organization operated against the impulse to pure research. The need for research to function in the freest possible atmosphere militated against the necessity for cooperation inherent in the proper functioning of any complex organization. Librarians, working in a highly complex organization, were in no position to press forward the frontiers of knowledge: "Great librarians have been eminent in history or literature, but it is in spite of, rather than because of, their vast knowledge and responsibility for books."[98]

Even Frederick C. Hicks, who believed that reference librarians should have the PhD, declined to give unhesitating endorsement to the respectability of bibliograhic research. He maintained that the attitude of faculty members toward bibliography was such that it was completely unlikely that it would be allowed for doctoral research. As support, he brought forth the case of a student in zoology at Cornell who wished to elect subject bibliography as a minor but was opposed by his faculty. Hicks cited this as an example of faculty attitudes toward librarianship in general.[99]

The attitude of scholars to the pretentions of bibliography, then, was not promising to librarians who looked toward that form of research as a road toward a respected position in the academic community. Even such a man in the world of enumerative bibliography as Charles Evans found it difficult to secure the recognition that many felt was due him for his work. Only through the efforts of his friends was he able to procure an honorary doctorate from Brown University. Brown's president, Clarence A. Barbour, and the Board of Fellows concluded in 1934 that such work as *The American Bibliography* deserved at best an honorary Master of Arts. That was the degree they offered until convinced by Evans's influential friend Clarence Saunders Brigham, that a doctorate was the appropriate reward.[100]

Perhaps one of the most telling attacks on the scholarly aspirations of bibliographers was made by Charles Kendall Adams. When George Lincoln Burr became librarian of the White Library at Cornell in 1878, he began working on specialized catalogs of the holdings. These were annotated bibliographies that displayed impressive scholarship. One, on the Reformation, was published in 1889; a second, on the French Revolution, followed in 1894. Both were widely appreciated in the United States and Europe. But Adams, among others, thought this work a waste for a man of his talents. He wrote Burr on May 18, 1894, after the second effort had appeared: "It is a rather ungracious time to repeat what I have so often said, that I think you have too large and precious abilities to justify limiting them to the work of a bibliographer."[101]

By the end of the third decade of the twentieth century, the debate over the proper educational preparation of academic librarians was largely over. By that time a consensus had been reached, at least by the institutions, that some form of training as represented by the course of study given by the library schools was desirable. The ALA's 1926 survey of libraries found few formalized requirements for full-time positions in academic libraries, though. Only a handful of libraries included in the survey specified any definite qualifications for appointment and these for only a few positions. The University of Washington, under the influence of William E. Henry, was alone in reporting a fully developed set of requirements for professional-level employment. The lowest level of appointment required three years of college and one year of library school as well as two foreign languages.

But the survey found that library education was well entrenched in these libraries. Almost 44 percent of all full-time employees of the 114 academic libraries surveyed held either the one-year or two-year level of certification from a library school. Most held only the one-year certificate. An additional 13 percent had undergone at least a six-month training class. It must be noted in this context, that the proportions are biased to an unknowable degree. The survey, like the entire profession, as Williamson noted, made no distinction between clerical and professional levels of service. It can be assumed with some confidence that a large proportion of those without library training were employed in positions that could not have demanded the services of a professional librarian.[102]

This was the conclusion reached by Azariah S. Root in 1919. He had surveyed thirty-four institutions at the request of the American Library Association's Committee to Investigate Salaries. These colleges and universities reported employing ninety-eight people who were library school graduates, sixty-five trained in summer schools or apprentice classes, and eighty-seven completely untrained except at their jobs. Root expressed disappointment in these results, but asserted that this indicated "that those parts of library work which require somewhat detailed and technical training such as cataloging, have been largely cared for by people with library school experience." Reference was another area found to have a high proportion of library school trained people "while order department work, delivery desk work, and the like, are more likely to be handled by people with lesser training."[103]

But the situation was improving. Charles H. Compton accepted the definition of the rank of assistant as synonymous with professional grade when he prepared a survey for the ALA

Committee on Salaries, Insurance, and Annuities in 1929. Compton found that assistants in college libraries tended to have higher salaries than those in public libraries and attributed this to their higher educational qualifications. He found that ninety-three of the 110 assistants included in his survey held the bachelor's degree, and that seventy-eight of these had been graduated from library schools. He also found it significant that of the twenty-four staff members with less than two years' experience, eighteen were library school graduates. All of these were also college graduates. He concluded that "this indicates that college and university libraries are requiring full college graduates and in most cases library school graduates for all new members."[104]

Librarians holding both a college degree and a library school degree had frequently combined both and held the BLS awarded by many schools for some combination of a library school program with college study. Earl James McGrath included librarians in his 1938 historical study of administrative positions in American higher education from 1860 to 1933. He found the only library directors holding the doctorate from 1860 to 1933 in the larger Eastern institutions. At the state universities, the standard was a bachelor's degree—usually the Bachelor of Library Science. Further, in these schools, the percentage of holders of the bachelor's degree who served as library director had risen from 25 percent in 1880 to 70 percent in 1933. He found a similar increase in the smaller Western institutions included in his study. He concluded that the percentage of doctorates held by the directors of the large Eastern schools was directly attributable to the process of appointing a faculty member as the administrative head of the library. In the state schools and the Western colleges, however, the practice early developed of appointing someone with library school training.[105]

Though the tendency existed to accept the necessity for library school training for academic librarians, by the early 1930s, it was not considered a requirement for a position. William Madison Randall of the University of Chicago Library School headed a group of college administrators, academic librarians, and representatives of professional organizations that was financed by the Carnegie Corporation to publish a report on libraries in liberal arts colleges in 1932. The report attempted to construct a general picture of the situation in the smaller colleges and surveyed 205 liberal arts colleges in America. This committee found that when a library director was sought by the colleges the authorities tended to look to academic credentials rather than professional training. The committee therefore concluded that librarians wishing to fit themselves for administrative positions should concentrate on their academic background rather than their professional training.

But it would seem that in reaching this conclusion, the committee may have approached the data with some bias. Of the 179 head librarians reporting, eighty-two (45.8 percent) had more than one year of professional training and fifty-seven of these held a bachelor's degree indicating the possibility of a high proportion of holders of the four-year BLS degree. An additional sixty-two (34.6 percent) had less than one year of formal library training and thirty-five (19.5 percent) had no professional training.[106]

At the larger and better-financed institutions, some form of professional training was recognized as necessary, at least for the more responsible positions. George Works surveyed Iowa State University, The University of California, the University of Cincinnati, Cornell, the University of Iowa, the University of Michigan, the University of Minnesota, the University of North Carolina, Oberlin, Stanford, and Yale, and found, as of March, 1927, that only seven of the fifty-seven department heads in the libraries were without any academic preparation. Nineteen of the fifty-seven held professional library degrees, the most common being the BLS awarded as a second degree which was held by fifteen of the nineteen.[107]

One class of schools, the smaller institutions funded by the Morrill acts, was in no position to demand much in either libraries or librarians at least until the 1930s. The larger land grant universities could, like the University of California, require an applicant for a professional position to present a bachelor's degree, library school training, and a knowledge of foreign languages. Most, however, could not. A 1930 survey of land grant colleges and universities found that 22.5 percent of the directors of the libraries did not hold even a bachelor's degree.

Further, ten of the head librarians of these institutions had no library experience before their appointments and five had undergone no library school training.

Charles Harvey Brown, librarian of Iowa State University, who conducted this survey for the Office of Education, pointed out that there were three classes of land grant colleges distinguished by the point at which the institutions began adequately funding their libraries. The libraries of the colleges just deplored showed little use and their budgets had not kept pace with needed increases. These were the ones that still, in 1930, were in the state of development that mandated teachers or clerks as caretakers of the collections. A second class of colleges had begun modernization since 1920 by erecting new buildings, employing professionally trained librarians, and dramatically increasing expenditures. Brown mentioned Iowa State, Louisiana State, and Oregon State as representative of this group. The third class like the universities of Illinois, California, Minnesota, and Nebraska, had developed a high level of sustained funding by or before 1900.[108]

Thus, by the end of the 1920s, the appropriateness of library education for at least some positions in academic libraries had won general acceptance by librarians and administrators of America's colleges and universities. Few of these, though, would be in complete agreement with the Drexel Library School director, Corrine Bacon, who opened an essay on the necessity for specialized training for academic librarians with a piece of doggerel on the importance of the schools:

A degree you may have from a college
Where wisdom you've quaffed at its source,
But no library'll trust to your knowledge
Till you've taken a library course.

You may love books and read them all day, Sir,
And be several removes from a fool,
But you can't run a library now, Sir,
If you've not been to library school.[109]

Many would concur that the training was important for a variety of reasons ranging from increased technical competency to improved status.

It is evident that formal training was never considered an absolute requisite for the higher positions of librarianship. But the more technical library positions required it, and the standing of the individual librarian in the profession came, in some way to be felt as determined by it. Whitman Davis, librarian of Mississippi State University, wrote Phineas Lawrence Windsor in 1910 inquiring about the requirements of the University of Illinois Library School. He was a 1904 graduate of Mississippi State and had been appointed librarian in 1904. He had attended a Chautauqua summer course in 1906, was president of the Mississippi Library Association, and had been to a few ALA annual conferences. In a real sense, his professional preparation was more complete than that of many of his peers. "But," he wrote Windsor, "I feel like I should have better standing among librarians If [sic] I could be graduated from your school."[110]

Though there is a great deal of subsequent correspondence from Davis to Windsor, Davis did not graduate from the Illinois school until 1933. This lack of professional training did not seem to have hindered his professional recognition: he was appointed to serve on the Advisory Committee on Library Facilities and Services for the *Survey of Land Grant Colleges and Universities* published in 1931; he was one of five members that included the library directors of the universities of Florida, New Hampshire, and Wyoming and a representative of the ALA. A profession that affirmed experience as equal to formal education could not ignore the value of its most experienced practitioners, though it must be added that the report for which Davis was in part responsible, tended to deplore the lack of formal training among land grant college librarians. The apology was offered that these librarians had been appointed long "before professional library education reached its present development."[111]

Thus, the development of formal instruction in librarianship was coupled with an increasing awareness by academic administrators that the library's place in the revitalized colleges and universities needed more than a simple caretaker for full realization. The burgeoning masses of materials collected and the necessity for order and organization lured the profession led by Melvil Dewey and his disciples to develop standardized forms and rituals that gave substance to the public library movement. Colleges and universities grew to accept formal training in these forms and rituals as appropriate for their librarians. Even its most perspicacious critic, Charles Clarence Williamson, concluded that it was a necessity for professional work. Admitting that he had long felt reservations toward it in a letter to William F. Yust in 1919, he confessed that "experience of nearly ten years has thoroughly changed my attitude toward library school training." Though the supply of trained librarians was severely limited, he inclined toward insisting on library school training for assistants: "I find myself more and more reluctant to consider the appointment of any person who has not had the training offered by a good library school."[112]

* * * * * *

As American higher education entered the twentieth century, faculty members and academic administrators became convinced that the new emphasis in American higher education demanded more in facilities and services than the libraries of the classical colleges could provide. Growing masses of materials created severe problems in access. The first naturally occurring solution was simply to keep the library opened for longer periods than was possible under the part-time professors and students who served as librarians of the classical colleges. To this end, the first full-time librarians were hired. But it was apparent that this simple step of providing someone with no special qualifications to maintain order and check out books was inadequate.

American higher education expanded in a number of directions at the end of the nineteenth century, one being the establishment of professional education in a variety of fields. The development of a point of professional focus for the growing public library movement in the American Library Association made it only natural that librarians as a group look to a higher education that could satisfy their needs. The establishment of a School of Library Economy at Columbia by Melvil Dewey in 1886 with the hesitant support of the American Library Association was a first step in defining professional education for librarians. That Columbia's trustees did not approve of the school or, ultimately, of the grating presence of Dewey himself, indicates that they were not ready to accept librarianship as an academic discipline. That they refused to allow support beyond that given the library and viewed Dewey's school as an internal affair of the library confirms this.

The notion that there was an appropriate path toward becoming a librarian enjoyed growing acceptance. Proselytizing leaders in the field, publication of information on library education in widely disseminated forms, and the active involvement of those who would be considered experts at the art of librarianship, all contributed to spread the idea that formal education was available and appropriate for the occupation. People like Katharine Lucinda Sharp and Melvil Dewey because of their prominence were asked for help by those with an interest in libraries. They invariably answered that the solution to problems in libraries lay in the employment of librarians trained to the profession. By 1920, fifteen schools proclaimed their ability to train students to assume a role as professional librarians. By the third decade of the twentieth century, the definition of professionalism for librarians included an element of formal training that demanded study at a library school.

The development of library education and the concerns of the ALA in the promotion of the library spirit are inextricable. Dewey, as a moving force in both developments, influenced the relationship of one to the other. Dewey's intense concern with utility conditioned the forms of pedagogy that library education assumed—just as it influenced the concerns of the ALA. The public library movement became the central concern of both Dewey and the association, and because library education was directed toward practice rather than principle, the prime consideration in the training of librarians.

The programs of the schools as envisioned by Dewey and elaborated upon by his disciples were intensely practical. Dewey's commitment, at the conception of the school at Columbia, was to a purely technical program. This view was followed by succeeding schools at least until the redirection of library education occasioned by the conclusions of the Williamson Report and the intervention of the Carnegie Corporation. Various committees of the ALA and the AALS attempted to formulate and enforce some standard of training for librarianship, but were largely unsuccessful. Through the 1920s, library education remained an intensely practical process of acculturation that prepared prospective librarians in the professional forms and rituals.

Though the forms of this education were intensely practical, the ultimate aims were not. Library education, in the stage before the Williamson study, emphasized the practice of librarianship to the exclusion of any theoretical considerations. It relied on the entrance examinations and the rigors of the course to determine which students might be ordained at what Dewey considered the "moral" level of professionalism. Students would be properly imbued with the library spirit and, in addition to acquiring the technical competencies of organization and administration, would assume a missionary spirit that would further the library movement.

The quality of the early library schools perhaps deserved the reaction of Columbia's trustees. Williamson found only three—the Albany School and those of the Universities of California and Illinois—that required an undergraduate degree for admission. Others offered only certificates for varying amounts of work, or in the case of those associated with an academic institution, a bachelor's degree for some combination of college work with library school courses. The students were, on the whole, equally well equipped as the faculty that taught them and who had essentially the same academic credentials as they were awarding. The lack of any place within the academic organization for the schools and the absence of any similarity between the credentials of library school instructors and the faculty of other departments of the academic institutions precluded acceptance of the library schools as integral components of the academic community.

The relation of the ALA and the public library movement to academic librarians was such that academic librarians did not attempt to establish concern for their own special interests within the association. Rather, they accepted the emphasis of the ALA and shared the interest in public library development. But many perceived that library education, conditioned as it was by the needs of the public libraries, was inappropriate for the special interests of academic libraries.

There was much discussion among academic librarians about the appropriate forms of preparation for service in American colleges and universities. Many divergent visions of the proper solution were presented but there was a consensus that the credential to be awarded should be the doctorate. It was generally held that the PhD as the mark of academic competency was needed by academic librarians if they were to obtain the academic respectability necessary to perform their essential duties in the academic community.

But these early proposals betrayed a lack of understanding by academic librarians of the nature of graduate education as it had developed in the United States. The lack of any substantial interest from working librarians, the reluctance of the academic profession to accept the doctorate in librarianship, and the decision of the profession itself through the ALA's Board of Education for Librarianship that the appropriate preparation for academic librarians was an undergraduate education and a course in a library school, effectively ended the debate by the mid-1920s. Only through the active intervention of the Carnegie Corporation was the idea implemented at the University of Chicago beginning in 1928.

The failure of academic librarians to develop a formal preparation for their specialized area of librarianship derived in part from their failure to isolate a unique area of research. Rather than promote research into library operations or library problems, academic librarians generally agreed that systematic bibliography was their special province and concluded that bibliographic compilation should be the vehicle through which their scholarship would be recognized. But this level of research failed to win the academic community's support as evidence of sufficient scholarly attainment.

By the end of the 1920s, America's colleges and universities had accepted the value of trained librarians and were employing them in increasing numbers. Formal education was accepted as necessary, at least for the technical positions. The academic institutions, by hiring librarians who had been trained in library schools, affirmed the legitimacy of the preparation. Thus, the essentially undergraduate level and technical BLS became established as the appropriate credential for academic librarians.

Notes to Chapter 4

1. William Hugh Carlson, *The Library of Oregon State University: Its Origins, Management, and Growth, a Centennial History* (Corvallis, Ore.: 1966), pp. 16-17.

2. Elizabeth La Boone, "History of the University of Georgia Library," Master's thesis, University of Georgia, 1954, pp. 95-96.

3. Edith R. Mirrieless, *Stanford, the Story of a University* (New York: G. P. Putnam's Sons, 1959), p. 112.

4. Maurine Irwin, "History of the Ohio Wesleyan University Library, 1844-1940," Master's thesis, University of California, 1941, pp. 153-64.

5. Robert Ferguson Munn, *West Virginia University Library, 1867-1917*, unpublished doctoral dissertation, University of Michigan, 1961, p. 137.

6. Mary Elizabeth Nichols, "Early Development of the University of Mississippi Library," Master's thesis, University of Mississippi, 1957, pp. 28, 30; Ralph W. Hansen, "The Stanford University Library: Genesis 1891-1906," *Journal of Library History* 9 (April 1974): 146-47.

7. Benjamin Edward Powell, *The Development of Libraries in Southern Universities to 1920*, unpublished doctoral dissertation, University of Chicago, 1946), pp. 31-32.

8. Quoted in Jessica Chandler Potter, "The History of the University of Washington Library," Master's thesis, University of Washington, 1954, p. 22.

9. Burton J. Bledstein, *The Culture of Professionalism: The Middle Class and the Development of Higher Education in America* (New York: W.W. Norton & Co., Inc., 1976), p. 84.

10. Katharine Lucinda Sharp, "Librarianship as a Profession" *Public Libraries* 3 (January 1898): 5.

11. William Warner Bishop, "The American Library Association: Fragments of Autobiography," *Library Quarterly* 19 (January 1949): 38; Sydney B. Mitchell, *Mitchell of California: the Memoirs of Sydney B. Mitchell, Librarian, Teacher, Gardener* (Berkeley: California Library Association, 1960), p. 120.

12. John W. Burgess, *Reminiscences of an American Scholar: The Beginnings of Columbia University* (New York: Columbia University Press, 1934), pp. 217-18.

13. Fremont Rider, *Melvil Dewey* (Chicago: American Library Association, 1944), p. 21; Ray Trautman, *A History of the School of Library Service* (New York: Columbia University Press, 1954), pp. 3-4, 7.

14. American Library Association, Committee on the Proposed School for Librarians at the Columbia College, "Report," *Library Journal* 8 (September-October 1883): 293.

15. Sarah Katherine Vann, "Introduction," in Melvil Dewey, *Melvil Dewey: His Enduring Presence in Librarianship*, ed. Sarah Katherine Vann (Littleton, Colo.: Libraries Unlimited, 1978), p. 39.

16. Melvil Dewey, "School of Library Economy," *Library Journal* 8 (September–October 1883): 288.

17. Frederick Augustus Porter Barnard, "The Library and School of Library Economy: An Extract from the Annual Report of F. A. P. Barnard, S.T.D., LL.D., L.H.D., President of Columbia College, Made to the Trustees May 5, 1884," Columbia University, School of Library Service, *School of Library Economy of Columbia College 1887–1889: Documents for a History* (Columbia University, School of Library Service, 1937), p. 13.

18. Nicholas Murray Butler, *Across the Busy Years: Recollections and Reflections*, 2 vols. (New York: Charles Scribner's Sons, 1939–1940), 1:94–95.

19. Trautman, p. 16; W. Boyd Rayward, "Melvil Dewey and Education for Librarianship," *Journal of Library History* 3 (October 1968): 308; Melvil Dewey, "Report of the Columbia College School of Library Economy," Columbia University, School of Library Service, *School of Library Economy of Columbia College, 1887–1889: Documents for a History* (Columbia University, School of Library Service, 1937), p. 213.

20. Trautman, p. 22.

21. Charles Clarence Williamson, "Training for Library Work: A Report Prepared for the Carnegie Corporation of New York," *The Williamson Reports of 1921 and 1923* ed. by Sarah K.Vann (Metuchen, N.J.: Scarecrow Press, Inc., 1971), p. 106.

22. Louis C. Moloney, *A History of the University Library at the University of Texas, 1883–1934*, unpublished doctoral dissertation, Columbia University, 1970), p. 102; Winifred Linderman, *History of the Columbia University Library, 1876–1927*, unpublished doctoral dissertation, Columbia University, 1959, p. 274; Judith K. Meyers, "A History of the Antioch College Library, 1850 to 1929," Master's thesis, Kent State University, 1963, pp. 129–30; Ruth W. Clinefeller, "A History of Bierce Library of the University of Akron," Master's thesis, Kent State University, 1956, p. 70; Carl Milton White, *A Historical Introduction to Library Education: Problems and Progress to 1951* (Metuchen, N.J.: Scarecrow Press, Inc., 1976), pp. 94–95.

23. Williamson, p. 106.

24. Wayne Stewart Yenawine, *The Influence of Scholars on Research Library Development at the University of Illinois*, unpublished doctoral dissertation, University of Illinois, 1955), p. 48.

25. Laurel Ann Grotzinger, *The Power and the Dignity: Librarianship and Katherine Sharp* (New York: Scarecrow Press, Inc., 1966), pp. 54; 59–61; 78–86.

26. Mary Wright Plummer, "Brooklyn Library Training Class," *Library Journal* 16 (December 1891): 87.

27. Williamson, p. 30.

28. American Library Association, Committee on Library Training, "Report on Standards of Library Training," *Library Journal* 30 (September 1905): pp. 121–23.

29.   American Library Association, Committee on Library Training, "Report of Committee on Library Training," *Library Journal* 31 (August 1906): 177.

30.   Donald Gordon Davis, Jr., *The Association of American Library Schools, 1915-1968: An Analytic History* (Metuchen, N.J.: Scarecrow Press, Inc., 1974), pp. 24-25, 27; American Library Association, Board of Education for Librarianship, "First Annual Report of the Board of Education for Librarianship," *ALA Bulletin* 19 (July 1925): 235-48; White, pp. 218-19.

31.   William Isaac Fletcher, *Public Libraries in America*, Columbia Knowledge Series, no. 2 (Boston: Robert Brothers, 1894), p. 83; Marion Gilroy and Samuel Rothstein, *As We Remember It: Interviews with Pioneering Librarians of British Columbia* (Vancouver, B.C.: University of British Columbia School of Librarianship With the Co-operation and Assistance of the Library Development Commission of British Columbia, 1970), pp. 17-18; Herbert Putnam, "Education for Library Work," *Independent* 52 (November 22, 1900): 2773-776.

32.   American Library Association, Committee on Methods of Publicity for Library Schools, "Report," *Papers and Proceedings of the Thirty-Fifth Annual Meeting of the American Library Association* (Chicago: American Library Association, 1913), p. 350.

33.   Perry to Winsor, American Association of Library Schools Affiliated and Associated Organizations Subject File, 1913-1972, 85/2/6/ box 1, University of Illinois Archives; Roscoe Rouse, Jr., *A History of the Baylor University Library, 1845-1919*, unpublished doctoral dissertation, University of Michigan, 1962), p. 263; Melvil Dewey, *Librarianship as a Profession for College-Bred Women* (Boston: Library Bureau, 1886).

34.   Officer to Sharp, May 31, 1895, June 29, 1895, Sharp Papers, 18/1/20, box 1, University of Illinois Archives; Harkness to Sharp, January 22, 1895, *ibid.*

35.   Grotzinger, pp. 213-14; McKendree Hypes Chamberlin to Sharp, March 2, 1896, Sharp Papers, 18/1/20, box 1, University of Illinois Archives.

36.   "Columbia College School of Library Economy, Application for Admission," in Columbia University, School of Library Service, *School of Library Economy of Columbia College 1887-1889: Documents for a History* (Columbia University, School of Library Service, 1937), pp. 247-54.

37.   Moloney to Sharp, November 2, 1895, Sharp Papers, 18/1/20, box 1, University of Illinois Archives.

38.   Joseph Alfred Borome, *The Life and Letters of Justin Winsor*, unpublished doctoral dissertation, Columbia University, 1950, p. 45; Melvil Dewey, "Apprenticeship of Librarians," *Library Journal* 4 (May 1879): 147; Anna Salinas, "John Edward Goodwin: University Librarian," Master's thesis, University of Texas, 1966, p. 34.

39.   Library Workers Association, "Constitution of the Library Workers Association," *Library Journal* 45 (October 15, 1920): 839; Marian

Catherine Manley, "Aims of the L.W.A." *Library Journal* 46 (November 15, 1921): 943.

40 John Foster Carr, "A Greater American Library Association," *Library Journal* 45 (Oct. 1, 1920): 777.

41. Columbia College, Library, School of Library Economy, "Circular of Information, 1886-7," Columbia University, School of Library Service, *School of Library Economy of Columbia College 1887-1889: Documents for a History* (Columbia University, School of Library Service, 1937), p. 99.

42. Williamson, p. 92.

43. Paul Morris Parham, *Malcolm Glenn Wyer, Western Librarian: a Study in Leadership and Innovation*, unpublished doctoral dissertation, University of Denver, 1964, p. 56.

44. Melvil Dewey, "Library Instruction: Summary of Plans Proposed to Aid in Educating Librarians," *Library Notes* 2 (March 1888): 294.

45. Dewey, "Library Employment vs. the Library Profession," *Library Notes* 1 (June 1886): 50-51.

46. Dewey, "To Applicants for Admission," Columbia University, School of Library Science, *School of Library Economy of Columbia College, 1887-1889: Documents for a History* (Columbia University, School of Library Service, 1937), p. 116; Linderman, p. 170.

47. James L. Whitney, "Selecting and Training Library Assistants," *Library Journal* 7 (June 1882): 137-38.

48. Mitchell, *Mitchell of California*, p. 139.

49. American Library Association, Committee on Library Training, "Report of the Committee on Library Training," *Library Journal* 28 (July 1903): 93.

50. American Library Association, Committee on the Library School, "Report," *Library Journal* 12 (September–October 1887): 427.

51. "American Library Examination—Papers Set at Library School, Albany, New York," *Library World* 13 (August 1910): 86-90; Williamson, p. 40.

52. Ernest Cushing Richardson, "The Library School as It Should Be," *Library Journal* 15 (December 1890): 94.

53. Dennis Thomison, *A History of the American Library Association, 1876-1972* (Chicago: American Library Association, 1978), pp. 50-51.

54. Adam J. Strohm, "Do We Need a Post-graduate Library School?" *Public Libraries* 15 (February 1910): 54; Williamson, pp. 11-12.

55. Mary Wright Plummer, "Columbia College School of Library Economy from a Student's Standpoint," *Library Journal* 12 (September–October 1887): 363.

56. Mitchell, *Mitchell of California*, p. 131.

57. Williamson, p. 66.

58. Plummer, "Columbia College," p. 362; Idem, "Pages from the Note Books of Mary Wright Plummer on the Lectures for March 1887," Columbia University, School of Library Service, *School of Library Economy of Columbia College, 1887-1889: Documents for a History*

(Columbia University, School of Library Service, 1937), pp. 136–59; May Seymour, "Papers from the Note Books of May Seymour on the Lectures for March 1887," *Ibid.*, pp. 160–83.

59. Williamson, p. 149; Ella W. Clark to Sharp, August 18, 1896, Sharp Papers, 18/1/20, box 1, University of Illinois Archives.

60. Mabel Collins to Sharp, December 1, 1896, Sharp Papers, 18/1/20, box 1, University of Illinois Archives.

61. Vann, "Introduction," p. 32; White, *Historical Introduction*, p. 68.

62. U.S. Congress, Joint Committee on the Library of Congress, "Report under SCR 26, Relative to the Condition, Organization and Management of the Library of Congress, With Hearings: March 3, 1897," Senate Report 1573, 54th Cong., 2nd sess., 1897, p. 140.

63. Grotzinger, pp. 132–38.

64. Mary Wright Plummer, "Pros and Cons of Training for Librarianship," *Public Libraries* 8 (May 1903): 217.

65. American Library Association, Temporary Library Training Board, "Report of the Temporary Library Training Board," *ALA Bulletin* 18 (August 1924): 277–88.

66. Williamson, pp. 44, 46, 96.

67. ALA, Temporary Library Training Board, "Report," p. 276.

68. Williamson, p. 54, 99.

69. Eugene Russell Hanson, *Cataloging and the American Library Association, 1876–1956*, unpublished doctoral dissertation, University of Pittsburgh, 1974, p. 71.

70. Melvil Dewey, "Library Handwriting," *Library Notes* 1 (March 1887): 273.

71. Columbia College, Library, School of Library Economy, "Circular of Information 1884," Columbia University, School of Library Service, *School of Library Economy of Columbia College, 1887–1889: Documents for a History* (Columbia University, School of Library Service, 1937), p. 42; Carolyn Maria Hewins, "Report on the Library School As It Is," *Library Journal* 15 (December 1890): 91.

72. Charles H. Compton, *Memories of a Librarian* (St. Louis Public Library, 1954), p. 28.

73. Azariah Smith Root, "The Library School of the Future," *ALA Bulletin* 11 (March 1917): 158–59.

74. Aksel G. S. Josephson, "Preparation for Librarianship," *Library Journal* 25 (May 1900): 226; "The Williamson Report II: Comments from Librarians," *Library Journal* 48 (December 1923): 1005.

75. Quoted in Claud Glenn Sparks, *William Warner Bishop, a Biography*, unpublished doctoral dissertation, University of Michigan, 1967, p. 192.

76. "The Williamson Report: Comments from the Library Schools," *Library Journal* 48 (Jan. 1, 1923): 910.

77. Williamson, p. 54; Vann, p. 77.

78. Mary Beth Fleischer, "Credentials Awarded Through August, 1961, By Agencies Presently or Formerly Approved or Accredited By the

American Library Association," Master's thesis, University of Texas-Austin, 1963, pp. 20–21; Harriet E. Howe, "Two Decades in Education for Librarianship," *Library Quarterly* 12 (July 1942): 568.

79. American Library Association, College and Reference Section, "College and Reference Section," *ALA Bulletin* 17 (July 1923): 228; Charles E. Hale, *The Origins and Development of the Association of College and Research Libraries, 1899–1960,* unpublished doctoral dissertation, Indiana University, 1976, p. 52.

80. Vann, *Training for Librarianship,* p. 35.

81. Frederick C. Hicks, "Where Shall University College and Reference Library Assistants be Educated," *American Library Institute, Papers and Proceedings, 1918* (Chicago: American Library Association, 1918), p. 25.

82. American Library Association, Committee on the Proposed School of Library Economy, "Report," *Library Journal* 10 (September 1885): 292.

83. Charles Harvey Brown, "The Library," in Arthur J. Klein, *Survey of Land-Grant Colleges and Universities,* vol. 1, United States Office of Education, Bulletin 1930, no. 9 (Washington, D.C.: United States Government Printing Office, 1930), p. 692.

84. Josephson, "Preparation for Librarianship," pp. 226–27.

85. Josephson, "A Postgraduate School of Bibliography," *Library Journal* 26 (August 1901): 198–99.

86. Amy L. Reed, "A Graduate School of Librarianship," *American Library Institute, Papers and Proceedings, 1918* (Chicago: American Library Association, 1919), pp. 9–10.

87. Edith M. Coulter, "The University Librarian: His Preparation, Position and Relation to the Academic Department of the University," *ALA Bulletin* 16 (July 1972): 273.

88. Hicks, p. 15.

89. ALA, Temporary Library Training Board, "Report," p. 263.

90. Association of American Universities, "Report of the Committee on Academic and Professional Higher Degrees," *Journal of the Proceedings and Addresses of the Association of American Universities* 26 (October 31–November 1, 1924): 25–26.

91. American Library Institute, Committee on the Higher Education of Librarians, "Report," *American Library Institute Papers and Proceedings, 1919* (Chicago: American Library Association, 1920), p. 238.

92. ALA, Board of Education for Librarianship, pp. 244–45.

93. Ernest Cushing Richardson, "The Field of Library Science," *Public Libraries* 21 (May 1916): 210.

94. William Warner Bishop, "The Theory of Reference Work," *ALA Bulletin* 9 (July 1915): 134.

95. W. Dawson Johnston, "The Library as a University Factor," Association of American Universities, *Journal of Proceedings and Addresses of the Fifteenth Annual Conference* (Published by the Association, [1913]), p. 36.

96. Coulter, pp. 272–73.

97. Andrew Keogh, "Advanced Library Training for Research Workers,"
     *Papers and Proceedings of the Forty-first Annual Conference of the
     American Library Association* (Chicago: American Library Associa-
     tion, 1919), p. 166.

98. Granville Stanley Hall, "What Is Research in a University Sense, and
     How May It Best Be Promoted," Association of American Univer-
     sities, *Journal of Proceedings and Addresses of the Third Annual Con-
     ference February 25-27, 1902* ([Chicago]: Published by the Association,
     1901), p. 51.

99. Hicks, p. 23.

100. Edward G. Holley, *Charles Evans: American Bibliographer* (Urbana:
     University of Illinois Press, 1963), pp. 298-99.

101. Quoted in Roland H. Bainton, *George Lincoln Burr, His Life: Selec-
     tions from His Writings*, ed. Lois O. Gibbons (Ithaca, N.Y.: Cornell
     University Press, 1952), pp. 40-41.

102. American Library Association, *A Survey of Libraries in the United
     States*, 4 vols. (Chicago: American Library Association, 1926),
     1:260-64.

103. Azariah Smith Root, "College and University Library Salaries," *ALA
     Bulletin* 13 (May 1919): 79.

104. American Library Association, Committee on Salaries, Insurance, and
     Annuities, "ALA Research or Statistical Department," *ALA Bulletin*
     23 (August 1929): 271.

105. Earl James McGrath, *The Evolution of Administrative Offices in In-
     stitutions of Higher Education in the United States from 1860 to 1933*,
     unpublished doctoral dissertation, University of Chicago, 1938, p. 162.

106. William Madison Randall, *The College Library: A Descriptive Study
     of the Libraries in Four-Year Liberal Arts Colleges in the United
     States* (Chicago: American Library Association and the University of
     Chicago Press, 1932), pp. 56-58.

107. George Alan Works, *College and University Library Problems, A
     Study of Selected Group of Institutions Prepared for the Association
     of American Universities* (Chicago: American Library Association,
     1927), p. 90.

108. Brown, pp. 602-683.

109. Corrine Bacon, "Relation of the Library School to the School and Col-
     lege Library," *Public Libraries* 19 (November 1914): 396.

110. Davis to Windsor, December 2, 1910, Illinois, University, Graduate
     School of Library Science, Director's Office, Personnel Cor-
     respondence, 18/1/5, box 1, University of Illinois Archives.

111. *Who's Who in Library Service*, ed. C. C. Williamson and A. L. Jewett,
     2d ed. (New York: Wilson, 1943), p. 129; Arthur J. Klein, "Preface" in
     Arthur J. Klein, *Survey of Land-Grant Colleges and Universities*, vol.
     1, United States Office of Education Bulletin 1930, no. 9 (Washington,
     D.C.: U.S. Government Printing Office), p. xv; Brown, p. 682.

112. Quoted in Paul Albert Winckler, *Charles Clarence Williamson (1877-
     1965): His Professional Life and Work in Librarianship and Library
     Education in the United States*, unpublished doctoral dissertation,
     New York University, 1968), p. 172.

Neither Power Nor Dignity*

The status of librarians in the academic community is a complex phenomenon. The equality of librarians depended upon more than equivalent titles, though most librarians would seem to have been content with that. Working conditions, salaries, and social recognition were crucial considerations as well. But, perhaps the central issue was autonomy. For librarians to realize what they had come to view as their professional function, they needed control of their institutional activities. This, they failed to achieve. Although most academic librarians felt they deserved membership in the faculty by virtue of the functions they performed in America's colleges and universities, the level of training they brought to their jobs was insufficient to gain such recognition and their functions, as librarians came to define them, were not widely applauded by the academic community.

By the 1920s, it was obvious to librarians that their place in the academic endeavor was in no way comparable to that of the faculty. The reasons for this were complex, but one modern interpretation addresses itself to the problem of women working in a masculine society. Dee Garrison's recently published study of the feminization of American public librarianship emphasizes that much of the professional standing of librarians derived

*With apologies to Laurel Grotzinger

221

directly from the status of women in American society.[1] Since the last quarter of the nineteenth century, librarianship has been an occupation dominated—at least in numbers—by women. It has been, as have other jobs like social work and nursing, circumscribed in its autonomy and limited in potential rewards for the individual practitioner. It has been long recognized[2] that women in academic librarianship have suffered from the general effects of a male-dominated society as much as their sisters in the public library movement. Women in higher education and women academic librarians shared in the status of women in American society. The early enthusiasm with which male leaders of the emerging profession encouraged women entering into the work changed at least one major characteristic of America's librarians—sex.

American librarianship needed an enlarged, relatively well-educated, and cheap source of labor. Whatever else Dewey may have had in mind when he recruited women into the profession, that a competent woman cost less than a comparably qualified man was a major factor. Dewey was energetic in his efforts toward a strong beginning for his new school at Columbia. His address in 1886 before The Association of Collegiate Alumnae was an attempt to interest its members in the work and encourage them to attend his new school. Though he described the potential careers in librarianship in glowing terms, he warned his audience that because men could do more than women, as in the case of an emergency or tasks calling for heavy physical work, they would always command higher pay than women. In one of the most outrageous—or at least unfortunate—similes of Dewey's writings, he stated his case: The male librarian "adds something to his direct value just as a saddlehorse that is safe in harness and not afraid of the cars will bring more in nine markets out of ten than the equally good horse that can only be used in the saddle."[3]

Though the rhetoric is arresting, this was not a new sentiment in the academic library world. Fifteen years earlier, Andrew Ten Brook had successfully employed women at the University of Michigan as catalogers. He observed in his 1870-71 annual report that there were some tasks for which they were physically unsuited, but "in industry, and fidelity, and in quickness and accuracy of perception and execution," they were better than any man who would take the job. And, as an added positive factor, "they are ready to do faithful service at a much lower rate."[4]

The place of women in the American work force has traditionally been a difficult one, and the place of women in American higher education has been no exception. Large numbers of women have been employed in American colleges and universities in proportions greater than would be expected through the period under examination. From the 1870s through the 1920s, between 20 percent and 30 percent of the faculty members were women—but most of these were employed in the developing women's colleges.[5] These relative numbers, however, do not reflect the realities of the situation of academic women. The motivation of women to become faculty members of America's colleges and universities and their acceptance in the culture of American higher education are complex phenomena beyond the scope of this book. Discrimination in the academic world is a historical and, in light of recent research and reports, a persistent and pressing problem. The entry of large numbers of women into librarianship and the perception of library work as a proper occupation for women undoubtedly had an effect on the relation that developed between librarians and faculty members.

The place of the academic librarian in American higher education can not be attributed solely to the position of women in American society. Discrimination and a society founded on the assumed role of both sexes in continuing the world's work undoubtedly contributed to the place of a feminized occupation in an order dominated by men. But this cannot totally account for the subordinate position of librarians in the academic hierarchy. Librarianship in the classical college was a totally male occupation, but still was not highly respected. In the antebellum colleges, no particular status accrued to the librarian simply because he was the librarian. The status of the librarian derived from his other functions in the college. If he was a professor, or the president, his status was relatively high. If he was the janitor, or a student, his status was correspondingly low. As academic librarianship became a full-time occupation, the status of the librarian was defined by the academic community—both faculty members and administrators—as different from, and lower than, that of members of the faculty.

Even champions of women in the new profession like Justin Winsor contributed significantly to the problem of the librarian's image that has so frequently been recognized. Winsor strongly felt that women were indeed competent to withstand the strains and demands of the occupation, but he insisted on close supervision if they worked for him at Harvard. When Eliot assumed the presidency of Harvard, he abolished the elaborate code of regulations that governed students. Winsor reintroduced such a code for his staff. When he arrived at Harvard, he established written rules that, among other prohibitions and restrictions, forbade the women of the catalog department from going into parts of the library where someone might speak to them. These rules demanded strict adherence to work schedules and Winsor refused to allow visitors to call on staff members during working hours. To his credit, though, Winsor applied the same regulations to the men on the staff. He had inherited John Fiske who had failed to gain a permanent place on the faculty because of his radical views. Fiske's irregular habits did not please the new director. He would sometimes come in on Sundays to clear his desk of library matters so that he could devote the rest of the week to his studies. Winsor kept up a steady pressure and finally forced Fiske's resignation in December, 1878.[6]

The rules for staff conduct implemented at Harvard impressed many librarians. In 1902, William H. Tillinghast, assistant librarian at Harvard, published them in an abridged version in the *Library Journal*. After deleting those that would be applicable only to the Harvard staff, fifty-two separate items appeared. These ranged from an admonition to "take pains to push in catalog trays after using" to an assertion that definite rules were needed and must be enforced regarding "the length of time a book must be in circulation before it may be taken out by a member of the staff." They included rules for the use of reference books, rules governing lunch periods, and a hint that when it was absolutely necessary to speak to another worker in the library, whispering was much more distracting than conversing in "low but natural tones." Tillinghast emphasized that these rules were necessary in the proper function of the library and that a "full day's work is expected of everyone," so promptness and efficiency were of vital importance. His first general rule perhaps states his concern best:

> Begin work promptly, avoid interruption so far as possible, stop promptly at the closing hour. The entries on the time card are to be the times of actually beginning and quitting work, not the times of entering or leaving the building.

It is noteworthy that except for the heads of the order, shelf, catalog, and circulation departments, most of the assistants were on hourly wages.[7]

Winsor's attitude toward his subordinates was not unique. Ernest Cushing Richardson, librarian of Princeton, 1890–1925, felt that by securing competent people in supervisory capacities, he had discharged his obligation to the library and could fulfill his duty to the university by hiring the cheapest labor possible for the productive levels of librarianship. He is said to have prided himself on his plan to hire young women who, by living with their families, would content themselves with the lowest possible pay—some of them at only a few dollars a week. Because of this parsimony, Richardson rarely could attract trained librarians to Princeton. William Warner Bishop reported in 1946 that Richardson was amazed at the production of a Syracuse graduate who had somehow taken a job in the cataloging department. But Richardson was not impressed enough to offer a salary that would attract such a person in the future. As a direct consequence of Richardson's expressed attitude that "a good executive could take the place of brains in his subordinates" and the low salaries paid, Princeton had neither a strong nor a contented staff under his administration.

Perhaps none was as hard as Harold Lewis Leupp who became director of the library at the University of California in 1919. Leupp held strongly to the virtue of discipline and the morality of hard work and expected the same of his staff. He assumed that members of the staff would be at their desks punctually and forbade them to engage in conversation that was not directly related to their work. Leupp even prescribed a dress code that had the men in their coats at all times during working hours and required women to avoid bright colors and strong perfumes. He frequently indulged in temper outbursts when he found what he thought was inefficiency among his staff. Leupp kept a close watch over his workers and they were very aware of it.[8]

Academic librarians not at the higher administrative levels came to be viewed as workers by library directors, who saw their own role of administration as keeping the employees to the tasks at hand. Administrators allowed little or no discretion to the individual librarian who performed the daily duties that kept the library functioning. Instead, management imposed a rigid work environment that allowed no freedom for the staff to engage in activities not directed to the tasks assigned to them. The profession developed a distinct separation between the "rank and file" and the higher administrative personnel who assumed the leadership of the profession. The formation of the American Library Institute (ALI) in 1905 was the most obvious manifestation of this phenomenon. It was begun to promote the interests of learning and scholarship in the field of librarianship. Ernest Cushing Richardson observed on its founding that the purpose of the institute lay in encouraging "research, book publication and higher education in the field of library science and the promotion of libraries which aid research—the field, in short, of learned libraries and learning in library matters."

The ALI was proposed by Melvil Dewey and was to be limited in membership to ex-presidents of the ALA and a few leading librarians who were to be elected to the honor. Dewey found that the annual conferences had become so large (359 attended in 1905) that the true leaders of the profession could not make themselves heard over the babble. There was a pressing need for a forum of the elect to contemplate the scholarly side of library work away from the "large number of enthusiastic but inexperienced workers, who occasionally give a feeling of rapid decision and 'quick service' atmosphere to the meetings."

The ALI reflected a marked division among librarians and the recognition that an elite based on experience and position existed. This elite however, consisted mostly of Dewey's followers, not of an intellectual aristocracy of the profession. Indeed, higher administrators of academic libraries could not find the kind of professional environment for themselves that allowed them the freedom to pursue such dreams and were only sparsely represented in the membership of the ALI. In 1915, only eight of the forty-six members were academic librarians.[9] Even though academic librarians in the larger institutions had evolved an administrative function that placed them in positions of strong superiority over their workers, it was not recognized by the administrators and faculty members who sought their services. A distinction of sorts had emerged in the profession between library workers and library administrators, but the enhanced position of the higher levels was not recognized by the academic community that perceived library administration not as a scholarly activity but as one of the mundane activities necessary in higher education.

Academic librarians of all levels were not hired for their intellectual capacities, but for their technical expertise. The carefully constructed edifice erected by librarians to represent their academic respectability was simply ignored by the emerging academic profession. Statistical analysis is needed to document the nature of early academic librarianship, but even a cursory glance at the biographical directory of Albany's students from 1887 to 1926 reveals that the preponderance of graduates who could be considered academic librarians because of the libraries in which they spent major portions of their careers were catalogers. Three hundred thirty-one of a total of 1079 librarians listed as having attended the Albany school would probably be considered academic librarians under the loose definition that they spent a significant portion of their careers employed in academic libraries. Of this third of the Albany school's production of librarians, only sixty-three (19 percent) were reference librarians. Nine order librarians and 150 catalogers (48 percent) comprised the largest group of professionals. It is impossible to guess from the brief descriptions given what the nature of employment of thirty-five Albany students was, but seventy-five (22 percent) were simply described as *librarian*. In all probability, they were the only professionals on the staff, and cataloging the collection was a major part of their duties.[10]

Cataloging became the major professional activity of the new academic librarians. But cataloging—the ordering of chaos—was not an activity that commanded respect from the leaders of the new higher education. The decisions of cataloging, of course, allow a wide variety of interpretation and it would be difficult to conceive a schedule of classification that would please an entire faculty. Guy Stanton Ford, President of the University of Minnesota, touched on a concern central to the thinking of faculty members when he addressed the problem of library classification in 1913:

> A system of cataloguing that separates, on some antiquated classification, literature that should be massed together, sets of a single purpose, and material of the same character, is more than an annoyance—it is an actual hinderance. To find Domesday Book next to the reports of the city comptroller of New York; works on institutional and constitutional history separated by two stories from the national history to which they belong; Bismark's works next to John Adams because both are "works of statesmen"; animal psychology next to the herd books of the Animal Husbandry Department—such blunders do more than disturb academic peace of mind.[11]

Aside from most academic librarians lacking the background necessary to avoid some "blunders" that would be obvious to specialists in the various subjects, there would probably be little consensus among the faculty on the perfect system of classification. But classification of the books and periodicals in the library is one of the most visible aspects of the library's effectiveness and emerged as a permanent source of contention between faculty members and librarians.

Louis N. Wilson naively asserted in 1907 that he had found the perfect solution to this problem at Clark University where he was director of the library. Wilson had the heads of the departments of the university devise their own classifications for their subjects and, when new books came into the library, the department heads came to the library and classified them. Of course, Wilson did not demand any uniformity in the variety of schemes that were used. He felt, rather, that the advantages in having the faculty involved in the work of the library far outweighed any problems in consistency. In Wilson's view, "the librarian sees more of his colleagues than is usually the case, and friction between the library and any of the members of the faculty is unknown."[12]

But it was not only in the workings of the classification scheme itself that faculty members found a source of dissatisfaction. Cataloging has always been an expensive practice and many agreed with a member of a library committee who wrote to Hamilton Fish, a Columbia trustee on November 17, 1885, complaining of the problem:

> These specialists and cataloguers are like those Devil-Fish with long tentacles—once encircled in their arms, you are gone. The committee, of which I am a member, have been hard at work sounding bottom, with indifferent success. Professor Drisler tells me Columbia is in the same predicament, with 15 Assistant Cataloguers devouring your Library Fund in making a list of what you have! To the unregenerate mind there seems much foolishness in all this dilettantism.[13]

Cataloging and organizing, in the minds of many faculty members, were activities that were at best a poor substitute for the real purposes of the library—acquisition of materials. To many, anything that detracted from the library's ability to supply materials was detrimental to the essential function of the library, and salaries for catalogers and other librarians diverted money from the essential to the peripheral. The ratio of money spent for books and for personnel was a real concern of faculty members when they looked at the libraries of their institutions. When George Works considered the problems of university libraries in 1925, he found the relationship of financing for materials and for salaries had remained fairly constant from 1900 to 1925. But he also found that some faculty members firmly believed that expenditure for personnel was definitely increasing at the expense of the library's capacity to acquire books.[14]

This situation was responsible for the substitution of personality for intellect by librarians when they considered their functions in higher education. Professional demands for service to their educational clientele mandated that librarians frequently stoop to subterfuge in order to fulfill their professional functions and assume their place in the academic community. Justin Winsor observed in 1880 that the faculty members of the colleges were composed of a variety of different types of personalities. Some were "responsive and sympathetic"; others "repel and are self-contained." The librarian's central task was to adapt to each type of faculty member: "he fosters their taste; encourages their predilections; offers help directly where it is safe, accomplishes it by flank movements when necessary; does a thousand little kindnesses in notifying the professors of books arrived and treasures unearthed." But Winsor's concern was not so much in serving the faculty as enhancing the position of the librarian: "In this way suavity and sacrifice will compel the condition of brotherhood which is necessary and is worth the effort."[15]

But tact alone was not enough to compensate for the differences that both faculty members and administrators saw between themselves and librarians. The library was a major facility in the new learning and the scholars on the faculty had a major concern in how it was managed. Though some professionally trained librarians did acquire the authority to rule their domains, most performed their labors under the guidance of a faculty library committee that retained a great amount of control over the daily functions of the library. Phineas L. Windsor was one of the exceptions. When he became director of the library at the University of Illinois in 1909 after Katharine Lucinda Sharp, he found what he considered a totally inadequate book budget of $25,000. At Illinois it was customary for anyone involved in a research project to apply to the Library Committee of the Faculty Senate for funds for materials. As Windsor's competence came to be recognized on the campus, the committee increasingly turned to him for his judgment, and individual faculty members did also. When the dean of the graduate school, David Kinley, was appointed president in 1920, Windsor's continued autonomy was assured. Over the years, he had cultivated a strong working relationship with the new president in building one of the strongest research collections in the country.[16]

But most academic librarians found it impossible to develop a rapport that allowed this degree of autonomy. The survey conducted by the ALA in 1926 found that more than 80 percent of the reporting libraries were to some extent controlled by faculty members. In most cases, this control was exercised by a committee composed of faculty members, but in some it was a standing committee of the governing board. Interestingly, there was found a marked tendency to have no library committee in institutions holding fewer than 20,000 volumes. Seventy-five small institutions holding fewer than 20,000 volumes had library committees; twenty-one had none. This may have been because the library was still under the direct control of a faculty member—but it may indicate also that the library of under 20,000 volumes was not important enough for any real faculty interest.

In many academic libraries, the committee wielded real power in the areas of budgeting and allocation of the book funds. These functions, of course, represented the major source of power in the library from the faculty's perspective. The faculty library committee essentially represented the continuation of faculty control that earlier was embodied in the professor-librarian of the classical college. The library of Wake Forest presents a relatively typical case of the transfer of power. Though a full-time person took charge of the library in 1909, the professor who had been in charge remained in control with the title, "Curator of the Library." This post was abolished in 1919 and the professor was made chairman of the faculty library committee. This made little difference in the functions or the degree to which the library could act autonomously The committee still retained control of both the general budget and the expenditures of the library.[17]

Book selection and collection development were functions almost universally assumed by members of the faculty. Indeed, there was intense opposition at most institutions to interference by librarians in what was considered a faculty prerogative. At some—like the University of Delaware until 1938 when the activities of the library committee were limited to advisory functions—the faculty library committee controlled almost all operations of the library. Here, a seven-member committee composed of faculty representatives appointed by the president approved the budget, set hours of opening, and hired staff members in addition to approving subscriptions and purchases. The librarian had control only over the physical plant and responsibility for the direct supervision of the staff.[18] Even in places where the library staff had some role in the realm of selection, exercise of this authority was frequently impossible.

At Berkeley, only Joseph Cummings Rowell was allowed to select materials. He had at his disposal a sum of approximately 2 percent to 5 percent of the annual book budget to fill in sets and purchase reference materials. Until 1912, the staff members of the university library had no authority to initiate purchases. In 1912, the Library Staff Council appointed five staff members to read reviews in specified journals and recommend purchases. In 1913, the council decided that the members of the reference staff should go through antiquarian catalogs to recommend purchases. Lack of adequate staff time forced the eventual abandonment of these practices.

The extent of control exercised by library committees galled the professional sensibilities of many librarians. James Hulme Canfield, librarian of Columbia, 1899–1909, addressed the concerns of academic librarians in 1906. He saw that the large amounts of money expended for libraries would make a committee of trustees desirable, but questioned strongly the necessity for a faculty committee: "why a faculty committee, with its duties and powers as to library administration, any more than such a committee for the department of Latin or Biology?" The persistence of faculty library committees, Canfield felt, was due to the practice when "some dear old lady" was appointed librarian. The librarians of today, "experienced, well-trained, and worthy" as they were, needed no such overseer, and no librarian "could possibly regard such a committee as other than a large interrogation point against his or her competency."[19]

Most academic librarians failed to raise the same question as Canfield, realizing that the realities of academic life were such that the faculty considered responsibility for materials selection to be in its own domain as almost a sacred trust. Theodore Wesley Koch, librarian of the University of Michigan from 1905 to 1915 read a paper before the ALA Lake Minnetonka Conference in June, 1908, in which he questioned the practice of allowing the faculty much power in the disbursement of the budget. In the discussion that followed, Francis Drury of the University of Illinois reported that he had approached the "authorities" at Illinois about revising the process of book selection and

met with such intense opposition that I am sure it will not be utilized at the University of Illinois for several years. They said that they would never leave such discretionary powers to the librarian because it was an educational matter, that the whole educational policy of the university was based on the purchase of books and that it should be left in the hands of those who were shaping the policies.

Indeed, Illinois was probably much better off than most of the other land grant institutions. At least the librarian there had some idea of what was being acquired by the library.

Charles Harvey Brown's 1930 survey of the libraries of America's land grant colleges found that in twenty-two of the reporting institutions, faculty members and departments generally had the authority to purchase library materials independently of the library—in most cases, this authority was exercised without notifying the librarian. Only sixteen of the forty-eight institutions reported that the librarian had any authority in book selection.[20] The constraints upon the professional staffs of libraries to prevent them from performing what they had come to consider one of the primary professional functions of librarianship led many to adopt a form of service that echoed Winsor's earlier plea for tact. James Ingersoll Wyer repeated the earlier assertion that the role of the academic librarian was to serve the needs of the faculty and students even if these needs were not readily acknowledged by either professors or students. He, like Winsor, cautioned that subterfuge in such matters was by far the best policy:

> Just how much part the librarian has in the book selection is naturally not a subject that he will discuss with his professors. He will, however, if he is a good librarian, have a great deal to say, though just what he says or how and when he says it cannot be matters of exact statement. It must be done in a hundred different ways, tactfully, sometimes firmly, and even with occasional lapses from his best judgement. . . . Legitimate needs will grow out of student use of the library, needs unknown to any professor, unrelated to any course of study. These the librarian must supply.

Assertion of a right to control selection of materials for the library on the part of librarians was avoided by many librarians because of the intense belief—at least as perceived by librarians—that it would cause great difficulty from the faculty. Brown's survey found that some librarians felt any attempt by the librarian to supervise collection development would be "dangerous" to them, "a practice which would cause a vacancy in the position of librarian."[21]

Academic librarians believed that it was necessary to assume the control of selection. They had identified one of their principal functions as the general education of undergraduates, and the only resource they had to fulfill that function was through the collection. The faculty, in its affirmation of the necessity for specialization and publication, had abandoned the undergraduate student and, by insisting on control of the book budget, had effectively blocked librarians from their involvement in undergraduate reading. Allowing faculty members full control over areas of the book budget created great strains on the professional relationship between librarians and faculty members. Through the first fifty years of library development since the founding of the ALA, the public library movement had firmly established book selection as a primary concern of the new profession. Academic librarians who watched as the budget melted away each year due to the intense but undirected heat of the research efforts of individual faculty members while undergraduate students could find nothing suitable for their own needs in the library felt strongly that their professional obligations were being compromised by an authority that should have no privilege in the area. Alfred Clanghorn Potter, order assistant at Harvard, addressed the ALA in 1897. He complimented such men as Francis James Child for their selfless labor at building up the research facilities at Harvard. He noted that the librarian's duty in selection was twofold: to keep professors from spending the money "unwisely" and to bring to the individual faculty member's attention those titles that may not have crossed his path. But he cautioned strongly against "the hobby-horsical professor" who can do "as much injury to the library . . . as the negligent one, or the one who orders by fits and starts." Potter went on to embellish his theme. The subject specialist was suspect precisely because of his intense interest in his chosen area. Because of his preoccupation and his power in the area of selection, the library would invariably suffer because the professor

> will almost invariably develop its resources on this specialty at the expense of other sides of his subject. Perhaps the French professor

is an enthusiastic Molièreist, and has gathered many editions of Molière supplemented by a great mass of biographical and critical material. This collection is of undoubted value, and contains everything needed for a most profound study of the master of French comedy; but the student of modern French literature and criticism will find that his wants have been scantily provided for.

Potter ultimately sided with those who would make the process of ordering books as easy for the individual professor as possible. He urged academic librarians to "encourage the professors to order by using as little red-tape as possible" or to "at least keep it out of their sight." If a member of the faculty wanted the library to acquire a book, the librarian should not require a completed order card or a special form but should "take the orders gratefully in whatever way they prefer to give them—checked in a publisher's or bookseller's catalog, written in a letter or scrawled on a page torn from a pocket diary, or delivered by word of mouth." The librarian or the assistants can put them into a form usable by the library.[22]

Even though the need for this kind of service was generally recognized, librarians had little sympathy for the professor who retained full control over the budget and did not feel an obligation to develop a collection in the same way as a librarian would. James Hulme Canfield offered librarians the advice that they should gratefully honor the requests of professors who used the books that they ordered, selected them with some intelligence. and were diligent in getting their orders to the library on time. But he warned the librarian to "beware of the professor who orders little or nothing till toward the close of the fiscal year, and then comes in hastily with a long list to be ordered 'at once'—the list smelling suspiciously of recent publisher's catalogues, and on inspection found to be at least half duplicates of titles already on the shelves."[23]

Control over the collections they administered was another area that led to pronounced unease between faculty and librarians. One point of contention was the loan periods extended to the faculty. About half of the academic librarians contacted by the 1926 survey allowed professional staff members of the library the same borrowing privileges as they did to members of the faculty. But it is obvious that the librarians did not abuse the honor to the extent that they felt faculty members did. Brown's survey of land grant institutions cited complaints that books were unavailable for months and even years to students and junior faculty members because they were charged out to professors. Twelve of these schools had collections of materials out for over one year and some for as long as eight years. Most of the libraries recalled the books at the end of the year, but the practice was inconsistently applied and was a major source of friction between librarians and members of the faculty. The librarians were dissatisfied with the mechanisms at their disposal for repossessing their books or bringing to task faculty members who may have lost them. Of the forty-eight institutions reporting, only thirty-three did charge faculty members for lost books—but virtually none had any way of collecting.

Authority to purchase books was not the only conflict between librarians and faculty members. In some cases, the librarians felt that important decisions affecting their domain were made without proper consultation. Brown reported that one of the institutions he studied had come to the decision to offer graduate work in English—with no advice from any member of the library staff. The librarians found out about the decision—or that it was even being considered—only after it had been made, and the collection was, according to Brown's embittered reporter, totally inadequate for the task. He estimated that $50,000 would have been needed immediately to approach supporting such a program and this was not even considered in the planning.

Communications between faculty members and the library were never strong in the new universities. Brown also heard reports that instructors repeatedly failed to notify the libraries of assignments made so that the librarians could prepare for demands on the materials. He found that one librarian had gone so far as to approach the president of the college with statistics of the number of faculty members remiss in their duties in this area. The president took the faculty to task at the next faculty meeting and the problem was solved, for a time at least.[25] This may have been temporarily effective, but it would hardly endear the librarian to the faculty.

The required use of library materials by students demanded

by new methods of instruction was another source of concern. Charles Wesley Smith, associate librarian at the University of Washington, contended in 1924 that the destruction of the library's periodicals was attributable to increasing numbers of students assigned required readings by faculty members. Debate assignments, classroom discussions, and term papers had put the periodical runs into constant use. Because replacing missing, mutilated, or simply worn issues and articles was so difficult, he called for severe curtailment of their use.[26]

It was not only in the areas of acquisitions and preservation that the faculty placed unwanted obligations on the library and the librarian. Demands of other kinds were placed on the facility by those who had control that went far beyond what librarians had been prepared for by their profession. Alfred S. Cook, Chairman of the English Department at the University of California in 1884, convinced the regents that an exhibit of the book arts was an appropriate activity for the library. In accordance with this decision, the librarian, Joseph Cummings Rowell, was instructed to prepare the display. He sent out to local book collectors and called upon his correspondents in remote places for treasures. Rowell, however, was most anxious about the security for the event and felt himself compelled to sleep on the floor of the library for the eight days of the exhibit with a loaded pistol at hand. At the University of Chicago, both librarians and readers were put out by decisions not of their making in 1920 when they were perplexed by the lighting problems that developed when administrators solved their own problem of giving the university the proper patina of age and gravity. They had ordered that the stained glass windows in the reading room should never be washed in order to enhance the air of antiquity.[27]

The windows at Chicago and the decisions of faculties and administrators were not all that oppressed librarians. The desire for order and decorum that obsessed the keepers of public libraries also affected academic librarians. But frequenters of the chambers of the heart of the university were sometimes not all that the keepers of the library might wish. Even so great a library innovator as Katharine Lucinda Sharp had her prejudices. On October 28, 1905, she, as director of the University of

Illinois Library, answered a request from one of her assistants. Conduct or appearance that would distract or create a disturbance is, she wrote, sufficient cause to request anyone to leave the library. Miss Sharp confided that she felt the librarian was perfectly justified in protecting "the front steps and door" from any adverse effect on the high purposes of the library when she admitted, "I have asked smokers to leave these steps." She added that prompted by the complaint of her subordinate, she had written the editor of the campus newspaper requesting an editorial on the subject of decorum in the library feeling that "it would be more effective than a signed article from us."[28] The prospect of being evicted from the library steps while enjoying a cigar probably did not endear her to the faculty of Illinois. Katharine Sharp, like most academic librarians, was filled with a library spirit and sense of moral purpose that would not have allowed Canby's stein of beer or Kitteridge's cigar near the shrine of learning.

Academic librarians, in their desire to assume the mantle of gentility, also assumed one of the major functions of the professors of the classical college. Discipline and decorum had to be maintained among a clientele that would approach the shrine with impure hearts. Linda V. Duval, assistant librarian of Ohio Wesleyan University, made a plea in 1899 for a shortening of the rules of colleges' libraries that "were too lengthy for the perusal of a busy woman." She asserted that the proliferation of rules posted in the library were largely unnoticed because of the "habitual carelessness of the students." She wanted a few short regulations that would do their part in "enunciating the three general principles of order, honor, and punctuality, and the student who loves nothing better than something catchy, something mottolike, will remember and heed." Quiet and order in the library were the two qualities that the librarian must encourage in students and the growth of these sentiments was "the librarian's strongest aid in subduing the noisy and boisterous" student.

A more serious area of confrontation for librarians lay in the faculty's inability to understand or utilize "bibliographical science." Academic librarians had long claimed bibliography as their major province of research, and reacted strongly to what they perceived as incompetence in the area among their colleagues on the faculty. At the ALA Ashville Conference of 1907, Willard Austen, a reference librarian at Cornell, took the members of the faculty sternly to task. The average faculty member, he asserted, had no conception of the importance of *bibliographical knowledge*—by which he meant the ability to find a book in a library: "anyone whose experience is large knows how many teachers there are whose use of a library reveals how deficient they are in this subject, and how often their bibliographical attempts work great hardship to others using their work."[29]

William Warner Bishop elaborated on this theme at the Lake Minnetonka Conference in 1908. Bishop was one librarian who strongly felt that the proper professional function of the trade was in the exercise of his "bibliographical knowledge," but he felt that too often this particular expertise was presumed upon by faculty members. Some of the requests for help, Bishop observed, were part of the professional obligation of the librarian. The librarian "is likely to be able, by reason of his familiarity with all sorts of catalogs, to run down titles obscurely quoted, and to perform other feats of library legerdemain in a fashion that not infrequently astonishes even the trained investigator." This ability, however, was often abused when discovered by faculty members, and the librarian frequently found that it led "to demands on his time that are totally unreasonable in view of the other responsibilities he must bear." Bishop reported: "In conversations with reference librarians I have found that the tendency of certain professors to make private secretaries out of them was a very real difficulty in their work."[30]

Planning library buildings was probably the area in which academic authorities most dramatically demonstrated that the librarian's was not a vital position in the institutional endeavor. Unlike the facilities of the various departments of arts and sciences, construction of a building to house the library involved large amounts of money, an administrative commitment, and the possibility of new sources of revenue through the sale of a name. As such, the decision to construct a new building to house the facility was probably the major decision made in its effect on the library. Indeed, it was usually considered so important that the librarian or the staff was rarely consulted.

William Warner Bishop's arrival at the University of Michigan was an exception to this rule. When he came to Michigan in 1915, he was given the rank of professor and an active role in planning a new building for the library. His predecessor, Theodore Wesley Koch, however, had been summarily dismissed by the regents, and had not been asked about his ideas on the matter. Koch's dismissal derived from his inability, to the minds of some faculty members, to administer the needs of a research library. In 1914, William L. Clements, a member of the Board of Regents of the University, considered giving his valuable collection of Americana to the library. Clements hesitated because he did not trust Koch. Koch was a scholarly man, but Clements felt that he ran a slovenly library and the sensibilities of Koch and Clements were at odds. Clements was a collector of books who wanted a rare book room for Michigan. Koch was a bookman of considerable knowledge and skill who had been asked by the ALA to prepare the exhibit for the "German Library Association" at its 1914 meeting in Leipzig. Koch, however, felt that at Michigan, the dispersal of the available funds made it necessary to consider the entire needs of the university and not be committed to the growth of a rare book collection. He felt that research needs must be subordinate to the needs of the university as a whole. He knew that the demands of a student "for all the editions of a minor author who may be the subject of a doctorate dissertation" were real and valid obligations of the university library, and the library must encourage research through providing the facilities, but he also maintained that these materials "ought not to be asked for at the expense of the all-round efficiency of the library."

Clements looked only to what he considered to be the defects of Koch and the Regents' Library Committee followed Clement's advice in planning a rare book room for Michigan. The committee went so far as to avoid telling Koch whom they had in mind for the curator of the room and finally took advantage of Koch's absence in Germany on the business of the ALA to plan a new library building. When Koch returned, he acted out of ignorance in his attempt to support the project. He tried to help in procuring a legislative appropriation for the new building by publishing pictures of the university's library along with pictures of the library buildings of Ohio State University, the Wisconsin State Historical Society, and the University of Wisconsin. Koch thought he had helped the efforts of his superiors, but the legislators found much of the picturesque in the old Michigan building, and Koch aroused much opposition to the plan for a new building. Clements was so exasperated that he called upon William Warner Bishop at the Library of Congress in April, 1915, to take over the librarianship at the University of Michigan.[31]

A far more typical example of practice can be found at the University of Texas. Nathaniel Lewis Goodrich became the director of the library after Phineas Lawrence Windsor left to assume his new post at the University of Illinois in 1909. Goodrich's relationship with the faculty was not as cordial as Windsor's, and after a few years, he had even abandoned the pretense of attending faculty meetings. A few months after Goodrich assumed office, the governor of Texas released the money that would allow the university to construct a new library building and the regents appointed a committee of three of their members and the president to design the structure. The committee went to New York and settled on Cass Gilbert who had designed the St. Louis Public Library building and a number of other public buildings. Gilbert was a designer of monuments who felt that only the actual operation of the facility should be left to the occupant, and consequently, Goodrich was not consulted at any stage in the design. Indeed, Gilbert repeatedly refused to listen to Goodrich when he proposed that library practice and obligations should have some effect on the final form of the structure. When the building was ready for occupancy, the allocation was so overextended that nothing was left for furniture or bookstacks.

At Bryn Mawr, the strong personality and taste of President M. Carey Thomas determined the shape of the library. She had become so captivated by the charms of Oxford University that she determined to reproduce the cloisters in Pennsylvania. The new library building constructed in 1903 was designed and executed without the advice of the librarian and when Isadore Gilbert Mudge assumed her duties as librarian construction had been in progress for six weeks. The administrators of Buchtel College turned to the Department of Home Economics for a design when they determined that a new building was needed in 1915. No librarians were consulted, and the architect's idea of the capacity of the stack area for 40,000 volumes was badly underestimated. The building was crowded at 20,000 volumes. At Columbia in the 1880s, Stanford and Chicago at the turn of the century, and many others, similar incidents occurred.[32]

Even when the librarian did work closely with the designer in planning a new building, the architect usually retained full authority in the final form that the building would assume. Ernest Cushing Richardson remembered in 1936 his part in the construction of the Pyne Library at Princeton. Though he had consulted with the architect on the practical details of library management and how they would affect the shape of the structure, aesthetic considerations led to a change about which he was not notified. The desire to have all buildings on the campus in keeping with the natural harmony of the landscape forced the architect to lower the structure of the library "in such ways as to throw all floors but the top one—five floors in all—out of level and made the use of trucks impossible without artificial run ways." The planned underground passage between the elevators of the north and south stacks was abandoned also "to the dismay of the working librarians." They foresaw, even though the architect did not, the difficulties that occurred when the south stacks were finally occupied.

The problems of Richardson and others were not isolated instances of administrative incompetence in planning new facilities for their libraries. Rather, it was a realization of the commitment of the institutions to the value of the library—a value unconnected to librarianship. The College and Reference Section of the ALA conducted a survey in 1907 of eighty colleges and universities and found that fifty libraries were housed in their own buildings. Librarians were consulted in only twenty-three of these fifty construction projects, and in fourteen of those cases their advice was either given little weight or ignored completely. In six of the fifty projects no librarian was employed by the institution at the time of planning the new building.[33]

Planning library buildings was only the most dramatic

manifestation of the attitude of administrators and faculty members toward their librarians. Salaries and conditions of employment, particularly working hours, were areas where the librarian's lot differed greatly from that of members of the faculty. The amount paid by academic institutions for the services of librarians is an essential index of the value placed on librarianship in an academic enterprise. There was, as there is today, a great deal of dissatisfaction among librarians over the remuneration received for their contribution. In the schools surveyed by George Works, a pattern of increasing parity was found between faculty and library salaries between 1910 and 1925. Works compared the salaries of head librarians to those of full professors and found that in 1910, the average salary of the professor was $2762[34] while it was $2147 for the position of head librarian. By 1925, the full professor averaged $4631, the head librarian, $4580. During the same period, the average for an assistant professor went from $1740 to $2768, and the head of the library went from $1090 to $2269.[35] But the group of libraries surveyed by Works probably was atypical of American higher education. Charles Harvey Brown found in his survey of land grant institutions that the salaries paid head librarians were less than those found by Works. On the whole, head librarians in those institutions were paid at about the level of associate professors at the same institutions. But some were paid at far lower levels.[36]

Many librarians felt strongly that the salaries offered the profession were insufficient to attract and retain competent people. William E. Henry, librarian of the University of Washington, lamented in 1919 the low salaries offered. He chose a more realistic point of comparison than that selected by others. Henry realized that "our best basis for judgement for salaries in library service is the salaries of high school teachers, for the educational requirements are usually about the same." He found that the staff of his library—those below the highest administrative levels—were not paid at a level that even approached the salaries of Seattle school teachers. In addition, Henry pointed out that his discrepancy was even more meaningful because of the difference in the work year—teachers worked only nine and one-half months of the year; librarians worked eleven.[37]

Working hours have been a point of contention among academic librarians since the Harvard Corporation reduced Sibley's vacations in 1847. The academic librarians of the early nineteenth century followed the schedules of the teaching faculty because they were teaching faculty. But by 1926, two-thirds of the larger academic libraries (those holding over 100,000 volumes) allowed their professional staff only one month vacation with pay. Among smaller libraries, the practice varied more and the staff were allowed from three months (the summer) to no paid vacation. By 1929, the work of the librarian was considered a year-round job. Sydney Bancroft Mitchell, of the University of California, reported on a survey completed in 1929. It found that only in rare cases was extra compensation given for work during the summer school. Mitchell concluded; "From the rare cases where extra pay was offered for summer employment, it was in connection with teaching at a summer library school."[38]

Overwork was a frequent cause for complaint by academic librarians. One anonymous college librarian turned to the *Library Journal* to voice discontent with the plight of academic librarianship in 1880:

> There are 500 students, 14,000 v., library and reading-room open for *six* hours every day in the week except the Sabbath, no card or printed catalog, and I am sole librarian. You know what this implies. I struggle along from receiving-desk to writing-desk, giving and receiving books, answering questions, suggesting themes, searching for directing search for information, selecting books for new purchase, cataloging, indexing current literature, and posting up on book lists, reviews, critiques, etc., for *I* believe that the librarian who does *not* read is lost. In addition to all this, I am required to have an eye on the reading-room and maintain order there.

This librarian ended with a request for advice to present the case to the trustees for shorter hours: "I believe that three hours a day would answer every purpose here—leaving me several hours of uninterrupted time for other work."

But the *Library Journal* was not a receptive forum for such a request. As official organ of the American Library Association's missionary library work, it could not approve of a reduction in opening hours in any library. Dewey directed the librarian to an earlier article of his on the topic of opening hours. Dewey did not perceive any real distinction between the situation of this college librarian and the needs of the village library which must be opened as long as possible for the convenience of the public. In the earlier piece Dewey observed that there were two problems in lengthening opening hours—lighting and staff. Electricity was quickly solving the first; the second posed no great problem: "in every village some one can be found with leisure, or having work to do that can be done in the library, who will attend at little or no charge, so that whenever any would-be-reader comes, he can be served and no time wasted."[39] Dewey's answer was perhaps inappropriate for the college library, but it was in keeping with the library spirit.

It was more than salaries, vacation hours, and overwork that disillusioned academic librarians with their lot in American higher education. Charles Herrick Compton was appointed director of the University of North Dakota upon his graduation from Albany with the BLS in 1908. But North Dakota did not live up to what he had been led to expect in library school, and in May, 1910, he resigned to take a reference position at the Seattle Public Library. Compton could not resist one parting shot at the faculty on the failings of the university library. On April 7, 1910, he addressed the entire faculty on "The Library in Relation to the University." Here, he took the university to task for its failure to provide a library that was "alive." He pointed to the true model of libraries—the public library—and bemoaned the inability of higher education to develop a similar force in learning: "It is a curious fact that the public library should have left the college library so far in the rear, for one has a right to expect that the college will be in the forefront when one considers how vital to intellectual progress the library of necessity is."

Compton owned that financial shortages had handicapped the effort, but found a more significant reason in the lack of autonomy and departmental status allowed the library and librarian: "the college library has not been a moving force ... because it has not been recognized that it had a separate existence, that it was a unit and that as a unit it had its own legs to stand on." Compton observed that the essential failure of the academic library lay in its subordination to other departments of the university and warned the faculty of North Dakota that unless the library attained autonomous departmental status, "the same as any other department, one cannot expect that it will show vigorous signs of life." With this address, Compton focused on the fault that derived from the division between faculty members and librarians. Faculty control would not permit the library to assume the kind of aggressive leadership in education that was the role of the public library, and consequently, academic librarians were hindered from full realization of their professional functions.[40]

All of this made it more difficult to approach what had become a central concern and desire of academic librarians—a sense of place in the academic community. Robert McEwen recognized this in 1942 when he observed that the central concern of librarians seeking faculty status was their lack of community with faculty members:

> the sense of group-belongingness most characteristic of the college campus is organized around the life of the faculty group, which group professionally share common interest in teaching and research. The college librarian naturally seeks social acceptance from this majority group. But the librarian is commonly excluded by the nature of his task from any complete acceptance in this fellowship.[41]

In this search, the trappings of academic respectability became important to librarians. Use of the honorary doctorate by faculty members and administrators had been abandoned as disreputable long before the turn of the century. By the early years of the twentieth century, even earned doctorates were dropped from use in the proceedings of scholarship. But, librarians who were thus honored *used* the titles. Frank P. Hill obtained an honorary Doctor of Letters from his alma mater, Dartmouth, in 1906. Dewey held two—one LL.D. from Syracuse, another from Alfred, awarded in 1902. Both used them to pepper the discussion of library education at the Ottowa conference. Ernest Cushing Richardson's only degrees after taking his BA from Amherst in 1880 were an in-course master's, an honorary master's awarded by Princeton in 1896, and an honorary doctorate awarded by Washington University in 1888. He used the title "Dr." in his writing, as did William Warner Bishop.[42]

It was not only in the formal areas of equivalency that librarians sought their reward. Social standing was also important. The community sought by academic librarians implied more than recognition in terms of the endeavor—it also required social recognition. But academic librarians were not, for the most part, accorded the social recognition they felt they deserved. A Brahmin, like Winsor, could be accepted into the social life of the faculty and even become a leader in such organizations as the Thursday Evening Club in Boston, but this acceptance had nothing to do with his work in the Harvard library, and most academic librarians were not accepted into the faculty social life of the institutions. Indeed, some apparently did not understand precisely what social equality meant. In 1960, Sydney Bancroft Mitchell fondly remembered that fifty years earlier at Stanford, social distinctions between members of the faculty and librarians did not exist. But his definition of social equality would seem to be deficient, at least in the area on which he based his judgment of equality: "the University Library had become a matrimonial agency for young faculty bachelors and, during our time, Professors LeRoy Abrams, Percy Martin, and Ira Cross found their wives there—and some others tried with less luck."[43]

It was widely recognized that librarians were not considered the equivalent of faculty members. Walter Lichtenstein, librarian of Northwestern University, addressed the central concern of the profession of academic librarianship in 1910 with the statement: "In general, it is not an exaggeration to say that very few library assistants in a university library occupy in reality, whatever it may be on paper, a position at all comparable to that of even the lowest ranks of university teachers." The rigid hours of work, absence of university vacations, and lack of perquisites awarded the teaching faculty made it impossible for librarians to be really part of the academic community, even if they did have official positions as faculty members: "In short," Lichtenstein concluded, "library assistants are regarded in the same light as are the stenographers, bookkeepers, etc., employed by the university." Though it was generally realized that librarians had higher training than that required of the clerical staff, members of the faculty did not recognize it as equivalent to their own and failed to agree that the librarians of the institutions contributed to the goals of colleges and universities in the same terms as did members of the faculty. Lichtenstein concluded: "Specialization in mechanical and administrative work will not be accepted as a substitute."[44]

It was not just the lack of recognition by individual faculty members that hindered academic librarians from assuming what they had come to consider their rightful place in the academic community. Recognition was denied by other groups with an interest in higher education. The Carnegie Foundation for the Advancement of Teaching began a program in 1905 of offering pensions to faculty members of American colleges and universities. These were established because it had "become clear . . . that the disadvantages which attach to the calling of teaching by reason of the small salaries paid must, in some way, be offset by a removal of the uncertainty of provision for old age and disability, if strong and ambitious men are to be drawn in sufficient numbers to that profession." But it was not until 1921 that the foundation was forced to answer the demands of groups other than college teachers for a share in the largesse. In 1921, the Executive Committee, "in response to numerous enquiries," ruled on a number of classes of academic employees that had petitioned for inclusion in the pension plan. But the committee refused to allow blanket approval to a class of academic workers that could be called *librarians*. They instead approved that "librarians, associate and assistant librarians were eligible for allowances." They specifically excluded "reference librarians, classifiers, cataloguers, superintendents of circulation, and library assistants." In the next phase, the committee placed this second group of library workers into perspective by also excluding "field secretaries, lady principals, and wardens of halls."[45] Thus, the foundation affirmed that professional librarians not in the administrative class were indeed different from teachers in America's colleges and universities. It must be acknowledged, though, that the foundation only gave written confirmation to a policy that had been followed for at least eleven years of granting pensions to the higher administrative personnel of academic libraries.

The refusal of the committee confirmed the decisions that had been made at many institutions when the question of granting faculty status to librarians had been broached. Academic librarians were not content to mutter their dissatisfactions to themselves. They frequently brought the injustice of their position to the attention of the authorities of their institutions—usually with indifferent results. Academic librarians, looking to their counterparts in public libraries, found a degree of freedom and recognition that they did not find in their own institutions. Their attempts to rectify this situation, however, met with no real support from the faculty or administrators of academic institutions. In university after university, librarians attempted to gain recognition for their professional staff and failed.

Columbia University was one of the few that early granted at least the sham of academic titles to librarians. In 1911, the trustees continued designating the library director as "Professor." They also bestowed the title "Associate Professor" on the assistant librarian and "Assistant Professor" on supervisors who had the grade of assistant librarian. Bibliographers were given the academic rank of Instructor. These did little more than brand Columbia librarians with the outward mark of faculty status. They were granted because the library had been unable to attract and retain competent staff members with the low salaries offered for library work. Another compelling consideration was the concern of the trustees that librarians be properly identified as faculty members in order to be eligible for the retirement provisions of the Carnegie Corporation for the Advancement of Teaching.

Since the time of Dewey, Columbia's trustees had agonized over the problem of defining the role and function of the library in the university. When Dewey left in 1888, George Hall Baker was appointed a temporary replacement. At that time, the trustees directed their library committee to consider whether the library should be under the direction of a member of the faculty and to suggest possible replacements. Little came of this, though, and Baker, who had been an assistant of Dewey, was elected to the permanent post of librarian by over half the faculty votes cast in 1889. Baker's status in the university was less than that enjoyed by Dewey, and the salary was decreased from $5000 to $3500. But in a reorganization in 1892, he was given greater power in the direction of the library than that held by Dewey.

Baker's tenure was short. He enjoyed relative autonomy in the direction of the library only until 1895, when a Library Council composed of three professors, the president, and the library director was established. The committee was directed to meet weekly, and was appointed by President Seth Low because he was dissatisifed with Baker's administration—or maladministration—of the library. Low felt that Baker's pre-occupation with the details of acquiring materials and catalog-ing had made him unable to give the library any real leadership. This committee functioned until 1899, when it received a letter from President Low detailing charges against Baker's manage-ment. Low asserted that the library had outgrown Baker's capacities and Columbia had need of someone with admin-istrative force and ability. Baker countered that during his ten years in office, the library had grown from relative obscurity to one of the finest in the country. But the dissatisfaction was too deep, he was forced into retirement by the trustees in 1899 as Librarian Emeritus at a stipend of $3000 per year.

Columbia next chose James Hulme Canfield to head the library. In Canfield, the faculty and administrators of Columbia found a man whose sensibilities and concerns were closer to their own. He was a Williams graduate who had been admitted to the bar in Michigan. His interest in higher education left him dissatisfied with law and he joined the faculty of the University of Kansas in 1877 to teach a wide variety of subjects. In 1891, he became president of the University of Nebraska and assumed the presidency of Ohio State University in 1895. He left this post in 1899 to become director of the library at Columbia. Can-field had been a long-time friend of Low's and when the oppor-tunity presented itself to Low to hire a competent and proven administrator to replace a man whose concept of librarianship was entirely in the area of housekeeping, Low took it.

Canfield was appointed librarian with the rank of professor. But he early expressed concern about the low status and lower salaries of his assistants—particularly those who had given long service and demonstrated high abilities. In 1902, he proposed in his annual report that his assistant librarian, then a vacant position, be classified an adjunct professorship and the reference librarians and supervisors be ranked as instructors. He would also have the catalogers ranked as at least tutors. His request was politely ignored. There is evidence that he was attempting to reopen the question in his last annual report in 1908.

Canfield's sudden death in 1909 forced Columbia again to reexamine its criteria for a head of the library. The committee considered an appointment from the faculty, but after contacting Herbert Putnam, John Shaw Billings, and other prominent librarians, opted for a trained, experienced library administrator who would, they hoped, fit well into the scholarly community at Columbia. They decided on William Dawson Johnston. Johnston was a Brown graduate who also held a master's degree from Harvard. He had taught history at the University of Michigan and at Brown. From 1900 to 1907, he assisted in the development of the social science schedules at the Library of Congress. He had lectured at Simmons College on bibliography from 1905 to 1907 and had been employed to recatalog the Bureau of Education collections from 1907 to 1909.

Johnston lasted only five years at Columbia. On December 9, 1913, the Library Committee concluded that he was incompetent and forced his resignation. For several years, there had been a series of complaints against Johnston about accounting at the main library for books in the departmental libraries, and the inability of the main library to supply books that were in branch or departmental libraries. Johnston demanded some sort of central control throughout his tenure and had aroused the active hostility of the law librarian who wanted complete autonomy for the law library.

Johnston's firing forced yet another reexamination of the university's policies toward the library. Shortly after he left, sixty members of the upper ranks of the faculty met with the president about the administration of the library. President Nicholas Murray Butler drafted a statement that seemed to be acceptable to all concerned. The document severely circumscribed the role of the director. Its principal purpose was to prevent the librarian from taking action independent of the Library Council. The council, composed of eight faculty members, and the president, was appointed on April 14, 1914. It immediately set to work and exercised authority down to the level of approving periodical subscriptions and voting to discontinue others.

The council finally resolved the controversy over whether the library should be under the control of a faculty member or a trained librarian by appointing Dean Putnam Lockwood, a professor of classics, to replace Johnston. The policy Dewey had established of offering strong reference service had been carried on by Canfield. Johnston expanded the reference department by securing a staff of reference librarians with subject specialties. But Lockwood and the faculty members newly in control of the library did not believe reference and reader's service were a major function of an academic library and the effort to strengthen the service was largely abandoned. Thus, Columbia went on record as denying the validity of the area essential to the growing professional awareness of academic librarians—the insistence on service to students and faculty members. The essential activity upon which academic librarians, such as William Warner Bishop, relied to support the desire of librarians for admission of "the non-teaching staff generally to full academic fellowship" was, in the case of Columbia, rejected.[46]

At Berkeley, relatively little concern was expressed by librarians about status before the 1920s. But after World War I, members of the professional staff increasingly questioned their appointments as "administrative employees." The librarians on the staff maintained that the qualifications demanded for their appointments—an undergraduate degree and one year of library school—and particularly, that a number of them were teaching courses in library work, removed them from the pale of administration and into the realm of faculty affairs. In 1920, the Board of Regents was requested several times to grant faculty rank and benefits to the professional staff of the library. But, aside from allowing for the director's membership in the faculty senate, no action was taken. The best the professional staff could obtain was consent for senior assistants to enroll in courses offered on the campus during working hours in 1922. Of course, they had to have the permission of the department heads.

But even this was a higher form of recognition than that obtained by librarians at other schools. John Edward Goodwin, library of the University of Texas from 1912 to 1923, felt throughout his term that the librarian deserved the rank and status associated with the title "Professor." After 1917, he experienced severe problems with attracting an adequately trained staff because of the low status of librarians at Texas and on May 11,1920, he addressed a letter to the president of the university, Robert Ernest Vinson, recommending that at least the heads of departments, the reference librarians, and the director be given academic rank. In September, the staff was given raises, but no change in status. His annual report for the year raised the problem again in a more formal way, but before the president could respond, the state legislature passed an appropriations bill that placed all librarians on a twelve-month contract reducing the two-month vacation they had enjoyed to two weeks. Goodwin protested strongly on the ground that recruitment was already difficult, and this action would render it impossible. The regents reconsidered and granted a one-month vacation to the professional staff.

Goodwin resigned in 1923 because he found the situation intolerable. Ernest William Winkler, associate librarian, was promoted to the librarianship. In addition to inheriting the financial problems that had plagued Goodwin, he retained Goodwin's deep belief in the necessity for faculty status for academic librarians. Winkler had as little success as Goodwin in obtaining this status. In 1926, he asked President Walter Marshall William Splawn at least to acknowledge that academic librarians had a case for being allowed faculty status. He was ignored. Later, in 1931, Winkler protested with outrage to President Harry Yandell Benedict when the state comptroller placed all librarians' salaries in the clerical category. Benedict did not think it anything to become upset about. By 1932, conditions were so bad that even with the Depression, Texas had only two librarians on the staff with professional degrees.[48]

But Texas was directly responsible for the granting of faculty status to at least one academic librarian. Louis Round Wilson, head of the University of North Carolina Library, had long been dissatisfied with his status in the academic community. Though he had gained the rank of associate professor in 1907 because he had taught classes in library technique in the summer sessions, this did not imply real equality. When he complained to President Francis P. Venable in 1903 that his salary was not equal to that of other faculty members, he was informed that he was not considered a faculty member because he did not have the kind of contact with students that *real* members of the faculty had.[49]

Wilson, however, brought pressure to bear on this situation. When Goodrich resigned from the University of Texas in 1911, he was charged with finding his own successor. Before Texas settled on Goodwin, Goodrich had tried to interest Wilson. But Wilson was cautious. He wrote to Goodrich inquiring about the status he could expect at Texas and Goodrich assured him it was hazy. Wilson took the Texas offer to Venable in 1911 and the president had to recant his belief that a librarian could expect only the rank of associate professor. Wilson obtained the rank of professor with an academic year contract, though he was not expected to use it and was to remain in Chapel Hill on a twelve-month basis.[50]

Appointing a member of the faculty to direct the library was a solution reached by a number of institutions. Though the necessity for trained librarians was widely recognized, there existed a strong distrust of the technician who could not lead the library in service to the academic community. Dewey's influence on library training was largely responsible for the form of technical introspection that library economy assumed through the early stages of library education, but even Dewey recognized the distinction between technique and leadership. He admitted that trained librarians were sometimes not the ones that should be in control of the destiny of a library in his address in 1886 before the Association of Collegiate Alumnae. Though all the details of library economy were necessary for the success of the venture,

> the great element of success is the earnest moving spirit which supplies to the institution its life. This should be the librarian, though often the one who bears that name is little more than a clerk and the real librarian will be found among the active members of the trustees or the committee, or possibly not officially connected with the library.[51]

Many institutions besides Columbia recognized this and drew their library directors from the faculty after bad experiences with obtaining librarians from other sources.

Harvard was faced with the inadequacy of a library director in 1910. Since Winsor's death, William Collidge Lane served as director of Harvard's library. He had served under Winsor since graduating from Harvard in 1881 until 1893, when he replaced Charles Ami Cutter at the Boston Athenaeum. When Winsor died in 1897, Lane was a natural choice as successor. Increased acquisitions and the pressing need for more staff and enlarged space left Lane, in the view of Harvard's faculty and administration, helpless. In addition, President Abbott Lawrence Lowell wanted a man who could command the respect of the faculty and rally their support to the library's cause. Professor Archibald Cary Coolidge had for years been active in library affairs. In 1909, Lowell asked him to take charge of the faculty's library council. Lane was left in charge of the staff, but it was clear that Coolidge was directing the administration. Coolidge formally assumed the post of librarian in February, 1910. Yet, Coolidge never considered himself a librarian. He avoided any contact with other librarians, even though his subordinates attended library conferences. When Richardson invited him to membership in the ALI in 1916, Coolidge declined, explaining that he was not a librarian and did not have the technical knowledge necessary to make a contribution to the institute.[52]

The Harvard Corporation may have had cause to regret abandoning the policy of placing the library under the control of a faculty member when Keyes Metcalf was hired in 1937 as a "skilled professional librarian" to continue the library development initiated by Coolidge. Metcalf early encountered difficulties because of his inability to realize that academic traditions and values were frequently irrational and ran counter to what he expected from administration.

John Shea, a laborer with, at best, a sixth-grade education, was employed to carry books from Gore Hall to the newly opened Widener Library in 1915. He so impressed everyone that he was put on the permanent staff of the university and given a title something like "Superintendent of Books." His major assigned duty was to open the library in the morning and lock it up at night. Shea had an office assigned to him in the basement of the library, but spent most of his time at the entrance of the Widener reading the morning newspapers. His great talent which endeared him to generations of graduate students and members of the faculty was that he *knew* exactly where anything was in the building—and could find it. This was no mean accomplishment in a library the size of Harvard's, and Shea, of course, could be approached more easily than the professional librarians on the Harvard staff. Metcalf was upset by the situation and removed Shea's title, insisting that it be given to a professional member of the library staff. Shea immediately resigned and Paul Buck, who was acting president during James Conant's absence, brought the matter before the next meeting of the Harvard Corporation. The group voted Shea a "Corporation" appointment with his old title which could be rescinded only by the corporation itself. At his retirement, Shea was awarded an honorary master's degree with the approbation of both students and faculty.[53]

The University of Chicago provides the best example of disillusioned faculty reacting against librarians from their ranks assuming responsibility for the major facility of research. Though Chicago later affirmed that librarianship did indeed possess enough intellectual content to be worthy of the doctorate, it must be remembered that this was essentially through the active intervention of the Carnegie Corporation and not from any indigenous appreciation of the discipline.

Chicago's first librarian was inherited from the old Baptist Union Theological Seminary (The Morgan Park Seminary). Zella Allan Dixson was a Mt. Holyoke graduate who was widowed shortly after her marriage. She turned to librarianship in order to support herself and, after study at Dewey's school at Columbia, became one of the peripatetic catalogers that characterized early academic librarianship, accepting a series of positions around the country classifying libraries on the Dewey Decimal System. In 1888, she accepted a permanent job as librarian at Dennison after having reclassified that library, but moved on to the Seminary in Chicago in 1890. When the Seminary was incorporated into the new University of Chicago, Harper did not think her capable enough to assume the job as librarian, and approached Dewey for recommendations. Dewey came to Chicago in 1892 and Harper offered him the job at $7000 per year, but Albany raised the amount they were willing to pay and Dewey held out for $8000 from Harper.

It was not only money that concerned Harper. Dewey had at first indicated his extreme interest in the position, but his ardor had cooled on his return to Albany. Though he had soon concluded he did not want the position, he kept Harper hanging while initiating a series of correspondence with many members of the library community. Well after Dewey had decided against the offer, he approached Charles Ami Cutter about coming to Chicago as head of the library. According to Dewey's plan, Cutter was to assume actual administrative duties while Dewey retained responsibility at the policy level. Dewey's indecision and attempts to seek advantages in the offer of the directorship undoubtedly had a bad effect on Harper's view of professional librarians. Finally, Harper found Dewey's demands too much and solved the problem by appointing Mrs. Dixson assistant librarian at $1500, leaving the head post open.

Harper had also attempted to secure a scholar as director of the library. Possibly even before he contacted Dewey, he had approached Herbert Baxter Adams of the History Department of Johns Hopkins for recommendations, but Adams failed in finding a suitable candidate. One of his students expressed reluctance to accept such a position. John Martin Vincent, a Hopkins graduate in 1890, was in Europe attempting to secure a reputation through publishing at the time he was notified by Adams that the position was open. He considered the possibility, but wrote to Adams on February 15, 1892, expressing his misgivings:

I suppose the affair of the Chicago Library—the search for a librarian—has blown over. I am not opposed to such a career as that, and feel that my studies lead up to such a position. I have moreover been taking notes of things in the Library line over here, but I should prefer to be a professor of history and political science sometime as there is more freedom.

Harper's failure to enlist the services of either an experienced librarian or a scholar perhaps induced him to despair of finding a more suitable person than Mrs. Dixson.[54]

Harper seems to have abandoned the library for some time,

under the press of other matters. When Henry S. Burrage approached him in 1903 about a position in the library for his son, Harper was candid about the prospect:

> The most discouraging element in connection with the work of the University of Chicago is the library. We have neglected it beyond all description. We are paying salaries that are only half what they ought to be and we have a staff only half as large as it ought to be. At present it is not considered a matter of very great honor to be a member of our library staff. When we are going to be able to change this nobody knows. The immediate outlook is far from encouraging. Under these circumstances I doubt whether your son would care to be identified with us.[55]

But, perhaps Harper's discouragement was not so much in the position as in the candidate presented. There is some evidence that he was actively looking for a man to replace Mrs. Dixson in 1903.

From the beginning, she failed to establish a working relationship with the faculty of Chicago. She was quarrelsome and tended to regard disagreements as personal attacks. She also spoke out on a wide variety of subjects without regard to the accuracy of the facts she presented or the grammar with which they were conveyed. Her attempt to offer correspondence courses in librarianship from the university was condemned by the ALA College and Reference Section and by the faculty of Chicago. Even her attempt at publishing, *The Comprehensive Subject Index to Universal Prose Fiction* (N.Y.: Dodd, Mead, 1897), was soundly panned by its reviewers. After noting that "the positive inaccuracies of the work are so glaring that they cannot be allowed to pass unnoticed," the reviewer in the *Dial* proceeded to catalog them. The quixotic indexer, William McCrillis Griswold, could not resist the temptation and turned a review of a reference work that "will take the lead for carelessness and ignorance" into a listing of its sins in his anonymous review for the *Nation*.[56]

By 1910, faculty dissatisfaction was so strong that her resignation was forced. She had learned that Harper's successor, Harry Pratt Judson, planned finally to fill the position of library director and she had long threatened her resignation if this was done. Judson felt strongly that the position of director should be a faculty one because the faculty should control the library. In 1910, Ernest DeWitt Burton, Chairman of the Department of New Testament Theology, was named acting director and it soon became apparent that his appointment would be permanent. Burton had long been an active opponent of Mrs. Dixson on library and other matters and made no effort to retain her services.

Burton realized that he needed competent support in running a library. When he took the position, he presented Judson with a reorganization plan that called for four administrative divisions for the library: acquisitions, cataloging, a "reader's division," that was more circulation than reference, and a binding and shelf division assigned the physical care of the books. Burton's plan called for one of the heads of these divisions, if he was "a strong enough man," to assume the post of assistant director in charge of technical control and the "important function of mutual interpreter" of the library to the faculty—and the faculty to the library. In addition to this, he retained his position in his department, and was also called upon for a variety of different duties associated with the university. So, when appointed, he recruited James Christian Meinich Hanson, then at the Library of Congress, to accept the position of associate director. The position carried the rank of professor and a salary of $4000 per year. Because of Burton's outside interests, Hanson's position, while subordinate, "was in a way also Acting Director." But Burton's outside activities placed strong demands on the resources available to Hanson for the business of the library. Burton was a prolific writer who managed to keep several secretaries busy with his manuscripts. When he and other members of his department found how capable Hanson's secretary was, even the Saturday afternoons that Hanson had tried to reserve for library business were taken by the demands for typescripts of faculty manuscripts. Hanson finally had to resort to having the library correspondence attended to by a private office near the campus that specialized in typing and stenography.

Hanson encountered numerous frustrations in a situation where the library was rigidly controlled by the faculty. Burton had little appreciation for the subject so close to Hanson's heart—cataloging. Hanson, in describing Burton's work, observed that after a long day of departmental, administrative, and committee assignments, he would appear in his office in the library in the evening "quite ready to take up any problems that might be waiting his attention." Burton enjoyed attacking problems of administration, but abhorred anything to do with bibliography and cataloging. Hanson remembered: "He once told me that he had never consulted a card catalog, had always had his secretary or someone else do it for him."[57]

Hanson's lack of authority in the administration of the library is what seemed to bother him the most. He had been against the system of departmental libraries so beloved by the faculty since he arrived. In 1917, he felt compelled to write Burton that he feared some day he might receive the blame of the administration for the expensive duplication of materials and equipment in the plethora of departmental collections:

> Are they not likely to say that here was a person who had devoted thirty years of his life to special study of library problems and was, therefore, called here for the particular purpose of pointing out possible improvements in library administration, and that he had failed to make it clear to members of the Library Board and Committees of Faculty just what certain policies, now in force, might lead to?[58]

Hanson expressed a fear that may have been common among librarians in his position. The knowledge to improve without the authority to act upon that knowledge tended to create a feeling of helplessness and fear that blame would ultimately be assigned where it did not rightfully belong. But Hanson did not realize—or perhaps had forgotten—that he had not been hired at Chicago to exercise his judgment at this level of policy. Burton was appointed to his position to take charge of this level of decision by Judson explicitly to represent the interests of Chicago's faculty. With his appointment, the decision was made and affirmed that the judgment of a librarian "who had devoted thirty years of his life to special study of library problems" was irrelevant to the needs of Chicago's intellectual life.

* * * * * *

Librarians felt a strong responsibility to what they saw as their mission of insuring the success of the educational enterprise, but found they had limited authority to make it successful.

The entrance of women into librarianship at the end of the nineteenth century was a major turning point of American librarianship. The need for a rapidly expanded labor force in the field was brought about by the public library movement. Leaders of the new profession encouraged women to enter because of the larger role of librarians envisioned by the ALA and the public library movement.

The new group of librarians produced by the library schools became the workers in the newly expanded field. A distinction quickly developed between these new entrants and the older librarians. Library directors viewed their role in management as keeping library workers to the tasks at hand and developed elaborate systems of rules and regulations to insure that the work was produced. The lot of the workers in this new enterprise was not comfortable. They were controlled by rigid forms of management that prevented them from exercising any discretion in their duties and were rewarded with a wage level that enforced a life of impoverished servitude.

The formation of the American Library Institute in 1905 was a manifestation of this developing schism between the select few that perceived themselves as leaders and the mass of librarians who cluttered the meetings of the ALA. The ultimate inability of academic librarians to attain a major role in the ALI is at least partially attributable to their relation with their own governing authorities.

Academic institutions did not hire librarians produced in the schools or trained in libraries because of their intellectual capabilities but for their technical abilities. In higher education, trained librarians were first needed because of the demand for skilled catalogers. But cataloging was never perceived as an intellectual activity by faculty members or academic administrators. Indeed, many members of the academic community felt that the elaborate mechanism developed for bibliographic control drained resources from what should be the proper function of the library—acquiring materials. The tension between faculty members and librarians in the academic community forced many librarians to recognize that an unobtrusive, pleasant personality was as much or more important for the librarian than any intellectual attainment. Consequently, tact and circumspection in dealing with members of the faculty became high values in the work of academic librarians.

Faculty members were reluctant to turn the library over to these new trained specialists. As the part-time faculty members in charge of the library gradually gave way to the newly trained librarian, faculty members retained control—in some cases to a great extent—through faculty library committees. Library committees frequently exercised close control over the operations of the library and consequently, over the professional activities of librarians. Librarians thought that many of the decisions made for them would be better made by them.

Selection of materials for the collection was a major source of contention between academic librarians and the faculty. Librarians had taken much of what they held to be their professional function from the public library movement. Book selection in the public library, was a major professional activity. For academic librarians to fulfill what they saw as their role in higher education, they had to control the acquisitions budget. Faculty members, however, maintained that their own research needs were the proper object of the library's collecting activities and demanded the support of the library. As librarians watched the funds that should have gone to promote reading and culture among undergraduate students go instead to the purchase of esoteric and expensive materials for the research interests of individual faculty members, they came to believe that their basic professional obligation was being subverted by a group with special interests that countered the true purpose of higher education.

The amount of control librarians exercised over the collections themselves was another source of difficulty. In the 1920s, only about half of American academic libraries allowed their librarians the same circulation privileges they allowed the faculty. The policies of circulating materials to faculty members was felt, by many, to be too liberal. Librarians frequently complained that they had no mechanisms at their disposal to repossess the books held by faculty members, and this situation created hardships for students and junior faculty. It also, undoubtedly, created pressures on librarians to produce what they claimed to have in their catalogs when the materials themselves were beyond their power to recall.

Communication between faculty members and librarians was never clear. Faculty members, in the eyes of librarians, too often made demands on the library that librarians could not fill. Frequently enough to make it a general failing, teachers made assignments and failed to notify librarians so that they could prepare for the demands of students. Further, the required use of the library's resources by the new forms of teaching increased wear on materials difficult to replace. Demands for special projects and decisions affecting library buildings made without consideration of the effects on library service and work became issues that sharply divided librarians from their faculty colleagues.

Perhaps the most significant ongoing source of dissatisfaction among librarians lay in the faculty's inability to understand and follow the niceties of bibliography. Academic librarians had laid claim to "bibliographic science" as their special area of intellectual expertise and were impatient when faced with faculty members who in their opinion, were not competent in their efforts to describe and locate books and periodicals in the library.

The most dramatic area in which the attitude of faculty members and administrators toward academic librarians was manifested was in the preparation of a new library building. This represented a major commitment of the institution to the idea and value of a library, and usually was considered of such critical importance that librarians were frequently not consulted. When they were, their advice was often ignored.

The peripheral place of librarians in the academic enterprise was made obvious to them in their salaries and conditions of employment. Salaries at all levels rarely matched those of members of the faculty. By the end of the 1920s, librarianship was considered a year-round job. Faculty members could take summers off and, of course, had regular academic vacations at the end of terms; librarians were usually allowed only a one-month vacation with pay.

These differences made the central concern of librarians—a sense of place in the academic community—more difficult to approach. They were accorded neither equality in the official academic hierarchy nor social recognition in the academic community. A few, like Justin Winsor or Phineas Lawrence Windsor, could gain such status. At the higher administrative levels, some small gains were made, as when the Carnegie Foundation for the Advancement of Teaching granted pensions to administrative librarians in 1921. But even here, the lower ranks of librarians were pointedly relegated to the class of clerical workers necessary for the prosaic tasks of academic life.

Through the early decades of the twentieth century, many librarians approached the issue of gaining faculty status with their administrators, but were rebuffed. Librarians' arguments to justify their claims to faculty rank were not convincing enough to gain it for them. Only in cases where the lure could attract or retain a valuable person was the demand for faculty rank successful. Louis Round Wilson's attempt to obtain the rank of professor at the University of North Carolina availed him nothing until the threat of an offer from the University of Texas forced North Carolina to capitulate. Wilson, though, did not gain all the privileges of his new rank.

A distrust of trained librarians by both faculty members and administrators led many institutions to appoint a faculty member to direct the library. Dissatisfaction with William Coolidge Lane at Harvard forced the president to place him under the control of Archibald Cary Coolidge in 1909. At Columbia, the kind of librarian the university needed was a subject of much debate. After Dewey, the decision was reached that a man of solid scholarship was needed. It took eleven years of what was perceived as mismanagement by Dewey's successor, George Hall Baker, until an adequate man was found in James Hulme Canfield. Canfield's death in 1909 saw a reversal of the decision to put the library in the hands of a scholar, and William Dawson Johnston was hired. Johnston, however, lasted only five years when he was ousted for incompetence and the faculty appointed one of their own ranks to the post.

At the University of Chicago, William Rainey Harper early decided the "trained" librarian he had inherited from the old Morgan Park Seminary was inadequate for the task at hand. He approached Melvil Dewey, but Dewey feigned interest in the post while attempting to turn the offer to his own advantage and Harper abandoned the idea of gaining a leading librarian. He also seems to have failed at gaining a man of proven scholarship for the position and had to make do with the person at hand. Rather than appoint her as director of the library, Harper gave her the position of assistant librarian and left the head position open. It was not until after Harper's death that a new president appointed a director from the faculty. Ernest DeWitt Burton, the new librarian, operated the library in much the same way as the old librarians of the classical colleges and retained his other duties. He devoted only a small part of his time to the library, leaving the technical problems to his principal assistant, James Christian Meinich Hanson. But, to Hanson's dismay, Burton retained all control of the major decisions.

Thus it was established that librarianship was a minor position in the academic hierarchy. Technical proficiency was necessary, but the actual decisions that affected the ability of the library to serve the academic community were in the hands of the faculty—either through faculty library committees or by the appointment of a faculty member to direct the library. Trained librarians came to be viewed as a distinct class of academic worker whose status in the academic community was essentially subordinate. At larger institutions, some librarians at the higher administrative levels did acquire a position in some ways comparable to that of faculty members, but this was rare and usually based on other accomplishments than that of simply being a competent librarian.

Notes to Chapter 5

1.   Dee Garrison, *Apostles of Culture: The Public Librarian and American Society, 1876–1920* (New York: Macmillan Information, 1979).

2.   James Ingersoll Wyer, "Women in College Libraries" *School and Society* 29 (Feb. 16, 1929): 227–28.

3.   Melvil Dewey, *Librarianship as a Profession for College-Bred Women* (Boston: Library Bureau, 1886), pp. 20–21.

4.   Quoted in John Cushman Abbott, *Raymond Cazallis Davis and the University of Michigan General Library 1877–1905*, unpublished doctoral dissertation, University of Michigan, 1957, p. 54.

5.   Jessie Bernard, *Academic Women* (University Park: The Pennsylvania State University Press, 1964), pp. 39–40.

6.   Joseph Alfred Borome, *The Life and Letters of Justin Winsor*, unpublished doctoral dissertation, Columbia University, 1950, pp. 265, 364–67.

7. William H. Tillinghast, "Some General Rules and Suggestions for a Library Staff" *Library Journal* 27 (October 1902): 871–75.

8. William Warner Bishop, "Princeton 1902–7: Fragments of Autobiography" *Library·Quarterly* 16 (July 1946): 216; Kenneth Gerard Peterson, *The History of the University of California Library at Berkeley, 1900–1945*, unpublished doctoral dissertation, University of California, 1968), pp. 124–25.

9. Ernest Cushing Richardson, "The Field of Library Science" *Public Libraries* 21 (May 1916): 211; Mary Eileen Ahren, "The American Library Institute," American Library Institute, *Papers and Proceedings, 1917* (Chicago: American Library Association, 1918), pp. 147–48; Garrison, pp. 156–58.

10. New York Library School Association, *New York State Library School Register, 1887–1926* (New York: New York State Library School Association, Inc., 1928).

11. Guy Stanton Ford, "The Library and the Graduate School," Association of American Universities, *Journal of Proceedings and Addresses of the Fifteenth Annual Conference* (Published by the Association, 1913), pp. 42–43.

12. Louis N. Wilson, "Correlation of the Library and Other Departments of Colleges and Universities" *Public Libraries* 12 (June 1907): 220.

13. Quoted in Winifred Linderman, *History of the Columbia University Library, 1876–1927*, unpublished doctoral dissertation, Columbia University, 1959), p. 142.

14. Kenneth J. Brough, *Scholar's Workshop; Evolving Conceptions of Library Service*, Illinois Contributions to Librarianship, no. 5 (Urbana: University of Illinois, 1953), p. 116; George Alan Works, *College and University Library Problems, A Study of a Selected Group of Institutions Prepared for the Association of American Universities* (Chicago: American Library Association, 1927), p. 35.

15. Justin Winsor, "The College Library," *College Libraries as Aids to Instruction*, U.S. Bureau of Education, Circular of Information no. 1, 1880. (Washington: Government Printing Office, 1880), pp. 8–9.

16. Wayne Stewart Yenawine, *The Influence of Scholars on Research Library Development at the University of Illinois*, unpublished doctoral dissertation, University of Illinois, 1955), p. 76.

17. *ALA Survey*, vol. 1 (Chicago: American Library Association, 1926), p. 160; James M. Nicholson, Jr., "A History of the Wake Forest College Library, 1876–1946," Master's thesis, University of North Carolina, 1954, pp. 59–63.

18. S. H. Bauersfeld, "The Growth and Development of the University of Delaware Library, Newark, Delaware, 1833–1965," Master's thesis, Catholic University of America, 1967, pp. 58–59.

19. Peterson, "History of the University of California Library," p. 45; James Huline Canfield, "The Modern College Library" *Education* 27 (November 1906): 132.

20. Theodore Wesley Koch, "Apportionment of Book-funds in College and University Libraries," *Papers and Proceedings of the Thirtieth Annual*

Meeting of the American Library Association (Boston: American Library Association, 1908), pp. 341–47; Charles Harvey Brown "The Library" in Arthur J. Klein, *Survey of Land-Grant Colleges and Universities*, United States Office of Education Bulletin 1930 no. 9, vol. 1 (Washington: United States Government Printing Office, 1930), p. 674.

21. James Ingersoll Wyer,*The College and University Library*, Reprint, *Manual of Library Economy*, chap. IV (Chicago: American Library Association Publishing Board, 1911), p. 10; Brown, "The Library," p. 651.

22. Alfred Clanghorn Potter, "The Selection of Books for College Libraries," *Papers and Proceedings of the Nineteenth General Meeting of the American Library Association* (Chicago: American Library Association, 1897), pp. 41–42.

23. Canfield, "Modern College Library," p. 134.

24. Brown, "The Library," p. 632.

25. *Ibid.*, pp. 690, 635.

26. Charles W. Smith, "The Vanishing Supply of Research Periodicals" *Library Journal* 49 (Feb. 1, 1924): 117–19.

27. Benjamin Putnam Kurtz, *Joseph Cummings Rowell, 1853–1938* (Berkeley: University of California Press, 1940), p. 33; Charles Haynes McMullen, *The Administration of the University of Chicago Libraries, 1892–1938*, unpublished doctoral dissertation, University of Chicago, 1949, p. 126.

28. Sharp to Simpson, October 28, 1905 in Sharp Papers, University of Illinois Archives, folder "Sharp Correspondence, 1891–1901" (18/1/20, box 2).

29. Linda M. Duval, "The Ethics of the College Library" *Public Libraries* 4 (November 1899): 422; Willard Austen, "Educational Value of Reference Room Training for Students," *Papers and Proceedings of the Twenty-Ninth Annual Meeting of the American Library Association* (Boston: American Library Association Publishing Board, 1907), p. 275.

30. William Warner Bishop, "Amount of Help to be Given to Readers," *Papers and Proceedings of the Thirtieth Annual Meeting of the American Library Association* (Boston: American Library Association Publishing Board, 1908), p. 331.

31. Claud Glenn Sparks, *William Warner Bishop, A Biography*, unpublished doctoral dissertation, University of Michigan, 1967, pp. 176–80; Margaret Nadine Finlayson Maxwell, *Anatomy of a Book Collector: William L. Clements and the Clements Library*, unpublished doctoral dissertation, University of Michigan, 1971, pp. 83–103; Theodore Wesley Koch, "The University Library" *Library Journal* 40 (May 1915): 323.

32. Lewis C. Moloney, *A History of the University Library at the University of Texas, 1883–1934*, unpublished doctoral dissertation, Columbia University, 1970, pp. 180–90; John Neal Waddell, *The Career of Isadore G. Mudge: A Chapter in the History of Reference Librarianship*, unpublished doctoral dissertation, Columbia University, 1973, pp. 106–197;

Ruth W. Clinefeller, "A History of Bierce Library of the University of Akron," Master's thesis, Kent State University, 1956, p. 60; Linderman, pp. 73–75; Ralph W. Hanson, "The Stanford University Library: Genesis 1891–1906" *Journal of Library History* 9 (April 1974): 149; McMullen, p. 79.

33. Quoted in the Princeton Alumni Weekly, *The Harvey S. Firestone Memorial Library* (Princeton, 1949), pp. 7–8; American Library Association, College and Reference Section, Committee on College and University Library Statistics, Preliminary Report, *Papers and Proceedings of the Twenty-Ninth Annual Meeting of the American Library Association* (Boston: American Library Association Publishing Board, 1907), p. 261.

34. At Stanford, Tulane, Cornell and the universities of California, Illinois, Iowa, Minnesota, North Carolina, and Oregon.

35. At Iowa State, Cornell, Stanford, the universities of California, Illinois, Minnesota, and North Carolina; *Works*, pp. 133–34.

36. Brown, "The Library," p. 685.

37. William E. Henry, "Living Salaries for Good Service" *Library Journal* 44 (May 1919): 283–84.

38. ALA, *Survey*, 1:268; Sydney Bancroft Mitchell "Salary Statistics: University and College Library Salary Statistics" *ALA Bulletin* 23 (March 1929): 57.

39. College Librarian, "Library Hours" *Library Journal* 5 (June 1880): 171; Melvil Dewey "Library Hours" *Library Journal* 4 (December 1879): 449.

40. Charles H. Compton *Memories of a Librarian* (St. Louis Public Library, 1954), pp. 31–39; Idem, "The Library in Relation to the University" *Library Journal* 35 (November 1910): 495–96.

41. Robert W. McEwen, "The Status of College Librarians" *College and Research Libraries* 3 (June 1942): 257.

42. Chalmers Hadley "What Library Schools Can Do for the Profession," *Papers and Proceedings of the Thirty-Fourth Annual Meeting of the American Library Association* (Chicago: American Library Association, 1912), p. 155; Ernest Cushing Richardson, "Antediluvian Libraries" *Library Journal* 15 (December 1890): 40; Sparks, p. 313.

43. Borome, p. 440; Sydney Bancroft Mitchell, *Mitchell of California; the Memoirs of Sydney B. Mitchell, Librarian, Teacher, Gardener* (Berkeley: California Library Association, 1960), pp. 185–86.

44. Walter Lichtenstein, "The Question of a Graduate Library School" *Library Journal* 43 (April 1918): 234.

45. Henry S. Pritchett, "The Policy of the Carnegie Foundation for the Advancement of Teaching" *Educational Review* 32 (June 1906): 83; Carnegie Foundation for the Advancement of Teaching *Sixteenth Annual Report* (The Corporation, 1921), p. 5.

46. Linderman, pp. 408, 184–86, 245–46, 249–51, 275–76, 365–66, 441–45; James Everett Skipper, *The Ohio State University Library, 1873–1913*, unpublished doctoral dissertation, University of Michigan, 1960, pp. 132–33; Samuel Rothstein, *The Development of Reference Sources*

Through Academic Traditions, Public Library Practice and Special Librarianship ACRL Monograph no. 14 (Chicago: Association of College and Reference Libraries, 1955), pp. 35–36; William Warner Bishop, "The Contribution of the Library to College Teaching" *Library Journal* 54 (March 15, 1929): 255.

47. Peterson, "History of the University of California Library," p. 234.
48. Moloney, pp. 230–33; 272–74, 285.
49. Maurice Falcolm Tauber, *Louis Round Wilson: Librarian and Administrator* (New York: Columbia University Press, 1967), pp. 27, 34–35.
50. Moloney, pp. 210–11; Tauber, pp. 142–43.
51. Dewey, *Librarianship as a Profession for College-Bred Women*, p. 10.
52. William Bentinck-Smith, *Building a Great Library: The Coolidge Years at Harvard* (Cambridge: Harvard University Press, 1976), pp. 24–27, 155.
53. Howard Mumford Jones, *Howard Mumford Jones: an Autobiography* (Madison: University of Wisconsin Press, 1979), pp. 189–91.
54. McMullen, pp. 31–34; Francis Louis Miksa, *Charles Ami Cutter: Nineteenth Century Systematizer of Libraries*, unpublished doctoral dissertation, University of Chicago, 1974, 1:261–62; Herbert Baxter Adams, *Historical Scholarship in the United States, 1876–1901: As Revealed in the Correspondence of Herbert B. Adams* W. Stull Holt (Ed.), The Johns Hopkins University Series in Historical and Political Science, ser. 56, no. 4 (Baltimore: The Johns Hopkins Press, 1938), p. 180.
55. Quoted in McMullen, p. 65.
56. *Dial* 23 (November 1, 1897), p. 253; *Nation* 66 (April 14, 1898): 288.
57. McMullen, pp. 104–107; Edith Scott, *J. C. M. Hanson and His Contribution to Twentieth Century Cataloging*, unpublished doctoral dissertation, University of Chicago, 1970, p. 561; James Christian Meinich Hanson, *What Became of Jens? A Study in Americanization, Based on the Reminiscences of J. C. M. Hanson, 1864–1943*, ed. Olvind M. Horde (Decorah, Iowa: Luther College Press, 1974), pp. 220–23.
58. Quoted in McMullen, p. 113.

A Conclusion

The status of librarians in the academic community has been defined by the value structure of American higher education. Academic librarians consistently failed to understand that the university movement had developed means of official and unofficial recognition and reward that differed greatly from that which librarians had adopted. By the 1920s, the forms that characterize American higher education had substantially evolved. The moribund classical colleges had given way to the university. Though many small liberal arts colleges remained committed to undergraduate education, the best of their faculty could easily be lured away by offers from Chicago, Johns Hopkins, or Illinois. Recognition of the importance of undergraduate instruction did not obscure the reality that values that characterize American higher education were derived from the university ideal.

Scholarship and research became the essential element in this new value system. Increasingly narrow specialization and work in relatively limited fields of knowledge constricted the intellectual horizons of the teacher from what they had been in the classical college. Faculty members were no longer expected to teach the entire spectrum of the curriculum, but to devote their energies to the intense study of a small portion of the world. The valued member of the academic community was one whose work led him beyond the known and into the search for new truths. Since the nature of specialization was such that few could adequately evaluate the contribution of the individual researcher, publication became the means by which the work of the scholar was weighed. The university movement had turned

271

from the classical colleges' commitment to making young boys into Christian gentlemen, to affirm that productive specialization which pushed forward the frontiers of knowledge was the proper function of the faculty. The age that associated piety with scholarship had passed and, within limits, no matter how variegated their personal habits or religious views, the professors who published the results of their sound research were the ones respected by their colleagues in their disciplines and in their institutions.

In the period of the classical college, the librarian's role was a minor one at best. The colleges could maintain their educational efforts without a library except for a few books and journals that some professor needed but could not afford. As the university movement gained momentum, the library became increasingly important. The new universities and colleges demanded productive scholars for their faculties and the library became an important attraction for them. "Access" became the shibboleth of the institutions when they approached the problem of hiring a librarian.

At first, the problem was defined in simple terms. If the library was opened longer hours, it would satisfy the need for access created by the new educational methods. But this soon proved inadequate. Colleges then turned to librarians trained by the schools begun by Melvil Dewey and carried on by his disciples. By choosing these technically trained people as academic librarians, the colleges and universities affirmed that they valued technical proficiency and ability to maintain control of the mass of material over any high degree of scholarship for librarians.

The kind of education accepted by librarians and by academic institutions differed radically from that expected of faculty members. Indeed, the form of library education as it was begun by Dewey and promoted by his disciples was, in essence, a manifestation of the spirit of the public library movement. Dewey's missionary spirit led librarianship to develop a professional identity in the American Library Association that resoundingly affirmed the importance of the public library in American life. The purpose of library education as envisioned by Dewey and his acolytes and realized in the schools at Albany, Illinois, and

elsewhere was to further the cause of the public library by training librarians to the techniques of the work and the enthusiasm
of the calling.

Librarians trained by the schools and reinforced by the concerns of the American Library Association came to feel that
they had a central role to play in higher education—indeed,
some asserted that it was a role greater than even that of the
faculty. Deriving their vision from the public library movement,
they defined their purpose in relation to the void they perceived
had been left by the passing of the classical college. The intense
specialization of the graduate schools, the development of
undergraduate majors that pushed specialized course work to
ever-lower levels in the curriculum, and the emergence of areas
of new academic specialization and vocational preparation led
many academic librarians to the conviction that a major concern of undergraduate education had been abandoned. They
began to seek a function that they perceived to be identical to
that of the teaching faculty when they assumed the task of
directing the general cultural reading of the students and helping them find a way through the mass of material required by
the scholars and researchers on the faculty. Because they were
involved in an activity that was directly concerned with higher
education and scholarship, academic librarians came to consider
their work as a scholarly pursuit. With this conviction, they
looked back to the nineteenth century when librarians were professors in the classical colleges. Without awareness that the
condition that obtained in that period was due to the single,
limited purpose of the colleges and the financial necessity for
college teachers to assume a variety of duties, academic librarians recalled a golden age when the communal spirit of higher
education gave the librarian a more significant place in the
academic hierarchy. Librarians defined their functions in educational terms, the faculties and administrations of the institutions viewed the librarian as an organizer and administrator
thus leading to a conflict of roles which has not been resolved
satisfactorily.

Academic librarians were, however, self-consciously aware of
the differences between themselves and members of the faculties of their institutions. In salaries, working conditions, and

recognition, they were not equal. Their response was to develop a vision of the role of the librarian in the academic community that relied heavily on the importance of the library and a general feeling that the former high place the librarian had enjoyed in the classical college had somehow been unfairly abandoned by the university movement.

It is reasonable to conclude that both the external forms and the activities of academic librarians were involved in their developing dissatisfaction with their status in American higher education. The influence of the public library movement and education for librarianship conditioned academic librarians to see their professional role as analogous to that of the college teacher. In public libraries, this analogy was directed toward the high school teacher. Academic librarians absorbed the vision of library service conditioned by the public library movement and applied it to their own occupation. Their role as teachers of books coupled with the pervasive view that they had somehow been displaced in the academic scheme by the new specialists on the faculty forced them to examine the preparation necessary for their occupation. The most professionally directed librarians concluded that the doctorate was necessary for academic librarians. But, this conclusion was not reached from any awareness that academic librarianship itself was a specialization deserving study. It was a simple realization that the PhD was needed if librarians were to take their equal place on the faculties of America's colleges and universities.

Scholars in the new universities carried a basic proof of their competency. Librarians, not realizing that the symbol had substance, attempted to develop their own paths toward academic respectability through the doctorate in librarianship. The continuing discussion over the forms the degree should take was a very self-conscious debate that recognized the necessity for the form itself and then attempted to find a method to obtain the degree. Other recognized academic disciplines had evolved their research in an attempt to understand their own particular province of learning; academic librarians took the realm of books as the field they were expert in and accepted bibliography as the appropriate mode of research for the doctorate.

Bibliography, however, was not an activity that won the respect of scholars. Faculty members, for the most part, simply did not concur that it fit any real definition of research. Their disregard for the efforts of librarians was so pronounced that it led to a major differentiation between librarians and scholars. Faculty members failed to appreciate the demands of librarians for precise bibliographic descriptions. Librarians considered the inability of faculty members to apply "bibliographic science" to be evidence of scholarly incompetence. But the schism seems to have derived less from a genuine conviction of librarians that bibliography was a scholarly activity than from their need to lay claim to an area of knowledge and activity that they could identify as their own.

The feeling of academic librarians that they held a prominent place in the academic community undoubtedly played a significant part in their assertion that they deserved faculty rank on the basis of their teaching functions and their research duties. Whether their desire for this status derived from their sincerely held belief that they deserved equality or from the mythos that commanded them to control the "heart of the university" is essentially irrelevant. Both aspects arose concurrently and by the 1920s were ingrained into the professional awareness of academic librarians.

By that time, academic librarianship had failed to establish a consistent form as a profession. It had not approached a coherent theory beyond the attempt to apply to the peculiar problems of the academic library the missionary spirit of public library development as proposed by Dewey and the American Library Association. Rather than affirm the values of the academic community, librarians sought their own function in the enterprise of American higher education. Thus, they derived their own role from that which they perceived to be a major failing in the values of higher education and attempted to force it upon the academic institutions. Academic librarians existed in a state of professional ambivalence. They were not of the group that established the profession in its most distinct form —the public librarians—and they were excluded from the environment in which they labored—the academic community.

* * * * * *

Many questions are left unanswered. Obviously, much has happened to America and its institutions since the early decades of this century. Another world war, periods of national anxiety, and a recent trend of higher education to be more sensitive to the needs of American society have forced major transformations in American higher education. A realization that knowledge cannot be fragmented and pursued into narrow channels has resulted in the emergence of synthetic programs of study leading to degrees that certify the student as having mastered humanities, ethnic studies, the environment, and a wide variety of other interdisciplinary programs. There also have been major changes in the forms that characterize the education of librarians. The change from a program at the bachelor's level to a graduate degree has probably most influenced the position of librarians in higher education.

Faculty membership itself has also changed. The doctorate that became the mark of scholarship in the nineteenth century was a PhD. Since then, doctoral level work in a wide array of areas has been initiated, so that degrees of Doctor of Education (EdD), Doctor of Music (DMus), Doctor of Social Work (DSW), Doctor of Laws (JD), and Doctor of Library Science (DLS), among others, have won some degree of academic respectability. Recently, the professional degree of Doctor of Arts (DA) has been awarded by some institutions as a credential specifically designed for teachers of undergraduates. The PhD is maintained as the most valued form of the doctorate, but there are challenges in the still amorphous field of higher education for a degree designating the proper preparation of teachers. These degrees exist and have some form of academic acceptance, but the true extent of realization of the efforts has yet to be properly identified. Much more research is needed in the area. The question of how a PhD is compared with other doctorates and how this distinction is realized in the status of the holder in the academic community has yet to be determined.

It seems quite obvious that a degree at the master's level does not equal a doctorate. The tendency of some academic library directors to require second master's degrees in "subject" areas for professional staff positions probably has not enhanced the position of academic librarians. Educational credentials at that level seem not to be greatly respected by either faculty members or administrators. In insisting on such levels of preparation, academic librarians continue to affirm that broad knowledge is more important to their work than any ability to conduct research. This trend must be considered in any further investigation into the culture of academic librarianship.

Three additional developments in academic librarianship need further investigation to truly define the profession. In the 1930s, Louis Shores began the evolution of an idea that emerged as the "Library-College Movement." This attempt to vitalize the role of the academic librarian represented a major emerging force in efforts of librarians to define their identity in higher education. Though the movement failed to win acceptance in America's institutions of higher learning, it has been and still is a factor in any consideration of modern academic librarianship.

The second development is the idea that academic librarianship has transcended the realm of books and has moved to establish a science of information. The Library-College Movement attempted at least at some levels to lead academic librarianship into the area of educational technology. Information retrieval represents a further projection into the realm of scholarship. The attempt by academic librarians to manipulate information rather than provide requested sources represents a new dimension in the evolution of American academic librarianship.

The nature of research in librarianship is another area that must have attention. The establishment of the library school at the University of Chicago and the subsequent development of doctoral programs at other universities demonstrate that librarianship has emerged as a discipline with its own body of research and knowledge. The evolution of research in library schools has had an effect on academic librarianship. In addition to providing a model of research for the academic community to evaluate, it has encouraged a significant number of research activities by academic librarians. The question of whether published research is sufficient in itself to enhance the status of the working librarian in higher education must be attempted.

The present work defines the basic forces and events that have conditioned the origins of American academic librarianship. As a profession distinguishable from that of members of the faculty and from other types of librarians, it has failed to become fully defined. It is hoped that this attempt will encourage further efforts toward defining and evaluating the role and function of the librarian in America's colleges and universities.

Selected Bibliography

Abbott, John Cushman. *Raymond Cazallis Davis and the University of Michigan General Library 1877-1905.* Unpublished doctoral dissertation, University of Michigan, 1957.

"An Act Denoting Public Lands to the Several States and Territories Which May Provide Colleges for the Benefit of Agriculture and the Mechanic Arts." U.S. Office of Education. *Report of the Commissioner of Education for the year 1890-91* vol. 1. Washington, D.C.: Government Printing Office, 1894, pp. 582-84.

Adams, Henry. *The Education of Henry Adams.* Edited by Ernest Samuels. Boston: Houghton Mifflin Company, 1974.

Adams, Henry. *Letters of Henry Adams (1858-1891).* Edited by Worthington Chauncey Ford. Boston: Houghton Mifflin Company, 1930.

Adams, Herbert Baxter. *Historical Scholarship in the United States, 1876-1901: As Revealed in the Correspondence of Herbert B. Adams.* Edited by W. Stull Holt. The Johns Hopkins University Studies in Historical and Political Science, ser. 56, no. 4. Baltimore: The Johns Hopkins Press, 1938.

Adams, Herbert Baxter. *Thomas Jefferson and the University of Virginia.* U.S. Bureau of Education. Circular of Information No. 1, 1888. Washington: Government Printing Office, 1888.

Ahren, Mary Eileen. "The American Library Institute." In American Library Institute *Papers and Proceedings, 1917.* Chicago: ALA, 1918, pp. 147-56.

Allen, Don Cameron. *The Ph.D. in English and American Literature.* New York: Holt, Rinehart & Winston, 1968.

American Association of University Professors, Committee on College and University Teaching. *Report of the Committee on College and University Teaching.* Washington, D.C.: The Association, 1933.

American Association of University Professors, Committee Q. "Required Courses in Education." *AAUP Bulletin* 19 (March 1933): 173–200.

American Library Association. *A Survey of Libraries in the United States,* 4 vols. [n.d.] Chicago: American Library Association, 1926.

American Library Association, Board of Education for Librarianship. "First Annual Report of the Board of Education for Librarianship." *ALA Bulletin* 19 (July 1925): 226–63.

American Library Association, College and Reference Section. "College and Reference Section." *ALA Bulletin* 17 (July 1923): 227–29.

American Library Association, Committee on Library Training. "Report of the Committee on Library Training." *Library Journal* 28 (July 1903): 83–101.

American Library Association, Committee on Library Training. "Report on Standards of Library Training." *Library Journal* 30 (September 1905): 121–23.

American Library Association, Committee on Library Training. "Report of the Committee on Library Training." *Library Journal* 31 (August 1906): 175–77.

American Library Association, Committee on Methods of Publicity for Library Schools. "Report." In *Papers and Proceedings of the Thirty-Fifth Annual Meeting of the American Library Association* (Chicago: American Library Association, 1913); p. 350.

American Library Association, Committee on Salaries, Insurance, and Annuities. "A.L.A. Research or Statistical Department." *ALA Bulletin* 23 (August 1929): 270–77.

American Library Association, Committee on the Classification of Library Personnel. *Budgets, Classification and Compensation Plans for University and College Libraries; Report of the Committee on Classification of Library Personnel of the American Library Association, December 1928.* Chicago: American Library Association, 1929.

American Library Association, Committee on the Library School. "Report." *Library Journal* 12 (September–October, 1887), pp. 426–28.

American Library Association, Committee on the Proposed School for Librarians at Columbia College. "Report." *Library Journal* 8 (September–October 1883): 293–94.

American Library Association, Committee on the Proposed School of Library Economy. "Report." *Library Journal* 10 (September 1885): 291–94.

American Library Association, Temporary Library Training Board. "Report of the Temporary Library Training Board." *ALA Bulletin* 18 (August 1924): 257–88.

"American Library Examination—Papers Set at Library School, Albany, N.Y." *Library World* 13 (August 1910): 86-90.

American Library Institute, Committee on the Higher Education of Librarians. "Report." In *American Library Institute Papers and Proceedings, 1919.* (Chicago: American Library Association, 1920), pp. 233-41.

Askew, Thomas A. Jr. *The Liberal Arts College Encounters Intellectual Change: A Comparative Study of Education at Knox and Wheaton Colleges, 1837-1929.* Unpublished doctoral dissertation, Northwestern University, 1969.

Association of American Universities. "Report of the Committee on Academic and Professional Higher Degrees." *Journal of the Proceedings and Addresses of the Association of American Universities* 26 (Oct. 31-Nov. 1, 1924): 25-27.

Association of College and Research Libraries, Committee on Academic Status. *Faculty Status for Academic Librarians: A History and Policy Statement.* Chicago: American Library Association, 1976.

Atkinson, Carroll. *Pro and Con of the Ph.D.* Boston: Meador Publishing Company, 1945.

Austen, Willard. "Educational Value of Reference Room Training for Students." In *Papers and Proceedings of the Twenty-Ninth Annual Meeting of the American Library Association.* Boston: American Library Association, 1907, pp. 274-77.

Babbitt, Irving. *Literature and the American College, Essays in Defense of the Humanities.* Boston: Houghton, Mifflin and Company, 1908.

Bache, Alexander Dallas. "A National University." *American Journal of Education* 1 (May 1856): 477-79.

Bacon, Corrine. "Relation of the Library School to the School and College Library." *Public Libraries* 19 (November 1914): 396-98.

Bainton, Roland H. *George Lincoln Burr, His Life: Selections from His Writings.* Edited by Lois O. Gibbons. Ithaca, N.Y.: Cornell University Press, 1952.

Barnard, Frederick Augustus Porter. "The Library and School of Library Economy. An extract from the Annual Report of F. A. P. Barnard, S.T.D., LL.D., L.H.D., President of Columbia College, Made to the Trustees May 5, 1884." Columbia University, School of Library Economy. *School of Library Economy of Columbia College 1887-1889: Documents for a History.* Columbia University, School of Library Science, 1937, pp. 11-17.

Barnard, Frederick Augustus Porter. "On Improvements Practicable in American Colleges." *American Journal of Education and College Review* 1 (January 1856): 174-85; (March 1856): 269-84.

Barnard, John. *From Evangelism to Progressivism at Oberlin College, 1866-1917.* Columbus, Ohio: Ohio State University Press, 1969.

Barzun, Jacques. *Teacher in America.* Boston: Little, Brown & Company, 1945.

Bauersfeld, S. H. "The Growth and Development of the University of Delaware Library, Newark, Delaware, 1833-1965." Master's thesis, Catholic University of America, 1967.

Baughman, Nancy C. (Vermilya). "A History of the Otterbein College Library Westerville, Ohio, 1858-1955." Master's thesis, Western University, 1955.

Bean, Mary Vernace. *Development of the Ph.D. Program in* [sic] *United States in the Nineteenth Century.* Unpublished doctoral dissertation, Ohio State University, 1958.

Bentinck—Smith, William. *Building a Great Library: the Coolidge Years at Harvard.* Cambridge: Harvard University Press, 1976.

Bernard, Jessie. *Academic Women.* University Park: Pennsylvania State University Press, 1964.

Bidlack, Russell Eugene. *The University of Michigan General Library: A History of Its Beginnings, 1837-1852.* Unpublished doctoral dissertation, University of Michigan, 1954.

Bishop, William Warner. "The American Library Association: Fragments of Autobiography." *Library Quarterly* 19 (January 1949): 35-45.

Bishop, William Warner. "Amount of Help to be Given to Readers." In *Papers and Proceedings of the Thirtieth Annual Meeting of the American Library Association.* Boston: American Library Association Publishing Board, 1908, pp. 327-32.

Bishop, William Warner. "Changing Ideals in Librarianship." *Library Journal* 44 (January 1919): 5-10.

Bishop, William Warner. "The Contribution of the Library to College Teaching." *Library Journal* 54 (March 15, 1929): 254-55.

Bishop, William Warner. "Our College and University Libraries—a Survey and a Program." *School and Society* 7 (Sept. 18, 1920): 205-214.

Bishop, William Warner. "Princeton 1902-7: Fragments of Autobiography." *Library Quarterly* 16 (July 1946): 211-24.

Bishop, William Warner. "The Theory of Reference Work." *ALA Bulletin* 9 (July 1915): 134-39.

Bledstein, Burton J. *The Culture of Professionalism: The Middle Class and the Development of Higher Education in America.* New York: W. W. Norton & Co., Inc. 1976.

Boll, John Jorg. *Library Architecture 1800-1875: A Comparison of Theory and Buildings with Emphasis on New England College Libraries.* Unpublished doctoral dissertation, University of Illinois, 1961.

Borome, Joseph Alfred. *The Life and Letters of Justin Winsor.* Unpublished doctoral dissertation, Columbia University, 1950.

Breedlove, Joseph Penn. *Duke University Library, 1840-1940: A Brief Account with Reminiscences.* Durham, N.C.: Friends of Duke University Library, 1955.

Briggs, Walter B. "Reference Work in Public and College Libraries: A Comparison and a Contrast." *Library Journal* 32 (November 1907): 492–95.

Bronson, Walter C. *The History of Brown University 1764–1914.* Providence, R.I.: Published by the University, 1914.

Brooks, Van Wyck. *The Life of Emerson.* New York: E. P. Dutton, 1932.

Brough, Kenneth J. *Scholar's Workshop: Evolving Conceptions of Library Service.* Illinois Contributions to Librarianship, no. 5. Urbana: University of Illinois, 1953.

Brown, Charles Harvey. "The Library." In Klein, Arthur J. *Survey of Land-Grant Colleges and Universities,* vol. 1. United States Office of Education. Bulletin 1930, no. 9. Washington, D.C.: United States Government Printing Office, 1930, pp. 609–713.

Brown, Jerry Wayne. *The Rise of Biblical Criticism in America, 1800–1870; the New England Scholars.* Middletown, Ct.: Wesleyan University Press, 1969.

Brubacher, John S., and Willis Rudy. *Higher Education in Transition: A History of American Colleges and Universities, 1636–1956.* 3d ed. New York: Harper & Row, 1976.

Bruce, Philip Alexander. *History of the University of Virginia, 1819–1919: The Lengthened Shadow of One Man.* 5 vols. New York: The Macmillan Company, 1921.

Bryson, Gladys. "The Emergence of the Social Sciences from Moral Philosophy" *Ethics* 42 (April 1932): 304–323.

Bureau of Public Personnel Administration. *Proposed Classification and Compensation Plans for Library Positions; Report of the Bureau of Public Personnel Administration to the Committee on the Classification of Library Personnel of the American Library Association.* Washington, D.C.: Bureau of Public Personnel Administration, 1927.

Burgess, John W. *Reminiscences of an American Scholar: The Beginnings of Columbia University.* New York: Columbia University Press, 1934.

Burton, Marion L. "Cooperation Between Universities." In *Transactions and Proceedings of the National Association of State Universities in the United States of America.* Edited by Frank L. McVey, 17 (1919): 45–68.

Butler, Nicholas Murray. *Across the Busy Years; Recollections and Reflections.* 2 vols. New York: Charles Scribner's Sons, 1939–40.

Canby, Henry Seidel. *Alma Mater: The Gothic Age of the American College.* New York: Farrar & Rinehart, Inc., 1936.

Canfield, James Hulme. "The Modern College Library." *Education* 27 (November 1906): 129–35.

Carlson, William Hugh. *The Library of Oregon State University: Its Origins, Management, and Growth, a Centennial History.* Corvallis, Ore.: 1966.

Carr, John Foster. "A Greater American Library Association." *Library Journal* 45 (Oct. 1, 1920): 775-79.

Chase, Harry Woodburn. "Making a University Faculty." In Association of American Universities. *Journal of Proceedings and Addresses of the Twenty-Sixth Annual Conference.* Chicago: Published by the Association, 1924, pp. 65-68.

Chessman, G. Wallace. *Denison: the Story of an Ohio College.* Granville, Ohio: Denison University, 1957.

Chiapetta, Michael. *A History of the Relationship between Collegiate Objectives and the Professional Preparation of Arts College Teachers in the United States.* Unpublished doctoral dissertation, University of Michigan, 1950.

Clark, Jay B. "The Odyssey of a University Library, 1869-1968." *Journal of Library History* 5 (April 1970): 119-32.

Clarke, Edith E. "Departmental Arrangement of College Libraries." *Library Journal* 14 (August 1889): 340-43.

Clemons, Harry. *The University of Virginia Library, 1825-1950: Story of a Jeffersonian Foundation.* Charlottesville: University of Virginia Library, 1954.

Clinefeller, Ruth W. "A History of Bierce Library of the University of Akron." Master's thesis, Kent State University, 1956.

"College Instruction and Discipline." *American Quarterly Review* 9 (June 1831): 283-314.

College Librarian. "Library Hours." *Library Journal* 5 (June 1880):171.

Columbia College. Library. School of Library Economy. "Circular of Information, 1886-7." In Columbia University, School of Library Service, *School of Library Economy of Columbia College 1887-1889: Documents for a History.* (Columbia University, School of Library Science, 1937); p. 61-105.

"Columbia College School of Library Economy. Application for Admission." In Columbia University, School of Library Science, *School of Library Economy of Columbia College 1887-1889: Documents for a History.* Columbia University, School of Library Science, 1937, pp. 247-54.

Come, Donald Robert. "The Influence of Princeton on Higher Education in the South Before 1825." *William and Mary Quarterly* 2 (October 1945): 359-96.

Commager, Henry Steele. *The American Mind; an Interpretation of American Thought and Character Since the 1880's.* New Haven: Yale University Press, 1950.

Compton, Charles H. "The Library in Relation to the University." *Library Journal* 35 (November 1910): 494-503.

Compton, Charles H. *Memories of a Librarian.* St. Louis Public Library, 1954.

Cooper, James Fenimore. *Letters and Journals.* Edited by James Franklin Beard. 6 vols. Cambridge: Belknap Press of Harvard University Press, 1960-1968.

Cordasco, Francesco. *The Shaping of American Graduate Education: Daniel Coit Gilman and the Protean Ph.D.* Totowa, N.J.: Roman and Littlefield, 1973.

Coulter, Edith M. "The University Librarian: His Preparation, Position and Relation to the Academic Department of the University." *ALA Bulletin* 16 (July 1922): 271-75.

Cowley, William Harold. *Presidents, Professors, and Trustees.* Edited by Donald T. Williams. San Francisco: Jossey-Bass Publishers, Inc., 1980.

Crenshaw, Ollinger, and William W. Pusey III. "An American Classical Scholar in Germany, 1874." *American-German Review* 22 (August-September, 1956): 30-33.

Curti, Merle Eugene, and Roderick Nash. *Philanthropy in the Shaping of American Higher Education.* New Brunswick, N.J.: Rutgers University Press, 1965.

Daniels, Joseph F. "Indeterminate Functions of a College Library." *Library Journal* 32 (November 1907): 487-92.

Davis, Donald Gordon, Jr. *The Association of American Library Schools, 1915-1968: An Analytical History.* Metuchen, N.J.: Scarecrow Press, Inc., 1974.

Davis, Raymond Cazallis. "The Relation of the Librarian to the Faculty." *Library Journal* 15 (December 1890): 140-41.

Davis, T. K. "College Library and the College." *Library Journal* 10 (May 1885): 100-103.

Denison, John Hoplins. *Mark Hopkins: A Biography.* New York: Charles Scribner's Sons, 1935.

Dewey, Melvil. "Apprenticeship of Librarians." *Library Journal* 4 (May 1879): 147-48.

Dewey, Melvil. *Librarianship as a Profession for College-Bred Women.* Boston: Library Bureau, 1886.

Dewey, Melvil. "Libraries the True Universities for Scholars as Well as People." *Library Notes* 1 (June 1886): 49-50.

Dewey, Melvil. "Library Employment *vs.* The Library Profession." *Library Notes* 1 (June 1886): 50-51.

Dewey, Melvil. "Library Handwriting." *Library Notes* 1 (March 1887): 273-82.

Dewey, Melvil. "Library Hours." *Library Journal* 4 (December 1879): 449.

Dewey, Melvil. "Library Instruction: Summary of Plans Proposed to Aid in Educating Librarians." *Library Notes* 2 (March 1888): 286-306.

Dewey, Melvil. "Melvil Dewey's Introduction." In Melvil Dewey, *Dewey Decimal Classification and Relative Index*, vol. 1. 17th ed. N.Y.: Forest Press, Inc., of Lake Placid Club Educational Foundation, 1965.

Dewey, Melvil. "Relation of the Colleges to the Modern Library Movement." Association of College and Preparatory Schools of the Middle States and Maryland, *Proceedings, 1891*, vol. 4. (Globe Printing House, 1891), pp. 78-83.

Dewey, Melvil. "Report of the Columbia College School of Library Economy." In Columbia University, School of Library Economy, *School of Library Economy of Columbia College 1887-1889: Documents for a History*. Columbia University School of Library Service, 1937, pp. 205-218.

Dewey, Melvil. "School of Library Economy." *Library Journal* 8 (September-October 1883): 285-91.

Dewey, Melvil. "To Applicants for Admission." In Columbia University, School of Library Economy. *School of Library Economy of Columbia College, 1887-1889: Documents for a History*. Columbia University. School of Library Service, 1937, pp. 116-17.

Diehl, Carl. *Americans and German Scholarship, 1770-1870*. New Haven, CN: Yale University Press, 1978.

Downs, Robert Bingham. "The Role of the Academic Librarian, 1876-1976." *College and Research Libraries* 37 (November 1976): 491-502.

Downs, Robert Bingham. "Status of Academic Librarians in Retrospect." *College and Research Libraries* 29 (July 1968): 253-58.

Dupree, A. Hunter. *Asa Gray 1810-1888*. Cambridge, Mass.: The Belknap Press of Harvard University Press, 1959.

Duval, Linda M. "The Ethics of the College Library." *Public Libraries* 4 (November 1899): 421-24.

Eddy, Edward Danforth, Jr. *Colleges for Our Land and Time: The Land Grant Idea in American Education*. New York: Harper & Brothers, 1957.

Edwards, Edward. *Memoirs of Libraries Including a Handbook of Library Economy*. 2 vols. London: Trubner & Co., 1859.

Eliot, Charles William. "Inaugural Address of Dr. Eliot." In Eliot, Charles William, *Charles W. Eliot the Man and His Beliefs*. Edited, with a biographical study, by William Allan Neilson. New York: Harper & Brothers, Publishers, 1926.

Eliot, Charles William. "The New Education: Its Organization." *Atlantic Monthly* 23 (February 1869): 203-220; (March 1869): 358-67.

Eliot, Charles William. *University Administration*. Boston, Houghton, 1908.

Ely, Richard T. "American Colleges and German Universities." *Harper's Magazine* 61 (July 1880): 253-60.

Engley, Donald B. "The Emergence of the Amherst College Library, 1821-1911." Master's thesis, University of Chicago, 1947.

Epler, Stephen Edward. *Honorary Degrees/a Survey of Their Use and Abuse*. Washington, D.C.: American Council on Public Affairs, 1943.

Fish, Carl Russell. *The Rise of the Common Man, 1830-1850*. A History of American Life, vol. 6. New York: Macmillan Company, 1929.

Fleischer, Mary Beth. "Credentials Awarded Through August, 1961, by Agencies Presently or Formerly Approved or Accredited by the American Library Association." Master's thesis, University of Texas —Austin, 1963.

Fletcher, William Isaac. "Modern Librarianship." *New Hampshire Library Commission Bulletin* 3 (December 1902): 185-87.

Fletcher, William Isaac. *Public Libraries in America.* Columbia Knowledge Series, no. 2. Boston: Robert Brothers, 1894.

Flexner, Abraham. *The American College, A Criticism.* 1908. Reprint. New York: The Arno Press and The New York Times, 1969.

Flexner, Abraham. *Daniel Coit Gilman, Creator of the American Type of University.* New York: Harcourt, Brace & Company, 1946.

Ford, Guy Stanton. "The Library and the Graduate School." In Association of American Universities, *Journal of Proceedings and Addresses of the Fifteenth Annual Conference* published by the Association ([1913]); pp. 38-46.

Foster, Frank Hugh. *The Seminary Method of Original Study in the Historical Sciences.* New York: Charles Scribner's Sons, 1888.

Franklin, Fabian. *The Life of Daniel Coit Gilman.* New York: Dodd, Mead & Company, 1910.

Fuess, Claude M. *The College Board; its First Fifty Years.* New York: College Entrance Examination Board, 1967.

Furnas, J. C. *The Americans: A Social History of the United States, 1587-1914.* New York: G. P. Putnam's Sons, 1969.

Garrison, Dee. *Apostles of Culture: the Public Librarian and American Society, 1876-1920.* New York: Macmillan Information, 1979.

Gilman, Daniel Coit. "Historical Address." In Cornell University, *Exercises of the Opening of the Library Building . . . October 7, 1981.* Ithaca, N.Y.: Cornell University, 1891, pp. 40-54.

Gilman, Daniel Coit. *The Launching of a University and Other Papers.* New York: Dodd, Mead & Company, 1906.

Gilman, Daniel Coit. *University Problems in the United States.* New York: The Century Co., 1898.

Gilroy, Marion, and Samuel Rothstein. *As We Remember It: Interviews with Pioneering Librarians of British Columbia.* Vancouver, B.C.: University of British Columbia School of Librarianship with the co-operation and assistance of the Library Development Commission of British Columbia, 1970.

Goodspeed, Edgar F. *As I Remember.* New York: Harper & Brothers, 1953.

Goodspeed, Thomas Wakefield. *The Story of the University of Chicago.* Chicago: University of Chicago Press, 1925.

Green, Samuel Swett. "Personal Relations between Librarians and Readers." *Library Journal* 1 (Nov. 30, 1876): 74-81; 123-24.

Griffin, Richard W. "Student Days at Davidson College, 1838-1857, in Letters to the Rev. G.H.W. Petrie." *Presbyterian Historical Society Journal* 40 (September 1962): 181-86.

Grotzinger, Laurel Ann. *The Power and the Dignity, Librarianship and Katherine Sharp*. New York and London: Scarecrow Press, Inc., 1966.

Gurlanick, Stanley M. *Science and the Ante-Bellum American College*. American Philosophical Society. Memoirs, vol. 109. Philadelphia: The American Philosophical Society, 1975.

Hadley, Arthur Twining. "The Library in the University." *Public Libraries* 14 (April 1909): 115-17.

Hadley, Chalmers. "What Library Schools Can Do for the Profession." In *Papers and Proceedings of the Thirty-Fourth Annual Meeting of the American Library Association*. Chicago: American Library Association, 1912, pp. 147-58.

Hadley, Morris. *Arthur Twining Hadley*. New Haven: Yale University Press, 1948.

Hale, Charles E. *The Origins and Development of the Association of College and Research Libraries, 1899-1960*. Unpublished doctoral dissertation, Indiana University, 1976.

Hall, Granville Stanley. *Life and Confessions of a Psychologist*. New York: D. Appleton & Company, 1923.

Hall, Granville Stanley. "What is Research in a University Sense and How May It Best Be Promoted." In Association of American Universities. *Journal of Proceedings and Addresses of the Third Annual Conference*. Chicago: Published by the Association, 1902, pp. 46-51.

Hamlin, Arthur Tenney. *The University Library in the United States: Its Origins and Development*. Philadelphia: University of Pennsylvania Press, 1981.

Hansen, Ralph W. "The Stanford University Library: Genesis 1891-1906." *Journal of Library History* 9 (April 1974): 138-58.

Hanson, Eugene Russell. *Cataloging and the American Library Association, 1876-1956*. Unpublished doctoral dissertation, University of Pittsburgh, 1974.

Hanson, James Christian Meinich. *What Became of Jens? A Study in Americanization, Based on the Reminiscences of J.C.M. Hanson, 1864-1943*. Edited by Olvind M. Houde. Decorah, Iowa: Luther College Press, 1974.

Harding, Thomas S. *College Literary Societies: Their Contribution to Higher Education in the United States, 1815-1876*. New York: Pageant Press International, 1971.

Harris, John Howard. *Thirty Years as President of Bucknell with Baccalaureate and Other Addresses*. Compiled and arranged by Mary B. Harris. Privately printed, 1926.

Hawkins, Hugh. *Pioneer: A History of the Johns Hopkins University, 1874-1889*. Ithaca, New York: Cornell University Press, 1960.

Henderson, Joseph Lindsey. *Admission to College by Certificate*. Teachers College, Columbia University Contributions to Education, no. 50. New York City: Teachers College, Columbia University, 1912.

Henry, William Elmer. "The Academic Standing of College Library Assistants and Their Relation to the Carnegie Foundation." In *Papers and Proceedings of the Thirty-Third Annual Meeting of the American Library Association.* Chicago: American Library Association, 1911, pp. 258-62.

Henry, William Elmer. "Living Salaries for Good Service." *Library Journal* 44 (May 1919): 282-84.

Hewins, Carolyn Maria. "Report on the Library School as It Is." *Library Journal* 15 (December 1890): 91-93.

Hicks, Frederick C. "Where Shall University, College and Reference Library Assistants Be Educated." In *American Library Institute, Papers and Proceedings, 1918.* Chicago: American Library Association, 1918, pp. 11-25.

Hinsdale, B. A. "Notes on the History of Foreign Influence upon Education in the United States." In *U.S. Commissioner of Education Report of the Commissioner of Education for the Year 1897-98,* vol. 1. Washington, D.C.: Government Printing Office, 1899, pp. 591-629.

Hislop, Codman. *Eliphalet Nott.* Middleton, Ct: Wesleyan University Press, 1971.

Hoff, Alethea. "A History of the Library of Western Maryland College." Master's thesis, Drexel Institute of Technology, 1954.

Hofstadter, Richard. *Anti-Intellectualism in American Life.* New York: Alfred A. Knopf, Inc., 1963.

Hofstadter, Richard. *Social Darwinism in American Thought.* Rev. ed. New York: George Braziller, Inc., 1959.

Hofstadter, Richard, and C. DeWitt Hardy. *The Development and Scope of Higher Education in the United States.* New York: Columbia University Press, 1952.

Holley, Edward G. "Academic Libraries in 1876." *College and Research Libraries* 37 (January 1976): 15-47.

Holley, Edward G. *Charles Evans: American Bibliographer.* Urbana: University of Illinois Press, 1963.

Houser, Lloyd J., and Alvin M. Schrader. *The Search for a Scientific Profession: Library Science Education in the U.S. and Canada.* Metuchen, N.J.: Scarecrow Press, Inc., 1978.

Howe, Harriet E. "Two Decades in Education for Librarianship." *Library Quarterly* 12 (July 1942): 557-70.

Hoyt, J. W. "An American University." U.S. Commissioner of Education *Report, 1870.* Washington: Government Printing Office, 1870, pp. 418-21.

Hudson, Jeanne Peery. "A History of the Roanoke College Library, 1842-1959." Master's thesis, University of North Carolina, Chapel Hill, 1963.

Hyder, Clyde Kenneth. *George Lyman Kitteridge: Teacher and Scholar.* Lawrence: University of Kansas Press, 1962.

Hyder, Clyde Kenneth. *Snow of Kansas; the Life of Francis Hunting-*

ton Snow with Extracts from His Journals and Letters. Lawrence: University of Kansas Press, 1953.

Irwin, Maurine. "History of the Ohio Wesleyan University Library, 1844–1940." Master's thesis, University of California, 1941.

James, Edmund Janes. "The National University in View of Present Conditions." In Transactions and Proceedings of the National Association of American Universities in the United States of America, vol. 16. Lexington, Ky: Transylvania Printing Co. (1918), pp. 129–36.

James, Henry. Charles W. Eliot President of Harvard University, 1869–1909. 2 vols. Boston: Houghton Mifflin Company, 1930.

James, William. "The Ph.D. Octopus." In William James. Memories and Studies. Edited by Henry James, Jr. London: Longman's, Green & Co., 1911.

Jameson, John Franklin. "The American Historical Association, 1884–1909." American Historical Review 15 (October 1909): 1–20.

Jewett, Charles Coffin. Appendix to the Report of the Board of Regents of the Smithsonian Institution Containing a Report on the Public Libraries. 31st Cong. 1st sess. Senate. Miscellaneous Document no. 120. Washington, D.C.: Printed for the Senate, 1850.

Johnston, W. Dawson. "The Library as a University Factor." In Association of American Universities. Journal of Proceedings and Addresses of the Fifteenth Annual Conference. Published by the Association, 1913, pp. 31–38.

Jones, Howard Mumford. The Age of Energy: Varieties of American Experience, 1865–1915. New York: The Viking Press, 1971.

Jones, Howard Mumford. Howard Mumford Jones: An Autobiography. Madison: University of Wisconsin Press, 1979.

Jones, Theodore Francis, ed. New York University, 1832–1932. New York: New York University Press, 1933.

Jordan, David Starr. The Days of a Man, Being Memories of a Naturalist, Teacher and Minor Prophet of Democracy. 2 vols. Yonkers, N.Y.: World Book Company, 1922.

Jordan, David Starr. "The Evolution of the College Curriculum." In David Starr Jordan. The Care and Culture of Men: A Series of Addresses on the Higher Education. San Francisco: The Whitaker and Ray Company, 1896., pp. 24–56.

Josephson, Aksel, G. S. "A Postgraduate School of Bibliography." Library Journal 24 (August 1901): 197–99.

Josephson, Aksel, G. S. "Preparation for Librarianship." Library Journal 25 (May 1900): 226–28.

Journal of the Proceedings of a Convention of Literary and Scientific Gentlemen, Held in the Common Council Chamber of the City of New York, October, 1830. New York: J. Leavitt and G. & C. Carvill, 1831.

Kennedy, M. St. Mel, Sister. The Changing Academic Characteristics of the Nineteenth Century American College Teacher. Unpublished doctoral dissertation, St. Louis University, 1961.

Keogh, Andrew. "Advanced Library Training for Research Workers." In *Papers and Proceedings of the Forty-First Annual Conference of the American Library Association.* Chicago: American Library Association, 1919, pp. 165–67.

Kirkpatrick, John Ervin. *Academic Organization and Control.* Yellow Springs, Ohio: The Antioch Press, 1931.

Kirkpatrick, John Ervin. *The American College and Its Rulers.* New York: New Republic, Inc., 1926.

Kitteridge, George Lyman. "Francis James Child." In Francis James Child, ed. *The English and Scottish Popular Ballads,* vol. 1 New York: Houghton-Mifflin and Company, 1882–1898, pp. xxii–xxxi.

Klapper, Paul. *College Teaching, Studies in Methods of Teaching in the Colleges.* Yonkers, New York: World Book Company, 1920.

Klein, Arthur J. "Preface." In Arthur J. Klein. *Survey of Land-Grant Colleges and Universities,* vol. 1. United States Office of Education Bulletin 1930, no. 9. Washington, D.C.: United States Government Printing Office, pp. vii–xxvii.

Koch, Theodore Wesley. "Apportionment of Book-Funds in College and University Libraries." In *Papers and Proceedings of the Thirtieth Annual Meeting of the American Library Association.* Boston: American Library Association, 1908, pp. 341–47.

Koch, Theodore Wesley. *On University Libraries.* Paris: Librarie Ancienne Honoré Champion Edouard Champion, 1924.

Koch, Theodore Wesley. "Student Circulation in a University Library." *Library Journal* 31 (November 1906): 758–61.

Koch, Theodore Wesley. "The University Library." *Library Journal* 40 (May 1915): 322–25.

Koopman, Harry Lyman. "The Functions of a University Library." *Library Journal* 19 (December 1894): 21–30; 151–52.

Kuhn, Madison. *Michigan State; the First Hundred Years.* East Lansing: Michigan State University Press, 1955.

Kurtz, Benjamin Putnam. *Joseph Cummings Rowell, 1853–1938.* Berkeley: University of California Press, 1940.

La Boone, Elizabeth. "History of the University of Georgia Library." Master's thesis, University of Georgia, 1954.

Lacy, Mary G. "The Opportunity of the Agricultural College Library." *South Atlantic Quarterly* 9 (January 1910): 78–82.

Le Duc, Thomas Harold André. *Piety and Intellect at Amherst College, 1865–1912.* New York: Columbia University Press, 1949.

Lehmann-Haupt, Helmut. *The Book in America; a History of the Making and Selling of Books in the United States.* 2d ed. New York: R. R. Bowker Company, 1951.

Library Workers Association. "Constitution of the Library Workers Association." *Library Journal* 45 (Oct. 15, 1920): 836–40.

Lichtenstein, Walter. "The Question of a Graduate Library School." *Library Journal* 43 (April 1918): 233–35.

Linderman, Winifred. *History of the Columbia University Library, 1876-1927.* Unpublished doctoral dissertation, Columbia University, 1959.

Longfellow, Henry Wadsworth. *The Letters of Henry Wadsworth Longfellow.* Edited by Andrew Hilen. 4 vols. Cambridge, Mass.: The Belknap Press of the Harvard University Press, 1966-1972.

Lovett, Robert W. "The Undergraduate and the Harvard Library, 1877-1937." *Harvard Library Bulletin* 1 (Spring 1947): 221-37.

Lowell, James Russell. *Letters of James Russell Lowell.* Edited by Charles Eliot Norton. 2 vols. New York: Harper & Brothers Publishers, 1894.

Lowrey, C. E. "University Library: Its Larger Recognition in Higher Education." *Library Journal* 19 (August 1894): 264-67.

McAnally, Arthur M. "Status of the University Librarian in the Academic Community." In Orne, Jerrold, ed., *Research Librarianship: Essays in Honor of Robert B. Downs.* New York: R. R. Bowker Company, 1971. pp. 19-50.

McEwen, Robert W. "The Status of College Librarians." *College and Research Libraries* 3 (June 1942): 256-61.

McGrath, Earl J. "The Control of Higher Education in America." *Educational Record* 17 (April 1936): 259-72.

McGrath, Earl James. *The Evolution of Administrative Offices Institutions of Higher Education in the United States from 1860-1933.* Unpublished doctoral dissertation, University of Chicago, 1938.

McMullen, Charles Haynes. *The Administration of the University of Chicago Libraries, 1892-1928.* Unpublished doctoral dissertation, University of Chicago, 1949.

Madsen, David. *The National University: Enduring Dream of the U.S.A.* Detroit: Wayne State University Press, 1966.

Manley, Marian Catherine. "The Aims of the L.W.A." *Library Journal* 46 (Nov. 15, 1921): 943.

Maxwell, Margaret Nadine Finlayson. *Anatomy of a Book Collector: William L. Clements and the Clements Library.* Unpublished doctoral dissertation, University of Michigan, 1971.

Metzger, Walter P. *Academic Freedom in the Age of the University.* New York: Columbia University Press, 1964.

Metzger, Walter P. "Academic Tenure in America: A Historical Essay." In Commission on Academic Tenure in Higher Education. *Faculty Tenure.* San Francisco: Jossey-Bass Publishers, Inc., 1973, pp. 93-159.

Meyers, Judith K. "A History of the Antioch College Library, 1850 to 1929." Master's thesis, Kent State University, 1963.

Michener, Roger. "Henry Wadsworth Longfellow: Librarian of Bowdoin College, 1829-35." *Library Quarterly* 43 (July 1973): 215-26.

Miksa, Francis Louis. *Charles Ami Cutter: Nineteenth Century Systematizer of Libraries.* 2 vols. Unpublished doctoral dissertation, University of Chicago, 1974.

Mirrielees, Edith R. *Stanford—the Story of a University.* New York: G. P. Putnam's Sons, 1959.

Mitchell, Sydney B. *Mitchell of California: The Memoirs of Sydney B. Mitchell, Librarian, Teacher, Gardener.* Berkeley: California Library Association, 1960.

Mitchell, Sydney B. "Salary Statistics: University and College Library Salary Statistics." *ALA Bulletin* 23 (March 1929): 57–59.

Moloney, Louis C. *A History of the University Library at the University of Texas, 1883-1934.* Unpublished doctoral dissertation, Columbia, 1970.

Mott, Frank Luther. *A History of American Magazines, 1741-1850.* Cambridge, Mass.: The Belknap Press of Harvard University Press, 1957.

Mott, Frank Luther. *A History of American Magazines, 1885-1905.* Cambridge, Mass.: The Belknap Press of Harvard University Press, 1957.

Mudge, Isadore Gilbert. "Stimulation of General Reading in the College Library." *Library Journal* 31 (November 1906): 764–68.

Munn, Robert Ferguson. *West Virginia University Library, 1867-1917.* Unpublished doctoral dissertation, University of Michigan, 1961.

Nethery, Wallace. *Dr. Flewelling and the Hoose Library: Life and Letters of a Man and an Institution.* Los Angeles: University of Southern California Press, 1976.

Newman, Robert P. "A Patron Saint for General Education." *AAUP Bulletin* 39 (Summer 1953): 267–80.

Nichols, Mary Elizabeth. "Early Development of the University of Mississippi Library." Master's thesis, University of Mississippi, 1957.

Nicholson, James M., Jr. "A History of the Wake Forest College Library, 1876-1946." Master's thesis, University of North Carolina, 1954.

Nightingale, Augustus Frederick. *A Handbook of Requirements for Admission to the Colleges of the United States with Miscellaneous Addenda, for the Use of High Schools, Academies, and Other College-Preparatory Institutions.* New York: D. Appleton and Company, 1879.

North, Ada. "A Western University Library." *Library Journal* 10 (June 1885): 124–25.

Oliphant, J. Orin. *The Library of Bucknell University.* Lewisburg, Pa: Bucknell University Press, 1962.

"Original Papers in Relation to a Course of Liberal Education." *American Journal of Science and Arts* 14 (1828): 297–351.

Parham, Paul Morris. *Malcolm Glenn Wyer, Western Librarian: A Study in Leadership and Innovation.* Unpublished doctoral dissertation, University of Denver, 1964.

Peterson, George E. *The New England College in the Age of the University.* Amherst, Mass.: Amherst College Press, 1964.

Peterson, Kenneth Gerard. *The History of the University of California Library at Berkeley, 1900-1945.* Unpublished doctoral dissertation, University of California, Berkeley, 1968.

Phillips, D. E. "The Elective System in American Education." *Pedagogical Seminary* 8 (June 1901): 206-230.

Pierson, George Wilson. *Yale College, an Educational History, 1871-1921.* New Haven: Yale University Press, 1952.

Plummer, Mary Wright. "Brooklyn Library Training Class." *Library Journal* 16 (December 1891): 87.

Plummer, Mary Wright. "Columbia College School of Library Economy from a Student's Standpoint." *Library Journal* 12 (September-October, 1887): 363-64.

Plummer, Mary Wright. "Pages from the Note Books of Mary Wright Plummer on the Lectures for March 1887." In Columbia University, School of Library Economy. *School of Library Economy of Columbia College, 1887-1889: Documents for a History.* Columbia University: School of Library Service, 1937, pp. 136-59.

Plummer, Mary Wright. "Pros and Cons of Training for Librarianship." *Public Libraries* 8 (May 1903): 208-220.

Porter, Noah. *A Plea for Libraries. A Letter Addressed to a Friend in Behalf of the Society for the Promotion of Collegiate and Theological Education at the West.* New York: S. W. Benedict, 1848.

Potter, Alfred Clanghorn, "The Selection of Books for College Libraries." In *Papers and Proceedings of the Nineteenth General Meeting of the American Library Association.* Chicago: American Library Association, 1897, pp. 39-44; 61-65.

Potter, Jessica Chandler. "The History of the University of Washington Library." Master's thesis, University of Washington, 1954.

Powell, Benjamin Edward. *The Development of Libraries in Southern Universities to 1920.* Unpublished doctoral dissertation, University of Chicago, 1946.

The Princeton Alumni Weekly. *The Harvey S. Firestone Memorial Library.* Princeton, 1949.

Princeton University Library. *College and University Library Statistics, 1919/20 to 1943/44.* Princeton, N.J.: Princeton University Library, 1947.

Pritchett, Herry S. "The Policy of the Carnegie Foundation for the Advancement of Teaching." *Educational Review* 32 (June 1906): 83-93.

Putnam, Herbert. "Education for Library Work." *Independent* 52 (Nov. 22, 1900): 2773-76.

Rainsford, George N. *Congress and Higher Education in the Nineteenth Century.* Knoxville: University of Tennessee Press, 1972.

Randall, William Madison. *The College Library: A Descriptive Study of the Libraries in Four-Year Liberal Arts Colleges in the United*

States. Chicago: American Library Association and the University of Chicago Press, 1932.

Randall, William Madison, and Francis L. D. Goodrich. *Principles of College Library Administration.* Chicago: American Library Association and the University of Chicago Press, 1936.

Rayward, W. Boyd. "Melvil Dewey and Education for Librarianship." *Journal of Library History* 3 (October 1968): 297–312.

"Receipts and Disbursements under the Act of August 30, 1892." In U.S. Office of Education. *Report of the Commissioner of Education for the Year 1890–91,* vol. 1 Washington, D.C.: Government Printing Office, 1894.

Reed, Amy L. "A Graduate School of Librarianship." In American Library Institute *Papers and Proceedings, 1918.* Chicago: American Library Association, 1919, pp. 8–10.

Rhees, William Jones. *Manual of Public Libraries, Institutions, and Societies, in the United States and British Provinces of North America.* Philadelphia: J. B. Lippincott Company, 1859.

Richardson, Ernest Cushing. "Antediluvian Libraries." *Library Journal* 15 (December 1890): 40–44.

Richardson, Ernest Cushing. "Co-operation in Lending among College and Reference Libraries." *Library Journal* 24 (July 1899): 32–36.

Richardson, Ernest Cushing. "The Field of Library Science." *Public Libraries* 21 (May 1916): 205–211.

Richardson, Ernest Cushing. "The Library School as It Should Be?" *Library Journal* 15 (December 1890): 93–94.

Richardson, Ernest Cushing. "Place of the Library in the University." *ALA Bulletin* 10 (January 1916): 1–13; 45–48.

Rider, Fremont. *Melvil Dewey.* Chicago: American Library Association, 1944.

Ringenberg, William C. "College Life in Frontier Michigan." *Michigan History* 54 (Summer 1970): 91–107.

Roberts, Clarence N. *North Central College: A Century of Liberal Education 1861–1961.* Naperville, Ill.: North Central College, 1960.

Roberts, Isaac Phillips. *Autobiography of a Farm Boy.* Ithaca, N.Y.: Cornell University Press, 1946.

Robinson, Otis H. "College Libraries as Semi-Public Libraries: The Rochester University Library." *Library Journal* 2 (October 1877): 57–60.

Robinson, Otis H. "College Library Administration." In U.S. Office of Education. *Public Libraries in the United States of America; Their History, Condition, and Management.* Part I. Washington, D.C.: Government Printing Office, 1876, pp. 505–525.

Root, Azariah Smith. "College and University Library Salaries." *ALA Bulletin* 13 (May 1919): 77–80.

Root, Azariah Smith. "Future Development of College and University Libraries." *Library Journal* 39 (November 1914): 811–15.

Root, Azariah Smith. "The Library School of the Future." *ALA Bulletin* 11 (March 1917): 157–60.

Ross, Earle D. *Democracy's College: The Land-Grant Movement in the Formative Stage*. Ames, Iowa: Iowa State College Press, 1942.

Ross, Edward Alsworth. *Seventy Years of It; An Autobiography*. New York: Appleton-Century Company, 1936.

Ross, Murray G. *The University: The Anatomy of Academe*. New York: McGraw-Hill Book Company, 1976.

Rothstein, Samuel. *The Development of Reference Services through Academic Traditions, Public Library Practice, and Special Librarianship*. ACRL Monographs no. 14. Chicago: Association of College and Reference Libraries, 1955.

Rouse, Roscoe, Jr. *A History of the Baylor University Library, 1845–1919*. Unpublished doctoral dissertation, University of Michigan, 1962.

Rowell, Joseph Cummings. "Standards of Success." *Library Journal* 21 (March 1896): 110.

Rudolph, Frederick. *The American College and University: A History*. New York: Alfred A. Knopf, 1962.

Rudolph, Frederick. *Mark Hopkins and the Log; Williams College, 1836–1872*. New Haven: Yale University Press, 1956.

Rudolph, Frederick. "Who Paid the Bills." *Harvard Educational Review* 31 (Spring 1961): 144–57.

Ryan, W. Carson. *Studies in Early Graduate Education*. Carnegie Foundation for the Advancement of Teaching. Bulletin no. 30. New York: The Carnegie Foundation for the Advancement of Teaching, 1939.

Salinas, Anna. "John Edward Goodwin: University Librarian." Master's thesis, University of Texas, 1966.

Schmidt, George Paul. "Intellectual Crosscurrents in American Colleges, 1825–1855." *American Historical Review* 42 (October 1936): 46–67.

Schmidt, George Paul. *The Liberal Arts College; a Chapter in American Cultural History*. New Brunswick, N.J.: Rutgers University Press, 1957.

Schmidt, George Paul. *The Old Time College President*. Columbia University Studies in the Social Sciences, 317. New York: Columbia University Press, 1930.

Scott, Edith. *J.C.M. Hanson and His Contribution to Twentieth Century Cataloging*. Unpublished doctoral dissertation, University of Chicago, 1970.

Selden, William K. *Accreditation: A Struggle Over Standards in Higher Education*. New York: Harper & Row, 1960.

Severance, Henry Ormal. *History of the Library, University of Missouri*. Columbia: University of Missouri, 1928.

Seymour, May. "Pages from the Note Books of May Seymour on the Lectures for March 1887." In Columbia University, School of Library Economy. *School of Library Economy of Columbia College, 1887–1889: Documents for a History.* Columbia University. School of Library Service, 1937, pp. 160–83.

Sharp, Katharine Lucinda. "Librarianship as a Profession." *Public Libraries* 3 (January 1898): 5–7.

Shipton, Clifford Kenyon. "John Langdon Sibley, Librarian." *Harvard Library Bulletin* 9 (Spring 1955): 236–61.

Shryock, Richard Harrison. "The Academic Profession in the United States." *American Association of University Professors Bulletin* 38 (Spring 1952): 32–70.

Sibley, John Langdon. "Address Delivered before the A.L.A. at Boston." *Library Journal* 4 (July–August, 1879): 305–308.

Skipper, James Everett. *The Ohio State University Library, 1873–1913.* Unpublished doctoral dissertation, University of Michigan, 1960.

Smith, Charles W. "The Vanishing Supply of Research Periodicals." *Library Journal* 49 (Feb. 1, 1924): 117–19.

Smith, Dora. "History of the University of California Library to 1900." Master's thesis, University of California, 1930.

Smith, Wilson. *Professors and Public Ethics, Studies of Northern Moral Philosophers before the Civil War.* Ithaca, N.Y.: Published for the American Historical Association by the Cornell University Press, 1956.

Snow, Louis Franklin. *The College Curriculum in the United States.* New York: Teachers College, Columbia University, 1907.

Sparks, Claud Glenn. *William Warner Bishop, a Biography.* Unpublished doctoral dissertation, University of Michigan, 1967.

Stein, John H. "The Development of the Hiram College Library from the Literary Societies Which Formed Its Nucleus." Master's thesis, Kent State University, 1950.

Storr, Richard J. *The Beginnings of Graduate Education in America.* Chicago: University of Chicago Press, 1953.

Strong, Frank. "The Minimum Conditions, Environmental, etc., That Should Be Considered Favorable to Graduate Work." In *Transactions and Proceedings of the National Association of State Universities in the United States of America,* 1905, pp. 37–44.

Strohm, Adam J. "Do We Need a Post-Graduate Library School?" *Public Libraries* 15 (February 1910): 54–55.

Tappan, Henry P. *University Education.* New York: P. Putnam, 1851.

Tauber, Maurice Falcolm. *Louis Round Wilson, Librarian and Administrator.* New York: Columbia University Press, 1967.

Tebbel, John William. *A History of Book Publishing in the United States.* 3 vols. New York: R. R. Bowker Company, 1973–78.

Ten Brook, Andrew. *American State Universities, Their Origin and Progress; A History of Congressional University Land-Grants, a Particular Account of the Rise and Development of the University of Michigan, and Hints Toward the Future of the American University System.* Cincinnati: Robert Clarke & Co., 1875.

Tewksbury, Donald George. *The Founding of American Colleges and Universities before the Civil War; with Particular Reference to the Religious Influences Bearing Upon the College Movement.* 1932. Reprint. Hamden, Ct.: Archon Books, 1965.

Thomison, Dennis. *A History of the American Library Association, 1876-1972.* Chicago: American Library Association, 1978.

Thomson, Edward. *Letters from Europe: Being Notes of a Tour through England, France, and Switzerland.* Edited by D. W. Clark. Cincinnati: D. Swormstedt and A. Poe, 1856.

Thwing, Charles Franklin. *The American and the German University.* New York: Macmillan, 1925.

Thwing, Charles Franklin. *College Administration.* New York: The Century Company, 1900.

Tillinghast, William H. "Some General Rules and Suggestions for a Library Staff." *Library Journal* 27 (October 1902): 871-75.

Todd, Henry Alfred. "The Functions of the Doctor's Degree in the Study of Modern Languages." In Modern Language Association of America. *Proceedings of the Twenty-Fourth Annual Meeting.* Baltimore: The Association, 1907, pp. xlix-lxvii.

Trautman, Ray. *A History of the School of Library Service.* New York: Columbia University Press, 1954.

U.S. Congress. Joint Committee on the Library of Congress. "Report under SCR 26, Relative to the Condition, Organization and Management of the Library of Congress, with Hearings: March 3, 1897." Senate Report 1573, 54th Cong. 2d sess., 1897.

Utley, George Burwell. *The Librarians' Conference of 1853; a Chapter in American Library History.* Edited by Gilbert H. Doane. Chicago: American Library Association, 1951.

Van Santvoord, Cornelius. *Memoirs of Eliphalet Nott.* New York: Sheldon & Co., 1876.

Vann, Sarah Katherine. "Introduction." In Melvil Dewey. *Melvil Dewey: His Enduring Presence in Librarianship.* Edited by Sarah K. Vann. Littleton, Colo.: Libraries Unlimited, 1978, pp. 21-65.

Vann, Sarah Katherine. *Training for Librarianship before 1923: Education for Librarianship Prior to the Publication of Williamson's Report on "Training for Library Service."* Chicago: American Library Association, 1961.

Varg, Paul A. "The Land Grant Philosophy and Liberal Education." *Centennial Review* 6 (Fall 1962): 435-44.

Veblen, Thorstein. *The Higher Learning in America: A Memorandum on the Conduct of Universities by Business Men.* New York: B. W. Huebsch, 1923.

Vinton, Frederick. "College Libraries." In U.S. Department of the Interior. Bureau of Education. *Public Libraries in the United States of America; Their History, Condition and Management*, Part I. Washington, D.C.: Government Printing Office, 1876, pp. 60–126.

Waddell, John Neal. *The Career of Isadore G. Mudge: A Chapter in the History of Reference Librarianship.* Unpublished doctoral dissertation, Columbia University, 1973.

Wagner, Lloyd F. "A Descriptive History of the Library Facilities of Lafayette College, Easton, Pennsylvania, 1824–1941." Master's thesis, Catholic University of America, 1951.

Wayland, Francis. *Thoughts on the Present Collegiate System in the United States.* Boston: Gould, Kendall & Lincoln, 1852.

White, Andrew Dickson. *Autobiography of Andrew Dickson White.* 2 vols. New York: The Century Company, 1905.

White, Andrew Dickson. *A History of the Warfare of Science with Theology in Christendom.* 2 vols. New York: D. Appleton and Company, 1903.

White, Carl Milton. *A Historical Introduction to Library Education: Problems and Progress to 1951.* Metuchen, N.J.: Scarecrow Press, Inc., 1976.

White, Carl Milton. "Trends in the Use of University Libraries." In American Library Association. *College and University Library Service: Trends Standards, Appraisal, Problems: Papers Presented at the 1937 Midwinter Meeting.* Chicago: American Library Association, 1938, pp. 15–39.

Whitney, James L. "Selecting and Training Library Assistants." *Library Journal* 7 (June 1882) 136–39.

Williams, John Rogers. *The Handbook of Princeton.* New York: The Grafton Press, 1905.

Williamson, Charles Clarence. "Training for Library Work: A Report Prepared for the Carnegie Corporation of New York." In *The Williamson Reports of 1921 and 1923.* Metuchen, N.J.: Scarecrow Press, Inc., 1971.

"The Williamson Report: Comments from the Library Schools." *Library Journal* 48 (Jan. 1, 1923): 899–910.

"The Williamson Report—II: Comment from Librarians." *Library Journal* 48 (Dec. 1, 1923): 999–1006.

Wilson, Louis N. "Correlation of the Library and Other Departments of Colleges and Universities." *Public Libraries* 12 (June 1907): 220–21.

Wilson, Louis Round. "Organization and Administration of the College Library." *Library Journal* 36 (November 1911): 560–65.

Winckler, Paul Albert. *Charles Clarence Williamson (1877–1965): His Professional Life and Work in Librarianship and Library Education in the United States.* Unpublished doctoral dissertation, New York University, 1968.

Winsor, Justin. "The College Library." In *College Libraries as Aids to Instruction* U.S. Bureau of Education. Circular of Information no. 1,1880. Washington, D.C.: Government Printing Office, 1880, pp. 7-14.

Winsor, Justin. "The Development of the Library, Address at Dedication of the Orrington Lunt Library, Northwestern University, Evanston, Illinois." *Library Journal* 19 (November 1894): 370-75.

Winsor, Justin. "Library Lectures and Other Helps." *Library Journal* 3 (May 1978): 120-21.

Winsor, Justin, "Library Questions and Answers." *Library Journal* 3 (June 1878): 159.

Woodward, Fred E. *A Graphic Survey of Book Publication, 1890-1916.* U.S. Bureau of Education, Bulletin no. 14, 1917. Washington, D.C.: Government Printing Office, 1917.

Woodruff, Edwin H. "University Libraries and Seminary Methods of Instruction." *Library Journal* 11 (August-September, 1886): 219-24; 371-72; 435-36.

Works, George Alan. *College and University Library Problems, a Study of a Selected Group of Institutions Prepared for the Association of American Universities.* Chicago: American Library Association, 1927.

Wyer, James Ingersoll. *The College and University Library.* Preprint of *Manual of Library Economy* chapter IV. Chicago: American Library Association Publishing Board, 1911.

Wyer, James Ingersoll. "Women in College Libraries." *School and Society* 29 (Feb. 16, 1929): 227-28.

Yenawine, Wayne Stewart. *The Influence of Scholars on Research Library Development at the University of Illinois.* Unpublished doctoral dissertation, University of Illinois, 1955.

Young, Arthur P. "Daniel Coit Gilman in the Formative Period of American Librarianship." *Library Quarterly* 45 (April 1975): 117-40.

Index